PASSPORT READING
JOURNEYS™
BEGINNINGS

Expanded Learning
Voyager

LITERATURE CREDITS

"Salomón's Story" from *Tortuga*. Copyright © 1979 by Rudolfo A. Anaya. Published by University of New Mexico Press, Albuquerque. Reprinted by permission of Susan Bergholz Literary Services, New York. All rights reserved.

"Life Doesn't Frighten Me," copyright © 1978 by Maya Angelou, from *And Still I Rise* by Maya Angelou. Used by permission of Random House, Inc.

"'Mermaids' Fight to Save Florida Roadside Attraction" by Kimberly Ayers and Boyd Matson, *National Geographic on Assignment*, March 24, 2004. Reprinted by permission of National Geographic Society.

"Eleven" from *Woman Hollering Creek*. Copyright © 1991 by Sandra Cisneros. Published by Vintage Books, a division of Random House, Inc., and originally in hardcover by Random House, Inc. Reprinted by permission of Susan Bergholz Literary Services, New York. All rights reserved.

"On Turning Ten" from *The Art of Drowning*, by Billy Collins, © 1995. Reprinted by permission of the University of Pittsburgh Press.

"Dog Days" from *Don't Open the Door After the Sun Goes Down: Tales of the Real and Unreal* by Al Carusone. Text copyright © 1994 by Al Carusone. Reprinted by permission of Clarion Books, an imprint of Houghton Mifflin Company. All rights reserved.

From *The Circuit: Stories from the Life of a Migrant Child* by Francisco Jiménez. © Francisco Jiménez. Reprinted by permission of the author.

From "The Cement Truck" by Laurence Lasky. Published in *Literary Cavalcade*, May 1966. Copyright © 1966 by Scholastic, Inc. Reprinted by permission.

"Old Snake" from *This Big Sky* by Pat Mora. Reprinted by the permission of Russell & Volkening as agents for the author. Copyright © 1998 Pat Mora.

From *Hoops* by Walter Dean Myers, copyright © 1981 by John Ballard. Used by permission of Dell Publishing, a division of Random House, Inc.

"The Wendigo" from *Verses from 1929* by Ogden Nash. Copyright © 1934 by Ogden Nash. Reprinted by permission of Curtis Brown, Ltd.

"The Best Pasta Salad" from *Happy Days with the Naked Chef* by Jamie Oliver. Copyright © 2002 Jamie Oliver. Reprinted by permission of Hyperion. All rights reserved.

From *Cuba 15* by Nancy Osa, © 2003 by Nancy Osa.

"The Bloody Fangs: A Tale from Japan" from *Ask the Bones: Scary Stories from Around the World* selected and retold by Arielle North Olson and Howard Schwartz, copyright © 1999 by Arielle North Olson and Howard Schwartz. Used by permission of Viking Penguin, A Division of Penguin Young Readers Group, A Member of Penguin Group (USA) Inc., 345 Hudson Street, New York, NY 10014. All rights reserved.

From *The Beet Fields* by Gary Paulsen, copyright © 2000 by Gary Paulsen. Used by permission of Random House Children's Books, a division of Random House, Inc.

"Whatif" from *A Light in the Attic* by Shel Silverstein. Copyright © 1981 Evil Eye Music, Inc. Used by permission of HarperCollins Publishers.

"The Food Stylist's Art" by Doug Stewart, *Muse* magazine, Volume 9 Number 7 September 2005. Published by Carus Publishing Company, Cricket Magazine Group, 315 Fifth Street, Peru, IL, 61354.

From *Flight to Freedom* by Ana Veciana-Suarez. First Person Fiction published by Scholastic Inc./Orchard Books. Copyright © 2002 by Ana Veciana-Suarez. Reprinted by permission.

"Golden Glass" by Alma Luz Villanueva from *Hispanics in the U. S.: An Anthology of Creative Literature, Volume II*, edited by Francisco Jiménez and Gary D. Keller. Copyright © 1982 Bilingual Press/Editorial Bilingüe, Arizona State University, Tempe, Arizona. Reprinted by permission.

From "Sandy Skoglund" from *FOCUS: Five Women Photographers* by Sylvia Wolf. Copyright © 2006 by Sylvia Wolf. Reprinted by permission of Sylvia Wolf.

From "Bessie Coleman" from *American Profiles: Women Aviators* by Lisa Yount. Reprinted by permission of the author.

From "The Day It Rained Cockroaches" by Paul Zindel. Copyright © 1990 by Paul Zindel. First appeared in *The Pigman and Me*, published by HarperCollins. Reprinted by permission of Curtis Brown, Ltd.

ISBN 13: 978-1-4168-0885-5
ISBN: 1-4168-0885-X
190174

Copyright 2008 by Voyager Expanded Learning, L.P.

Printed in the United States of America   14 15 16 17 18 WEB 9 8 7 6 5 4
17855 Dallas Parkway, Suite 400 • Dallas, Texas 75287 • 1-800-547-6747

Table of Contents

Expedition 1
Connections

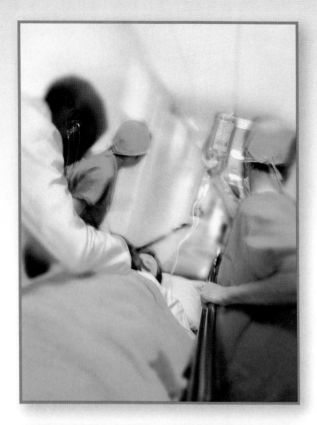

Expedition 2

Expedition 3

Expedition 4

Beating the Odds 45

Expedition 5

Fact or Fiction? 61

Expedition 6

Expedition 7

Expedition 8
Make It Right!

Expedition 9
Thinking Big

Expedition 10
E-World

Expedition 11
Motion and Emotion

Expedition 12

Watch Out!

Expedition 13

Coming of Age

Expedition 14
World at Work

Expedition 15
The Road Ahead

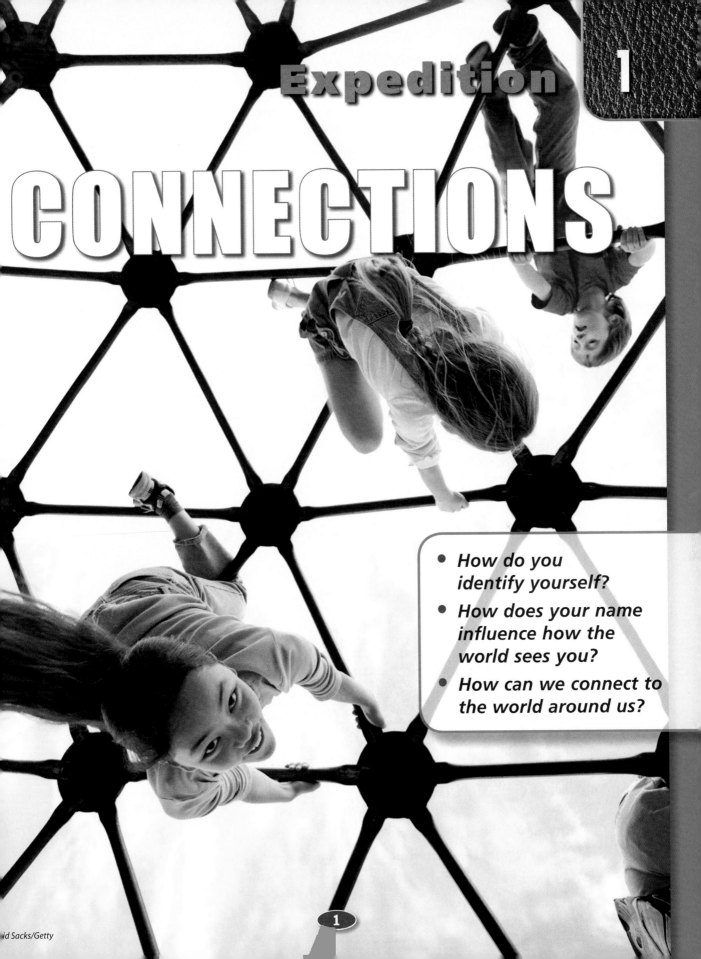

CONNECTIONS

- How do you identify yourself?
- How does your name influence how the world sees you?
- How can we connect to the world around us?

What's in a Name?

[1]**E**ddie kicked at the gravel as he crossed the school yard. School was over for the day. All around him kids were having fun while they waited for their buses. They laughed and shouted. Some played basketball or chatted with friends. Everyone seemed happy except Eddie.

2

²Eddie walked toward his best friend Leesha, who was reading a book under the big oak tree in front of the school.

³"What's with the frown?" she asked.

⁴"Nothing," he **grumbled** as he plopped down next to her.

⁵"Doesn't seem like 'nothing' to me. You must be having a bad day," she said.

⁶"No worse than usual," Eddie said. "Can I ask you a question?"

⁷"You just did," she said.

⁸"Very funny, Leesha." Eddie made a face at her.

⁹"So ask your question," she said.

¹⁰"How does a guy legally change his name?"

¹¹Leesha wrinkled her forehead. "Why in the world would you want to change your name?"

¹²"My name is so **ordinary** and boring," he said. "There must be a hundred Eddies in this school."

¹³"Oh, please," she said. "I only know one other Eddie."

¹⁴"Besides, my name doesn't **express** who I really am," Eddie said. "How could it? My parents gave it to me when I was born. I've changed a lot since then."

¹⁵"You think people stop changing when they get to middle school?"

Leesha said. "If you change your name every time your personality changes, nobody's going to know what to call you. It's your **character** that matters, not your name."

¹⁶"That's easy for you," Eddie said. "Your name is beautiful and **elegant**."

¹⁷"Whatever," Leesha said as she tried to hide a smile. "I don't always feel like a 'Leesha,' you know."

¹⁸"All right, I'll admit it," Eddie said. "I'm tired of people making fun of my name. I just can't hear 'Eddie Spaghetti' one more time!"

¹⁹"What's wrong with spaghetti?" Leesha said. "You love spaghetti."

²⁰"Maybe I could **persuade** my parents to change my name to Tony," he said.

²¹"Then they'll call you 'Tony Macaroni'," she said. "Kids are going to make fun of your name no matter what it is. Or they'll make fun of something else, like that crazy haircut of yours."

²²Eddie blushed at the joke. Just then, Leesha's mother drove up.

²³"Want to come to our house for dinner tonight?" Leesha asked as she got up to leave.

²⁴"That depends," Eddie said. "What are you having?"

²⁵"Spaghetti," Leesha answered.

Changing Names

¹There is something about you that almost everyone knows. What is it? It's your name. Your name is the first thing that most people learn about you. But have you ever thought about changing your name? If so, you are not alone. A lot of people like the idea of picking their own name.

A New Family, A New Name

²People change their names for many reasons. One of the most common reasons is marriage. Women usually take their new husband's last name when they marry. Sometimes, though, a couple makes up a new last name. Let's say Bob Smith and Mary Jones get married. They might change their last name to Smith-Jones. The new name **contains** both of their old names.

³Adoption is another reason people change their names. In most cases, adopted children take the last name of their new family. That's what former President Gerald Ford did. He was named Leslie Lynch King when he was born. Then his mother got divorced. Later, she married another man. She renamed her 2-year-old son after his new father. President Ford got more than a new last name. His whole name changed.

Making a Name for Yourself

[4]Entertainers often change their names too. Chances are some of the actors and singers you **admire** changed their names. They take new names for **professional** reasons. A name that is interesting or easy to remember can help them get jobs. A young man named Eric Morlon Bishop wanted to work in comedy clubs. He picked a new name that sounded like a woman's. "Back then, women comics were at a **premium** and got more mic time," he says. Club owners would book performers without even seeing their pictures. The owner would see a name like "Jamie" and think the performer was a woman. The name change worked. Eric got a lot of jobs at comedy clubs. Then he got a job on television. Soon he was starring in movies. Before long, his face was **familiar** to movie fans all over the world. You might know Eric better by his new name: Jamie Foxx.

[5]Rap artists almost always invent new names. A young rapper named Chris Bridges wanted a new name. He combined his first name with *ludicrous*. That word means "crazy or outrageous." The name he came up with was Ludacris. He says that the name describes his personality, his music, and everything about him.

Frank Micelotta/Getty

Jamie Foxx poses backstage after winning an Oscar award for best actor in the movie *Ray*.

A Name That Fits You

[6]People sometimes change their names for a simpler reason. They just don't like the name they were given at birth. They may think that it doesn't fit them. They might think that it sounds silly. Whatever the reason, they spend a lot of time thinking about new and better names. They might even try a new name with their friends. That helps them decide if they really like the new name. When they find a new name that they are **fond** of, they might change their name legally. That means filling out papers and appearing before a judge. It's a lot of work. But many people think a new name is worth the effort.

NICKNAMES

[7]A nickname is a new name that other people give you. A lot of basketball stars have nicknames. Nicknames are often made by shortening real names. That's how Tracy McGrady became T-Mac.

[8]Often the function of a nickname is to describe a player. In the 1950s, 7-footer Wilt Chamberlain was much taller than other players. It looked like he was standing on stilts. People started calling him "Wilt the Stilt." Michael Jordan was called "Air." Why? It was because he seemed to spend all of his time up in the air.

[9]Sometimes we don't even know a player's real name. For example, did you know that Magic Johnson's real first name is Earvin?

When Names Hurt

[1]**M**y name is Arno Girard. My family and I moved from France to America when Papa got a new job. I had already learned to speak English by reading books. I knew a lot of words, but I had not heard many people speak English. That's why I sometimes **pronounce** words the wrong way. I say English words the way I would say French words. For example, when I say *big*, it sounds like "beeg." That's what caused my problem.

[2]My first day at school started out fine. Then kids started to snicker at the way I spoke. I wasn't offended. I even laughed a little myself. I still figured that it would be easy to make new friends. Then the lunch hour came.

[3]First, no groups would let me sit at their table. Then they made jokes about the lunch Momma packed. "What's that—a bag full of snails?" one of the kids asked. Then the rest of them went "Ewww!" After that, another kid said, "It's probably frog legs." That made all the kids burst out laughing. Then some of them started calling me ugly names. I

began to **realize** that their jokes were not good-natured. This **discovery** hurt as bad as being punched.

[4]Finally, I sat at an empty table and ate by myself. The rest of the day was terrible. In the halls, kids whispered to one another and laughed. Some kids called me names. Others pushed me when I walked past. I felt hopeless. How could I **defend** myself against an entire school?

[5]Later that day, I told Momma how terrible school had been. She hugged me and reminded me of an old saying. "Sticks and stones may break my bones," she said, "but names will never hurt me." I used to believe that. But after my day at school, I was no longer sure it was true.

[6]The next day I tried to be invisible. I never raised my hand in class. I kept my head down as I moved through the halls. Then lunchtime came. I knew I would have to **settle** for an empty table. But there wasn't an empty table that day. As I stood there trying to figure out what to do, I heard the names again. The kids at the table next to me were laughing and pointing.

[7]Suddenly, a small girl at the end of the table stood up. She slammed her fist down on the table. The lunch trays jumped, and all the kids stopped laughing. The girl looked slowly around the table. Her eyes stopped briefly on each kid.

[8]"What is wrong with you?" Her quiet, **earnest** voice was so serious that nobody interrupted her. "You all know what it's like to be called names," she said. "You should be ashamed. Now move over and make room for Arno."

[9]For a moment, the cafeteria was completely quiet. Then the kids made room for me, and I sat next to the girl.

[10]"I'm Tina," she said. "I'll let all these other clowns introduce themselves. I'm sure they will all want to apologize."

[11]After that, things got much better at school. I started making friends. Before long, I was actually looking forward to lunch. One day I even brought snails, just so my friends and I could joke about it. Tina ate one, or at least she tried to.

[12]"Yuck!" she said as she spit the snail into a napkin. "These snails are for the birds!"

[13]Even I thought that was funny!

A Bullet Cannot Kill a Dream

Iqbal Masih

Anders Kristensson

Children work in a carpet factory in Attock, Pakistan.

Per-Anders Pettersson/Getty

¹The sixth-graders at Broad Meadows Middle School in Massachusetts were surprised. Their special guest that day in 1994 was about their age, but he was so much smaller than they were. His hands looked like they belonged to an old man. How was this **possible**?

Iqbal's Story

²Their guest was a boy from Pakistan. His name was Iqbal Masih. His story shocked them. Iqbal's family was very poor. They owed money to a man. The man threatened to hurt them if they didn't pay. So they sold Iqbal to a carpet maker for $12. Iqbal was just 4 years old.

³The carpet maker put chains on Iqbal. He forced him to tie tiny knots in carpets all day. If he slowed down, the carpet maker beat him. Iqbal

9

was never allowed to go to school. He was never paid for his work. The carpet maker did not even give him enough to eat. As a **result**, Iqbal grew much slower than other children.

[4]When Iqbal was 10, he ran away from the carpet maker. He told his story to those who would listen. These people told him that millions of children were treated just like he had been. They too worked all day without being paid. This made Iqbal very angry. He started speaking out against child slavery. That's why he was visiting the Broad Meadows class.

[5]The sixth-graders promised to help Iqbal fight child slavery. "There are kids around the world going through harder times than we ever will," said Amanda Loo, one of the students.

[6]When Iqbal returned to Pakistan, something terrible happened. He was shot and killed while riding a bike. He was probably murdered for telling people about child slavery. His tragic death **reminded** the students of what he had told them. "Iqbal told us his dream," said student Nicole Ferris. "He wished for freedom and education for all children. So we decided to build a school in Pakistan in Iqbal's memory."

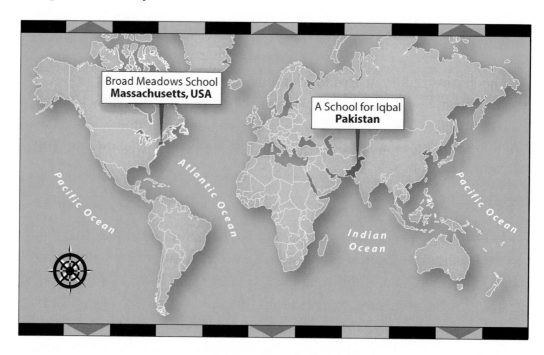

Naming a School for a Hero

Photos courtesy of Broad Meadows Sch

Students at A School for Iqbal

[7]People said the students of Broad Meadows could never raise enough money for a school. But the students would not **accept** this idea. They were determined to raise the money. First, they sent e-mails to schools all over the world. They told other students about Iqbal. They **urged** them to help build a school in his village in Pakistan. In each e-mail, they **suggested** a donation of $12. They asked for that amount because this was what the carpet maker paid for Iqbal. It was also Iqbal's age when he was killed.

[8]Next, they started writing to newspapers and government officials. They asked them to help end child slavery. The students worked day after day to raise money. They came to school early and stayed late. They worked on weekends and holidays.

[9]Finally, after a year of work, the students had raised $150,000. In Pakistan, that was enough to build a schoolhouse. They named it "A School for Iqbal." There was even enough money to hire teachers. When the school opened, hundreds of children attended. Many were going to school for the first time.

[10]After the school opened, there was money left over. The children used it to help parents in Pakistan buy their children back from men like the carpet maker. Many of those children then attended Iqbal's school.

[11]The story doesn't end there. Even now, the Broad Meadows students are continuing the work. They have joined with students from many other schools. The students raise money to build schools in other poor countries. As Broad Meadows eighth-grader Kristen Bloomer said, "It takes a little bit of time and a big heart to make a difference."

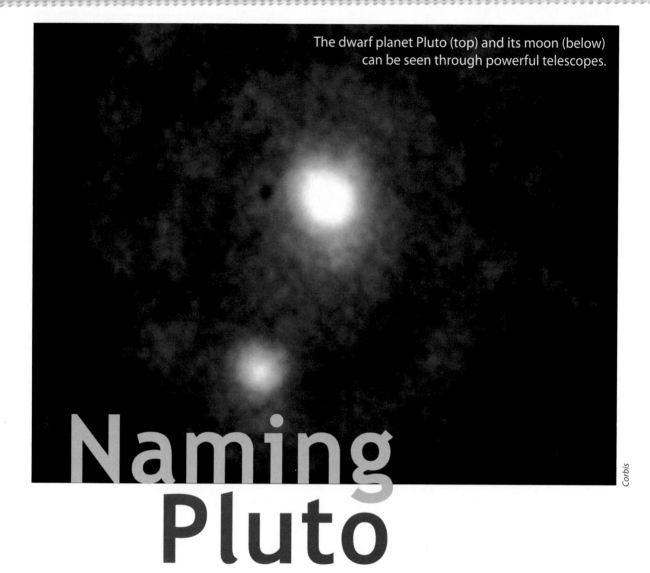

The dwarf planet Pluto (top) and its moon (below) can be seen through powerful telescopes.

Corbis

Naming Pluto

[1]You might know that Pluto is a dwarf planet in our solar system. You may also know that Pluto is Mickey Mouse's dog. But do you know which name came first?

Naming the Planet

[2]This distant, dwarf planet was discovered in 1930. Pluto is farther from the Sun than any known planet. It is also the smallest. It is too small and too far away to see without a telescope. Even early telescopes were not powerful enough to bring it into view.

12

From left to right are the Sun, Mercury, Venus, Earth, Mars, Jupiter, Saturn, Uranus, Neptune, and Pluto.

[3]After the planet was discovered, people wondered what to call it. Most of the planets that circle our Sun were named long ago. They were named for ancient gods in myths. For example, Mars appears red—the color of blood. It was named for the Roman god of war. Jupiter, the largest planet, was named after the Romans' most important god. Neptune looks as blue as seawater. It was named for the Roman god of the sea.

[4]People had many ideas for naming the new planet. The best idea came from Venetia Burney, an 11-year-old girl. The planet was far away and cold. It reminded her of the Roman underworld. Romans called the god of the underworld Pluto. On May 1, 1930, the planet was officially named Pluto.

Naming the Dog

[5]Pluto the dog appeared in his first cartoon in the same year the planet was discovered. At first, he was called Rover. Later, his creators decided to rename him in honor of the newly discovered planet.

[6]So now you know which name came first.

Pluto is a favorite Walt Disney character.

13

A BUG'S NAME

[1]Catherine got the idea in biology class. Mrs. Beale was talking about insects. She said that all insects have scientific names. The names are long and made up of Latin words. The long names end with the name of the species. Often, insects get their species name from people who discover them. That's what caught Catherine's interest.

[2]Catherine had a huge backyard with a lot of weird bugs. Surely one of those bugs was waiting to be discovered. Catherine was determined to find that bug. Her mom's birthday was next month. Naming a bug for her mom would be the best present ever!

[3]When Catherine got home, she flew up to her room. She grabbed her magnifying glass and ran out to the yard.

[4]"Let's see," she said. "Where would I hide if I were a bug that needed a name?"

[5]She looked in the flower bed. She searched along the garden fence. She studied the plants around the big oak tree. She found plenty of bugs. But they all looked like the bugs Mrs. Beale had shown them in class.

[6]She was about to give up when she saw something strange on a bush near the back door. She looked closely at one of the twigs with her magnifying glass. It had legs! Surely this was the bug she was looking for. She gently nudged the insect into a jar and ran inside.

[7]"Mom!" she yelled. "I discovered an insect! I get to name it!"

[8]Catherine's mom looked in the jar and smiled.

[9]"It's a walking stick," Mom said.

[10]"A what?" Catherine said.

[11]"A walking stick," her mom said. "They look just like sticks. They're hard to find unless you look closely."

[12]Catherine sighed. She was disappointed that she wouldn't get to name the walking stick. But Mrs. Beale always said that scientists rarely succeeded right away. Still, she kept trying. Catherine was determined to find an insect to name. She took her jar outside and released the walking stick. Then she started looking again.

Expedition

911

- How do people put themselves in danger to help others?
- What jobs help save lives?
- How can one event change a life?

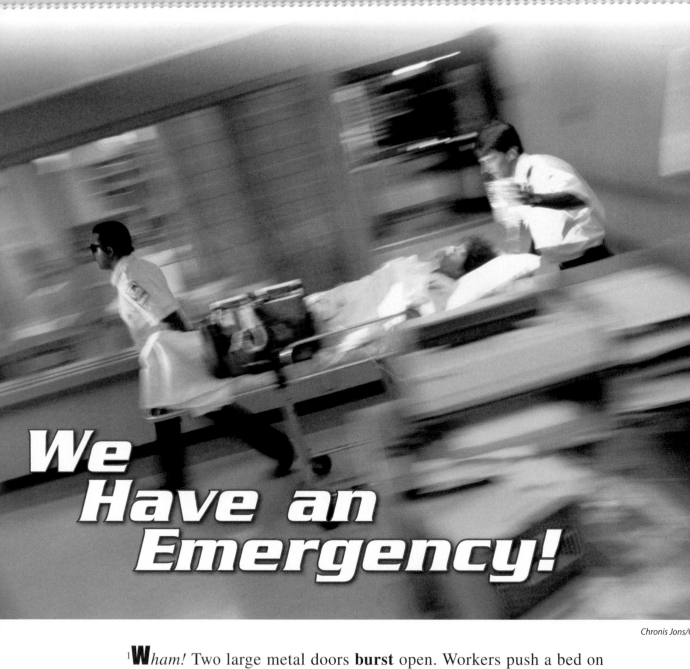

We Have an Emergency!

Chronis Jons/©

¹**W**ham! Two large metal doors **burst** open. Workers push a bed on wheels through the doorway into a world of white and gray. On the bed is a teenage boy. "Where am I?" he asks sleepily. He opens his eyes. The overhead lights are bright.

²"You're in the emergency room of a hospital," says one of the workers. The men move quickly through the hallway.

³"What happened?" asks the boy.

16

[4]"You fainted during a softball game," says the worker. The boy looks around as he is wheeled into a room. He hears a voice announce: "Dr. Garza to Room 5, *stat*!" The word *stat* means "move as fast as possible."

A Fast-Moving World

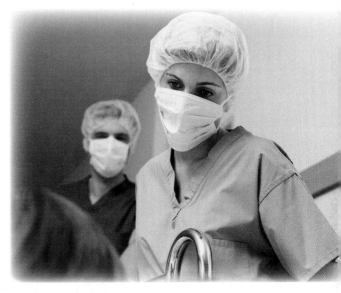

[5]A nurse and her helper are waiting for the boy in the room. Quickly, they turn on two machines. They use wires to connect the boy to the machines. One machine looks like a small TV screen. It keeps track of the boy's heart rate and breathing. A doctor enters the room. She greets the boy. Then she **examines** him. "Do you have any discomfort?" she asks. "Has this ever happened before?" The doctor writes notes on the boy's chart.

[6]The emergency room—or ER—is for patients who need **immediate** care. The sickest patients are seen first. An ER is a busy place. People rush around. Phones ring, lights blink, machines beep. Hospital workers call out to one another. "Move this bed to Room 4!" "My patient needs a blanket!" "Where's a wheelchair?"

An ER Doctor's Shift

[7]It's 3 p.m. The doctor just began her workday at the hospital. She will work for 8 hours or even longer, if **necessary**. She may see 30 patients today. She may not have time to eat. If she is lucky, she will get a bathroom break. She loves her job.

[8]The doctor finishes checking the boy. He fainted because he had not eaten all day. He will be fine. Next, she will see a man hurt in a car **accident**. She will treat a girl whose stomach **aches**. Then she will see a child with a broken arm. And that's just the first hour of her shift!

Shark *Attack*

Stuart Westmorland/

[1]At first, Jessie Arbogast did not see the dark shape darting toward him. The 8-year-old was splashing in the ocean off the coast of Florida. It was a hot July afternoon. Jessie had just finished the second grade. Now his family was on a trip to the beach. It was their summer vacation away from home. His brothers and cousins were there to have fun, too. They were with him in the water. The warm water where the group played was not deep.

[2]*Swish!* One of the boys felt something brush past his leg in the water. *What was that?* In the next **instant**, Jessie saw a large fin above the water. At that moment, a shark was headed straight toward Jessie! Rows of teeth like sharp knives flashed in the open mouth of the shark.

"He's Got Me!"

[3]"He's got me! Get him off! Get him off me!" Jessie yelled. Jessie's brothers and cousins began to scream. Jessie's uncle was on the beach. He heard the children's screams. Then he saw blood in the water. He knew that he had to act fast. He **scrambled** across the sand and into the water toward Jessie.

[4]The shark had Jessie's right arm in its jaws. The uncle grabbed the shark's tail and pulled. The 200-pound bull shark would not let go. The uncle tugged again. Finally, Jessie fell away from the shark.

[5]By then, Jessie's aunt and another person had entered the water. They carried Jessie to the sandy beach. Jessie's uncle still had the shark by the tail. The thought of letting go filled the uncle with **dread**. He knew that other people were still in the water. He had to get the shark out of the ocean. The shark twisted its body from side to side. The uncle held on tight.

[6]Jessie's aunt could see that her nephew was in terrible shape. His **condition** was very serious. The shark had torn out a hunk of Jessie's leg. Jessie's right arm was gone. The shark had bitten off the boy's arm 4 inches below the shoulder. Jessie was not breathing. His lips were white. The aunt tied beach towels around his arm and leg to try to stop the bleeding. She breathed into Jessie's mouth to save his life.

Will He Live?

[7]**Meanwhile**, as the others worked to save Jessie, the uncle dragged the shark to shore. Two park rangers arrived. One of them told everyone to stand back. Then he shot the shark

19

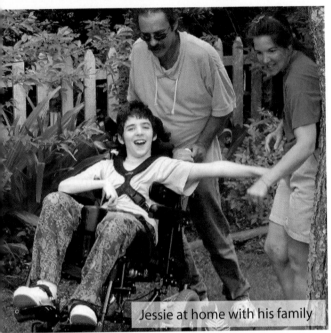
Jessie at home with his family

AP Images

four times in the head.

⁸The rangers opened the dead shark's mouth. They could see Jessie's arm deep inside. A lifeguard wrapped his own arm in a towel to protect it from the shark's teeth. Then he reached far into the shark's mouth. He pulled out Jessie's arm. The rangers then wrapped the arm in a towel and packed it in ice.

⁹By the time Jessie reached the hospital, he had lost almost all of his blood. He had been without enough oxygen for a long time. A nurse placed a needle in Jessie's arm and began sending blood into his body. Blood contains oxygen. This would give the oxygen that his body needed.

¹⁰The doctors were amazed that Jessie's arm had been so neatly torn off. They knew that shark bites are usually jagged. This would make it much easier to put the arm back on. Doctors worked for 11 hours. They sewed the muscle, blood vessels, and other parts back together. After this, they rubbed the arm to get the blood flowing. Then, they waited to see if blood would flow through Jessie's arm. Finally, the arm turned pink. The doctors smiled with **relief**. They felt much better. Blood was flowing again in Jessie's arm!

How Is He Now?

¹¹People all over the world sent cards and letters to Jessie and his family after the attack. Some people even sent money. After a month in the hospital, Jessie was finally able to go home. But 5 years after the attack, he is still recovering.

¹²Injuries to Jessie's arm and leg have now healed. But his brain was hurt, too. This injury was caused by his terrible blood loss. It continues to cause problems. Jessie still cannot walk on his own. He also has trouble talking. But he smiles and laughs with his brothers and sister. And he can move part of his wrist and some of the fingers on the arm that the shark almost got. All in all, people think of Jessie as a brave—and lucky—boy.

20

Helicopters to the Rescue

AP Images

Helicopter rescuers save two children from their flooded home after Hurricane Katrina.

¹**"P**lease help me!" The frightened woman sat alone on the steep roof of her house. Floodwaters rushed a few feet below her. A hurricane had brought the floods. The water had become polluted with garbage and oil.

²The woman had been **fearful** that she might die. *What if I fall off the roof? What if help doesn't come?* Help had come at last, though. A rescue helicopter circled above her. The noise it made filled the air.

³A rescuer stepped into a metal basket. Then the basket was lowered on a wire rope to the roof. The basket swung back and forth in the wind. "My husband is in the attic!" the woman shouted to the rescuer. "He is **unable** to walk." The woman pointed to a small hole in the roof. She had crawled onto the roof through the hole. The rescuer helped the woman into the basket. He signaled to another member of

21

the **crew** above. The basket was lifted upward. The woman held onto the basket. Finally, she was helped into the helicopter. Then the empty basket was sent back down to the roof.

[4]The rescuer **peered** through the hole in the roof. He could see the woman's husband. "Don't worry," he told the man. "I'll save you!" He made a larger hole in the roof with an ax. He used all his strength to pull the woman's husband onto the roof. Then he placed the husband in the basket. Soon the man joined his wife. The two were thankful to be alive.

[5]Later, the rescue team returned to the same neighborhood. They hoped to locate others in need. They soon would find more people trapped by the floods.

Emergency Rescues

[6]Helicopters have been used to save lives for 50 years. They have pulled people out of floodwaters. They have saved them from sinking ships. They have rescued people from tops of tall buildings that were on fire. They have reached people trapped at the bottom of cliffs.

[7]People are often lifted into a helicopter while it is in the air. This can look scary. But it saves time. The pilot doesn't have to find a place to land. Often there is just no place to land. That is true in a flood.

[8]Sometimes several people at a scene need to be helped. Who will be saved first? A rescuer decides which person will go first into the helicopter. This is usually the one most in need of medical help.

Dangerous Work

[9]Helicopter rescues are treacherous. A helicopter itself can be deadly. Its blades turn quickly. At full speed, they turn at more than 150 miles per hour. People have lost arms and legs from coming too near the spinning blades.

[10]Rescuers do their work while **dangling** from a helicopter. High winds can blow rescue workers into the side of a cliff. They might swing into electric wires while they are hanging by a rope. Sometimes there are even crashes on the way to or from a rescue.

Adastra/Getty

[11]Three main causes of crashes in helicopter rescues are:
- *Wind*—Helicopters are hard to control in strong winds. And heavy winds can send parts of roofs and other objects smashing into a helicopter.
- *Weather*—Rain, snow, and fog make it hard for pilots to see.
- *Wires*—Helicopters sometimes run into electric power wires. These wires can be hard to see. Trees, mountains, bridges, and steel towers are also dangers to pilots.

Saving Lives

[12]Helicopter rescue teams are trained to face these dangers. They practice many skills. They train to be fit and strong. Unlike many jobs, daring rescues are part of a normal day for these teams.

[13]One rescuer **relives** his memories of the work he did in Hurricane Katrina. Sometimes it is difficult to revisit these moments. He says that the people he rescued were picked up and dropped off quickly. There was not much time to talk to them. "But their handshakes, 'thumbs-up,' and big smiles let us know that they appreciate what we do. There's no better feeling than to save a life," he said.

Coast Guard Helicopter Rescues After Hurricane Katrina

U.S. Coast Guard helicopter teams helped rescue thousands of people from danger after Hurricane Katrina.

Total Lives Saved	6,470
Lives Saved by Helicopter Lifts	731
Number of Rescue Jobs	4,723
Number of Flight Hours	1,507

Robert Galbraith/Reuters/Corbis

Dying of HUNGER

[1] **"I**t's not fair!" Deion complained to Uncle Freddie. Deion was **arranging** dirt in neat rows in his uncle's backyard. Freddie wanted everything in good order for the vegetable garden. Uncle Freddie had helped Deion buy a bicycle. Deion was repaying his uncle by working in the garden all weekend.

[2] "What's not fair?" Uncle Freddie said. He stood up and stretched his back.

[3] "Some kids get burgers and fries for lunch," Deion said. "Their mothers buy fast food and then they drop it off at school. But I've got to eat cheese sandwiches almost every day. Do you think that's fair?"

[4] Uncle Freddie stared at Deion for a long time. Deion began to feel a little funny. "Come inside, boy," Uncle Freddie finally said. He gave a big sigh as he wiped dirt off his hands.

[5] Inside the house, Uncle Freddie told Deion to have a seat at the kitchen table. His voice was serious. *What's going on?* Deion wondered. He was starting to feel **nervous**. *Have I said something wrong?* It upset Deion to think that his uncle might be angry with him. Uncle Freddie went into his home office and returned with a picture. He handed the picture to Deion.

[6] Deion looked at the photo. It showed a small child lying in a woman's arms. Deion could not tell how old the child was. He couldn't tell whether it was a boy or a girl. The child looked very sick. Its eyes seemed huge. They were full of pain. Its ribs showed through the skin of its chest. The arms and legs of the child were as thin as pencils. "What's wrong with this baby?" Deion asked his uncle.

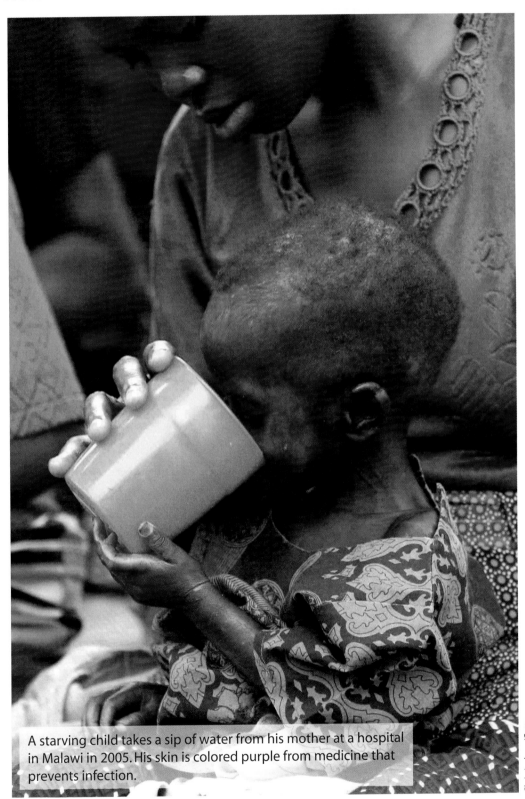

A starving child takes a sip of water from his mother at a hospital in Malawi in 2005. His skin is colored purple from medicine that prevents infection.

Chris Jackson/Getty

[7]"She's dying of hunger," Uncle Freddie said softly. "She lives in one of the poorest countries in Africa. Remember my friend Josie?"

[8]"The children's doctor?" Deion asked. He could not take his eyes off the photo.

[9]"That's right," Uncle Freddie said. "Josie took the picture. She just got back from Africa. She's trying to save these children. Other doctors are helping too."

[10]Uncle Freddie sat down next to Deion. He continued talking. "Josie saw another child die of hunger right before her eyes one day. She helped **bury** the little boy. The next day, seven children died."

[11]"This is terrible," Deion said. "Why can't they get enough food?"

[12]"Lots of reasons," Uncle Freddie said. He had a thoughtful look on his face. "These are very poor people. They don't have money to buy food. They have to grow it. Other countries send food. But sometimes these provisions don't reach the people who need it. The food gets lost or stolen. There are other reasons. At certain times of the year, there's not enough rain to grow crops.

And, insects destroy some crops."

[13]Uncle Freddie could see that Deion was curious. He explained more. "Josie says these times are called the 'hunger season.' The people are lucky if they get one meal a day. Sometimes that meal is a few leaves from a nearby tree or bush." Deion thought of the **aisles** of food in his town's supermarket.

[14]"I'm glad people like Josie are trying to help," Deion said. "I hate to think of anyone dying of hunger in Africa."

[15]"It's not just in Africa," Uncle Freddie said. "It happens in countries everywhere."

[16]Uncle Freddie looked out the kitchen window. Dark clouds boiled in the sky. "A **thunderstorm** is coming," Uncle Freddie said. "We won't be working in the garden this **afternoon**. Let's go to a movie instead. First, I'll fix us something to eat. What would you like?"

[17]Deion looked at his uncle. He still held the picture of the child in his hand. The photo felt as heavy as a big rock. "A cheese sandwich will be just fine," Deion answered.

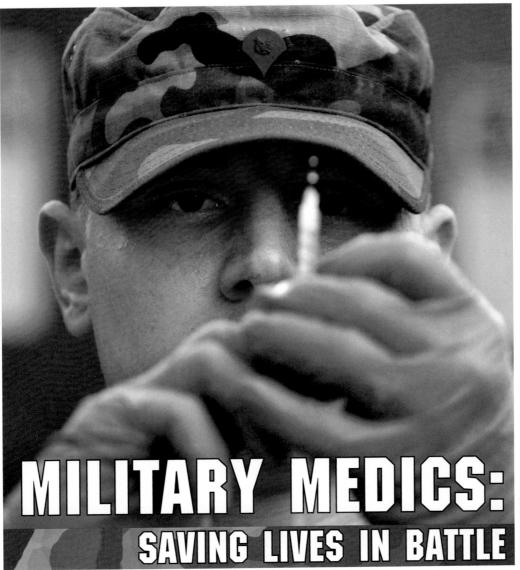

MILITARY MEDICS:
SAVING LIVES IN BATTLE

Paula Bronstein/Getty

¹You're riding in an Army truck on a dusty road when you hear a loud sound and see a flash of light. Suddenly you're lying in the road. You smell something unpleasant—like burned hair. You can't feel your right leg. Something warm is on your face. It's your own blood. You're frightened. *I don't want to die*, you think. Then everything goes dark.

²You wake up as two people are lifting you onto a stretcher. They're military medics. These people are trained to help wounded soldiers. They save lives in the middle of danger—while a war is going on around them. You feel thankful the medics have found you.

No Time to Waste

[3]Medics have to reach hurt soldiers fast. This is especially true when a wounded soldier is losing blood. Bomb blasts and gunshots can cause heavy bleeding, and a soldier will die if the bleeding is not stopped. Medics treat wounds on the battlefield if they can. If not, they will call for a helicopter. The helicopter will take the injured soldier to a hospital.

[4]Some medics travel with groups of soldiers and treat everything from the common cold to serious wounds. The medics travel with a truck of supplies, including blood. They are on the go with the soldiers nearly every day.

Who to Treat First?

[5]Medics decide which soldiers to treat first. They quickly look at each case. *Has the soldier lost an arm? Does she have serious burns?* Then they treat those who need the most immediate care. They have to act fast.

[6]Being a medic is a tough job. Not everybody could do such hard and dangerous work. The soldiers whose lives they save can never thank them enough.

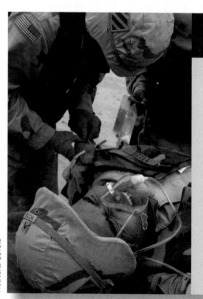

Reuters/Corbis

SAVING SOLDIERS' LIVES

Fewer U.S. soldiers are dying from wounds in wars. There are two main reasons. Military medics are trained better now. The medics also have improved ways of treating soldiers.

War	Years	Soldiers Who Died from Their Wounds
World War II	1930s and 40s	30%
Korean War	1950s	24%
Vietnam War	1960s and 70s	24%
Iraq Conflict	Early 2000	14%

I'm Hit!!

¹I heard the shots—pop! pop! pop!—like firecrackers. I remember dropping to the ground. I didn't feel any pain at first, but I felt something like warm water on my leg. Then I rolled over and saw the bleeding. "I've been hit!" I yelled to my buddies.

²Ansel was on the ground a few feet away. He wasn't moving. Roger and Ellis shouted that they were okay. They had ducked behind an

29

old stone wall. Both of them rushed out and dragged Ansel and me to safety behind the wall. That was really brave of them because they could've been killed.

[3]Ansel was badly hurt. He had been shot in the face and was having trouble breathing. Ellis began trying to help him.

[4]Roger took a special bandage out of his pack. There was a small hole in my pants leg where the bullet had gone in. Roger used the hole to rip open a bigger hole. He placed the bandage on my leg. The bandage stopped the bleeding. I was glad we had reviewed first-aid steps earlier that morning. We go over the steps many times each week.

[5]The medics got to us pretty fast. They put a rubber tube down Ansel's nose so he could breathe. They tried to make us as comfortable as they could. That was pretty thoughtful of them in the middle of all the danger.

[6]Soldiers who go into battle know there's a chance they might get hurt—or even killed. I'm lucky, and so was Ansel. We lived through it. And we didn't lose an arm or a leg. The Army will send me back into battle when my leg is healed. I just hope I stay safe.

WILD THING

- *What makes some animals so frightening?*
- *Why do animals behave in certain ways?*
- *In what ways do people and animals threaten each other?*

Invasion of the Snow Monkeys

¹In 1972, Japan gave 150 snow monkeys to scientists in Texas. The Texans didn't know how much trouble the monkeys could cause. The Japanese did though. They were giving away the monkeys because there were too many of them in Japan. Snow monkeys were invading homes, farms, and even temples!

Japan's Mischievous Monkeys

²The Japanese people loved snow monkeys. These animals had wise faces that made them look like little people. But there were too many monkeys and not enough food. That turned the sweet little monkeys into pests. They stripped fields and fruit trees bare. They sneaked into kitchens and took food from the table. Some stole candy from children! The monkeys were a big bother. Their mischief began to **disturb** people. A new law was passed to allow farmers to kill thousands of monkeys. People who cared about the monkeys were worried. They knew the snow monkeys needed **protection** or they would become extinct. They needed to go to a safe place. That's why scientists sent snow monkeys to a special ranch in Texas.

Monkey Trouble

[3]At first, the monkeys didn't like Texas. They missed their **natural** habitat. They longed for mountains and snow. They were hungry for their favorite plants. Texas was too hot and dry. Cactus and mesquite beans tasted odd. The monkeys were hungry and homesick. Some even died of **starvation**.

[4]In time, the monkeys adjusted to their new home with the scientists. They got used to the heat. They even liked their new diet. The troop grew to over 600! Soon the monkeys were up to their old tricks. At first, they would just **scamper** over the fence. Their quick escape let them search for food nearby. Then they learned to unlock gates. Next, they turned off the electric fence around the ranch. There was no stopping them after that. The monkeys ate neighbors' crops. They broke into

This snow monkey is curious about a scientist's camera.

Timothy Laman/National Geographic/Getty

barns and stole cattle feed. For fun, they climbed power poles and swung from electrical lines. They pulled antennas off cars. They made a mess in the cars. The cute little monkeys that ranchers had once liked were now unwanted pests.

A Better Home for the Snow Monkeys

[5]Some ranchers wanted to shoot the stray monkeys. Others just wanted the little troublemakers to stay home. They asked scientists at the monkey ranch to **construct** a better fence. But there was no money for a new fence. The monkeys continued to roam free. Then one day, four stray monkeys were shot. Everyone agreed that things had gone too far.

[6]Right away, animal lovers came to the rescue. Singer Wayne Newton held a benefit. Money poured in from all over. Soon, there were enough funds to build a wonderful preserve. A preserve is a place built to protect wildlife. The snow monkeys loved their new home. Today the monkeys still live at the Texas preserve. They share their home with baboons and green monkeys. As for Texas ranchers, they say the monkeys are great neighbors now that they've quit coming to visit!

GIANTS
of the Deep

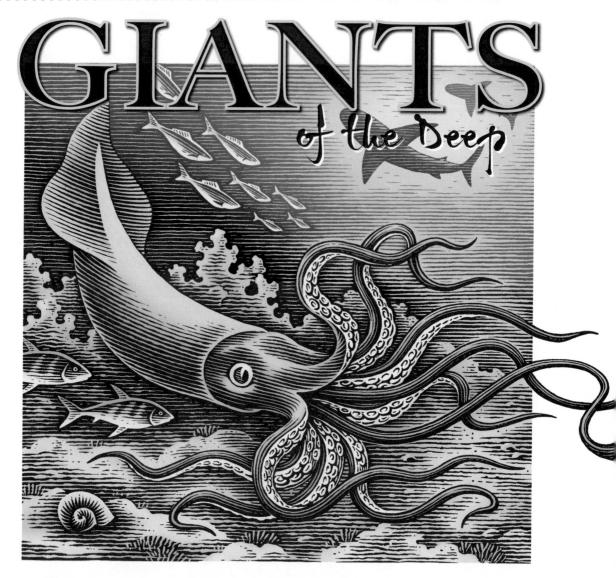

[1] **G**iant squids live a secret life. They stay away from **shallow** water. They prefer the deep, dark parts of the ocean. That makes them hard to find. Only about 50 have been spotted in the past 100 years! That's why we know little about these **mysterious** giants.

Super-Sized Squid

[2] The giant squid is a super-sized version of a small squid. Experts know this from studying dead ones that wash up on shore. A squid's body is a fleshy tube. It is pointed at the tail end. When the squid

swims, its tail goes first. Fins on the tail help the squid swim and turn. Near the open end of the tube is the squid's head. It has a large eye on each side. The squid's beak is just inside the tube. It is shaped like a parrot's beak. Eight legs are attached in a circle around the beak. There are also two tentacles. They are longer than the legs. Like the legs, they are covered with suckers. Each sucker is ringed with sharp hooks. These help the squid grab its **prey**. In all these ways, the giant squid is like a small squid. There is just one big difference. A giant squid is longer than 50 small squids placed end to end!

This 30-foot giant squid was caught off the coast of Tasmania.

William West/AFP/Getty

Get the BIG Picture!

[3]These descriptions may help you picture a giant squid:
- A giant squid can grow to be as long as a bus—or longer!
- The eyes of an adult giant squid are the size of basketballs. They are the largest eyes in the animal kingdom.
- A giant squid's tentacles could stretch from one side of a tennis court to the other.
- The beak of a giant squid is powerful enough to bite through steel cable.

The Giant in Battle

[4]Only one kind of whale, the sperm whale, is big enough to attack a giant squid. In fact, these **enormous** enemies prey on each other. One whaler said he watched a giant squid kill a 40-ton sperm whale. The

squid wrapped its tentacles around the whale. It squeezed until the whale was strangled. Then the squid **vanished**. It didn't stay around to eat the whale. Later, whalers pulled the whale from the sea. They discovered that the squid had not really won the fight. Its tentacles were still around the throat of the dead whale. The squid's head was inside the whale's belly! Both giants had fought to their deaths.

[5]People have told amazing tales of squid attacks. Many thought that sailors' stories about the giant squid were simply **legends**. Today we know that those old tales may be true. The stories told of a huge sea monster. It had many arms. It sank ships and ate sailors. Similar things have happened in modern times. In 1930, a Navy ship was attacked. A giant squid swam up and grabbed the ship in its tentacles. The squid squeezed, but it couldn't hold on to the smooth steel. The squid attacked again and again. At last, it got tired. It let go and slid under the ship. It died when it got caught in the ship's propellers. Sailors in World War II told of another attack. It was a terrible day. First, their ship sank. They survived, but then things got worse. A giant squid attacked them. Then came the worst of all. The squid ate one of their shipmates!

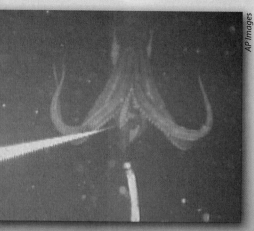

A remote-controlled camera captures a 26-foot giant squid. It was attacking bait off the coast of Japan's Bonin Islands in 2004.

AP Images

Chasing the Giant

[6]In September 2004, a live squid was photographed for the first time. For years, experts had tried to track down a live giant squid. Two scientists from Japan were the ones who finally did. The squid was in a very deep part of the ocean. The scientists used bait to attract the squid. When it came near, they took hundreds of pictures. The pictures showed that this squid was an active hunter. They showed just how the squid made its attack. But scientists have many questions that the pictures did not answer. It may be a long time before they can study a giant squid again. For now, the giant squid still lives its secret life!

36

The Komodo Dragon

[1]The Komodo dragon is a frightening creature. It is a lot like the **scary** dragons in fairy tales, but it is real. It lives today on the small island called Komodo. The beasts in fairy tales were huge, scaly lizards. They breathed fire and ate people. Everyone was afraid of them. The Komodo dragon is a huge, scaly lizard too. It can get as big as 10 feet long. And though this dragon doesn't breathe fire, its bite is deadly. It is a powerful hunter. It preys on animals as big as water buffalo. Many say that it eats humans too. All creatures are afraid when they know the Komodo is near!

Dragon Tales

[2]Komodo dragons are real, but many stories about them are not. One dragon story

dates back hundreds of years. The **ancient** story tells why the dragons eat outsiders but not people on the island. According to the **myth**, a spirit woman came to Komodo Island. She gave birth to twins. One was a Komodo dragon. The other was a human child. The dragon went to live in the wild. The human twin became the father of the island people. Because they wanted to care for their brothers, the islanders set out meat for the dragons. In return, the dragons didn't harm them. Other stories were spread by sailors who stopped at the island. Some told of huge land crocodiles. Others said there were dragons 20 feet long. There were even stories about monsters that exhaled steam.

The Look of a Monster

[3]A Komodo dragon's looks make it easy to see how all the wild tales got started. It looks like a cousin of the dinosaurs. The dragon is the largest lizard in the world. It has a thick, strong body. It is covered in scaly gray skin. Around the dragon's neck, the skin is loose and wrinkled. Its legs are bowed, and its feet are webbed. Long, sharp claws and teeth make it clear that the dragon is a serious predator. The dragon's face looks serious too. Small, dark eyes are set deep in the dragon's skull. Its wide mouth curves down. It looks like an angry frown. A long, yellow tongue flicks in and out of the dragon's mouth. It makes it look as if the dragon is breathing fire!

Feeding the Beast

[4]When a Komodo dragon gets hungry, it follows its tongue. The tongue has special sensors. They help the dragon smell its prey. To find dead meat, the dragon goes for a walk. As it walks, the dragon shifts its body sluggishly from side to side. It swings its head right and left. With each step, the dragon tests the air. It flicks its tongue in and out. The tongue picks up smells in the air. It can smell dead meat 2 miles away! The tongue carries the smells into the dragon's mouth. That sends a message to the brain. It tells the brain what smell is in the air. It also tells the direction from which smell is coming. If the smell is rotting meat, the dragon turns and moves toward it. Its tongue helps the dragon track the smell. When the dragon finds the dead animal, other dragons may be eating it. The dragon will join them. Komodo dragons live alone, but they share their meals.

[5]To hunt for live prey, the dragon stays in one place. It finds a hiding place and waits. The dragon flicks its tongue. It waits and watches. It is hungry for big animals like deer, wild pigs, and even horses. When prey comes near, the dragon begins a **savage** attack. It runs at full speed and knocks its victim down. The dragon opens its mouth wide. Long, jagged teeth sink into the animal's flesh. A bad smell fills the air. It comes from deadly germs in the dragon's mouth. The germs come from all the rotten meat the dragon eats. Once the animal is bitten, it is **doomed**. It cannot **avoid** death. If it escapes, the germs from the bite will kill it later. It will rot, and the dragon will find it. If the animal can't escape, the dragon will rip it to pieces. Either way, the animal will end up between the dragon's teeth. It has met the killer that never loses!

KOMODO DRAGON MAX FACTS

Maximum Body Length	10 feet
Maximum Body Weight	350 pounds
Maximum Life Span	50 years
Maximum Speed	12 miles per hour
Maximum Distance for Seeing Prey	1,000 feet away

Pot-Bellied Hero

[1]Lulu seemed like an ordinary pot-bellied pig. Like most piglets, she was cute, playful, and weighed about 4 pounds. She loved to eat, as most pot-bellied pigs do. She grew quickly. By her first birthday, Lulu weighed 150 pounds! But she was still a fun and loving pet. Lulu's owners, the Altmans, thought she was wonderful no matter how big she got. They just kept making the doggy door bigger so Lulu could get through it. Little did they know how vital that doggy door was. It was the door that would help Lulu save a life!

[2]The big emergency happened on August 4, 1998. Mrs. Altman suddenly collapsed on the floor. She was having a heart attack! She knew she needed help fast. Mrs. Altman managed to reach an alarm clock and throw it through a window. Her husband was away fishing, but she hoped that someone would hear the crash. By this time, Bear, the family dog, and Lulu were growing **anxious**. They could tell something was wrong. Bear barked and barked. Lulu came near Mrs. Altman and began to make a crying noise.

[3]No one heard the crash of the breaking window. Mrs. Altman tried calling for help. That's when Lulu stopped crying and took charge. She went to the doggy door and pushed her head and front legs through to the outside. Then something stopped her. It was the **bulge** around her middle! It seemed Lulu's stomach had grown too big for the doggy door again. But Lulu didn't give up. She tugged and pulled and squeezed. At last, her great belly popped through the doggy door. She squirmed until her **hind** end came through too. Then Lulu hurried toward the gate.

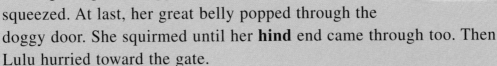

[4]Lulu had never left the yard by herself before. But she knew help was outside the gate. She had seen cars and people out there. So Lulu figured out how to open the gate. Then she trotted down to the street. Lulu looked at the passing cars. People waved and pointed, but no one stopped. How could she get them to help her?

[5]Lulu was worried about her owner. She went back to the house.

The big pig squeezed back through the doggy door. She found Mrs. Altman still on the floor. After checking on her, Lulu returned to the street. She tried to get drivers to stop, but she had no luck. Lulu kept checking on her owner. She went back and forth between the house and the street several times. Each time Lulu squeezed through the dog door, her belly got more scraped and raw.

Larry Lettera/Camera One

Lulu receives the Trooper Award from the president of the American Society for the Prevention of Cruelty to Animals.

⁶Finally, Lulu tried something new. She quit standing at the side of the road. Instead, she trotted into the street and lay down in front of the cars. That was hard to ignore! People slowed down and stared. One man stopped, but he couldn't tell what kind of animal Lulu was. He was afraid of her so he drove on. At last, one driver noticed Lulu's bleeding belly. The kind man stopped and got out of his car. Lulu immediately jumped up and ran to him. She tried to make him understand what she needed. Lulu **coaxed** the man to follow her. She looked back at him again and again as she moved toward the house.

⁷The man followed Lulu. At the house, he called out that the bleeding pig needed help. Mrs. Altman called back that she needed help too. The man phoned for an ambulance right away. In minutes, emergency workers arrived. They carried Mrs. Altman out on a stretcher. Lulu tried to follow them into the ambulance. Emergency workers had to push Lulu back and let her know that her job was done.

⁸Mrs. Altman was taken to a hospital where she had open heart surgery. Doctors explained to her just how **fortunate** she was. They said she was just minutes from death when help arrived. Mrs. Altman knows that Lulu saved her life. That **knowledge** makes her love her pudgy pet more than ever. She admits Lulu now gets more jelly doughnuts than most pigs do. But, clearly, Lulu is no ordinary pig!

Africa's Deadly Snakes

[1]Many deadly snakes hide in the wilds of Africa. Green snakes coil around tree branches. They disappear among the leaves. Spotted snakes hide on the forest floor. Their markings blend with the dried leaves and dirt. Some snakes hide in rock piles. Others dig their way into termite mounds. If people come near, most of these snakes stay hidden. They would rather not attack humans. Still, when threatened, many can harm or kill a person.

The Cobra

[2]African cobras hunt at night. They eat rats and other small animals. They also will attack large animals that threaten them. Cobras hide in animal dens or rock piles. They wait for prey to come near. To attack, a cobra lifts the front part of its body straight up. Then it opens a hood behind its head. It makes the cobra look bigger and scarier. Finally, it strikes. The cobra throws the lifted part of its body at its target. Then it bites its victim. When the cobra bites, poison squirts from its fangs. The poison goes into the nerves of the victim. That paralyzes the animal. It will have trouble breathing. Its heart may fail too. People who are bitten by cobras usually don't die, but they suffer terrible pain.

[3]The spitting cobra has an unusual skill. It can spit poison as far as 10 feet! This cobra's fangs work like squirt guns. Poison is squeezed into the fangs. Then it is forced out through tiny holes in the fangs.

The force sends drops of poison shooting through the air.

[4]The spitting cobra spits to defend itself. It has great aim. It shoots the poison right at its victim's eyes. The poison is very harmful to people. In some cases, people have been left blind for life!

The Black Mamba

[5]The most feared snake in Africa is the black mamba. It is mean and deadly. It is the fastest land snake in the world. A mamba on the run is quite a sight. It holds its head and the front of its body off the ground as it races along. The mamba can go 12 miles per hour!

[6]The black mamba lives in a rock pile, animal den, or termite mound. Like the cobra, it jumps out when prey comes near. It strikes at anything that moves. It even grabs birds out of the air!

[7]The black mamba is named for its scary mouth. It is purple and black inside. The mamba uses its mouth to scare away attackers. If a large animal comes near, the mamba lunges with its mouth open. If that doesn't work, the mamba strikes. It bites the animal again and again. Its poison is always deadly. It kills small animals in minutes. Large animals die within hours.

The Python

[8]Pythons are much bigger than cobras or black mambas. Some grow longer than 25 feet. They can weigh 250 pounds! Pythons don't have a hood or a black mouth to frighten enemies. Their size alone scares other animals away. They are the biggest snakes in Africa.

[9]A python can find prey that other snakes can't see. It has sensors that find heat. They lead the python to where a warm-blooded animal is hiding. The python grabs the animal in its teeth. But the python doesn't have poisonous fangs. It kills by squeezing. First, it coils around its prey. Then it squeezes so hard that the animal can't breathe. In minutes, the python's victim dies. Then the great snake opens its jaws wide. It swallows the animal whole. The python can eat large animals this way. It can even eat a whole person!

[10]It is no wonder that people fear Africa's deadly snakes!

BEATING THE ODDS

- What is athletic success?
- In what ways have athletes beat the odds to succeed?
- How can we overcome challenges?

The **Flying** Tomato

Shaun White competes at the 2006 Winter Olympic Games in Turin, Italy.

46

¹**S**nowboard champ Shaun White was born with a heart problem. It was a difficult problem to **overcome**. Shaun needed two operations before his first birthday. The operations left a 6-inch scar on his chest. But they fixed his heart problem. Even at this very young age, Shaun proved he could beat the odds.

²Shaun got on a snowboard for the first time when he was only 6 years old. His mom talked him into trying the snowboard. She hoped that it would keep him from skiing. "He was crazy on skis," his mom says. She thought that maybe on a snowboard he would sit down and go slow. Her plan didn't work. Shaun was just as crazy on the snowboard. He was doing jumps by the end of his first day on the board.

A Family Affair

³The White family lived in San Diego, where it almost never snows. Every weekend though, the family drove to the nearby mountains to find snow. Shaun, his brother Jesse, and his sister Kari would snowboard all day. At first, the Whites snowboarded for **pleasure**. They just had fun. Nobody worried about who was the best. But everyone could see that Shaun had a real aptitude for the sport.

⁴Soon Shaun began entering snowboarding contests. For 5 years, he won almost every **competition** he entered. By the time he was 13 years old, Shaun had become a professional **snowboarder**. "I wanted to be challenged," he says. There was also the promise of great wealth. A top snowboarder can earn a million dollars a year. Before long, Shaun was winning professional titles. Then he set his sights on the Olympics.

Triumph at the Olympics

⁵Shaun had to overcome problems just to get to the Olympics. First, he had to make the team. He tried in 2002, but he missed out by less than one point. Then Shaun hurt his knee. He spent months doing painful exercises every day. These **daily** workouts made his knee

stronger than ever. The hard work paid off when Shaun made the 2006 United States Olympic team.

⁶On his first run, Shaun fell during a landing. "I was so mad at myself," Shaun says. The fall left Shaun in seventh place. He had to finish in the top six to have a chance at the gold medal. On his second run, Shaun posted the best score of the day. He had made it to the finals.

⁷The dry mountain air gave Shaun a nosebleed just before the finals. Despite that, Shaun performed better than ever. In his first run, he earned a score that nobody could beat. Shaun had won a gold medal. "It hits you the next day," Shaun says. "You're like, 'Wow, did that seriously just happen?'"

⁸Now Shaun is one famous guy. His curly red hair draws attention everywhere he goes. Television hosts beg him to appear on their shows. Everyone in the sport knows who he is. But **fame** hasn't changed Shaun. He's still the same kid who loved snowboarding with his family. "This is the best year of my life," Shaun says. "I'm so happy my whole family's here. I know I won't have this again. It's amazing. Everybody's having such a good time."

2006 Winter Olympics Men's Halfpipe Snowboarding Results

Award	Name/Country	Best Score
Gold Medal	Shaun White/USA	46.8
Silver Medal	Danny Kass/USA	44.0
Bronze Medal	Markku Koski/Finland	41.5

Getty

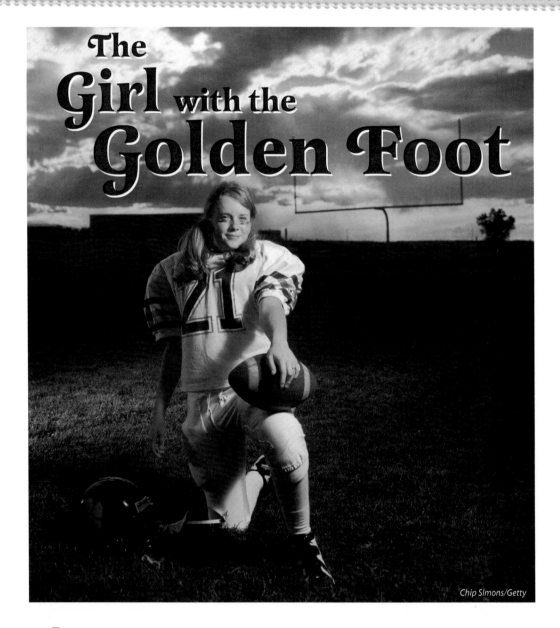

The Girl with the Golden Foot

Chip Slmons/Getty

¹**E**verything around Dayna seemed to slow down and go quiet at these moments. It was as if she were underwater. Dayna did not feel nervous. She knew exactly what to do: *Line up the soccer ball. Turn the foot. Swing the leg back and...THUNK!*

²As soon as the ball punched the net, sound returned to Dayna's ears. Her teammates were whooping for joy. A cheer was rising from the **audience** in the stands. "*Day-NUH, Day-NUH!*" Dayna beamed with relief and pleasure. The ball had gone just where she'd aimed it.

³At school the next day, Ms. Lopez called Dayna to her desk after class. "Coach Evans wants to speak to you," she said. "He's at the track." Dayna was mystified. *Why would the football coach want to talk to me?* She put her notebook in her backpack and went out to the track.

⁴A dozen boys were jogging around the track. Coach Evans stood in the grassy middle of the oval, his arms folded across his chest. He saw Dayna approaching and **hustled** across the track to meet her. "There's the girl with the golden foot!" he said. Dayna felt a little embarrassed.

⁵"How'd you learn to kick that way, with the top inside part of your foot?" the coach asked her.

⁶"I don't know," Dayna said. "I just started doing it, and it felt right."

⁷"I'll tell you what," began the coach, crossing his arms again. "We could use a player with your kicking skills on the football team. How about trying out to be our kicker?"

⁸That night, Dayna told her parents about the coach's invitation. "I'm going to the tryout next Saturday morning!" she said, amazed at herself. Her parents smiled. They offered to come to the tryout if she wanted them to.

⁹Later, Dayna went to her friend Mia's house to tell her the news. "You can't try out for the football team as a girl!" said Mia with a look of horror. "You'll have to **disguise** yourself as a guy. At least you'll have to act more like a guy. Otherwise,

you'll be teased to death." Dayna tried to argue. But Mia was persistent in her point of view.

[10]"Here's what you have to do," Mia began. "First, lower your voice a little. Then try **strutting** instead of walking like a girl." Mia demonstrated the walk. "And try to look tougher. Look like you'd punch somebody out if they tried to mess with you." Mia squinted her eyes to show toughness. "Pay attention to the little things," Mia continued. "For instance, wipe your nose with your sleeve. And don't forget to spit! Spitting is very important." Then Mia made Dayna practice all of these.

[11]Dayna's father borrowed a football. He helped Dayna practice kicking the ball in her backyard. She **adapted** easily to kicking a football. On Saturday, Dayna went to the tryout alone. She didn't want her parents to see her new way of acting.

[12]Coach Evans and the assistant coaches were at the field when Dayna arrived. So were a couple of football players, including Dayna's friend Ron. "Ready to begin?" Coach Evans asked Dayna.

[13]"Yup," Dayna replied in a low voice. She squinted her eyes. Ron looked curiously at Dayna. Coach had Ron hold the football for Dayna to kick. Dayna got a small running start. Then she kicked the ball. WHUNK! It went high and far.

[14]"Great kick!" said the coach.

[15]"Thanks!" said Dayna in her lower voice. She used her sleeve to wipe her nose before taking the next kick. She was trying to work up some spit when Ron took her aside.

[16]"You're acting funny," he whispered.

[17]"I'm just trying to fit in with the other players," Dayna whispered back.

[18]"You'll never fit in if you keep acting so weird," Ron told her. "Just be who you are. That's good enough. The team would love to have you as our kicker." Dayna took a deep breath. She thanked Ron. She was very glad she didn't have to spit.

[19]Dayna thought she looked a little funny in a football uniform. But she soon became **accustomed** to wearing it. No one on the team teased her about the way she looked or acted.

[20]On the night of the team's first game of the season, Dayna stood on the field, ready for the kickoff. The air felt electric. The stands were full. Dayna was eager for the game to begin. As she prepared to kick the ball, everything seemed to be in slow motion. Dayna was not nervous. She knew exactly what to do.

A Dream that Came True

AP Images

[1]Jason McElwain was an important member of his high school basketball team. But Jason didn't wear a uniform with a number. He wore a white shirt and a black tie. Jason was team manager of the Greece Athena Trojans in Rochester, New York. As manager, he did a little bit of everything. He helped keep score. He ran the clock. And he added a little something extra. "He's a cool kid," one of his teammates said. "He brings humor and life to the team." Jason loved being team manager. But he dreamed of something more. Like many kids his age, Jason wanted to be a basketball star. But would he ever get a chance to play in a real game?

Overcoming Autism

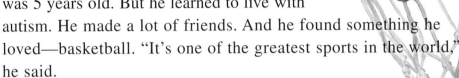

[2]Jason had a disorder called autism. The disorder made it hard for him to **interact** with others. Jason didn't even speak until he was 5 years old. But he learned to live with autism. He made a lot of friends. And he found something he loved—basketball. "It's one of the greatest sports in the world," he said.

[3]Jason was too small for the junior varsity team. So he took the job of team manager. Later, he took the same job with the varsity team. "Jason is an outstanding manager," said Coach Jim Johnson. "He's such a great help and is well liked by everyone on the team."

Put Me In, Coach

[4]In February 2006, Coach told Jason to put on a team uniform for the last game of the season. Coach said he would **attempt** to put Jason in the game. He would try, but he couldn't make any promises. It was an important game for the Trojans. They had to win to make the state basketball playoffs.

[5]Trojan fans chanted Jason's name. Some even waved pictures of Jason. As the Trojans built up a big lead, the fans shouted louder for Jason. With 4 minutes left, Coach put Jason in the game. As soon as the Trojans got the ball, a teammate passed it to Jason. Fans yelled for him to shoot. So he did. But his first shot was horrible. The ball didn't even touch the rim of the basket. Then he missed another shot. Coach wondered if he would **regret** his decision to let Jason play. But Jason's dad didn't share Coach's doubts. "The thing about Jason is he isn't afraid of anything," David McElwain said. "He doesn't care what people think about him. He is his own person."

Basket After Basket

[6]Jason's teammates gave him the ball again. This time he would not let his dream be **derailed**. His shot hit the basket. The crowd went crazy!

He quickly made another basket and then another. Once Jason started making shots, his **nervousness** disappeared. It seemed as if he couldn't miss the basket. "It was like a big old bucket, and I was just hitting them like they were free throws," Jason said. "I just felt relaxed."

⁷By the time the last seconds ticked off the clock, Jason had scored 20 points in just 4 minutes. "I was really hotter than a pistol," Jason said.

⁸After the game, his teammates carried him off the court on their shoulders. The crowd cheered wildly. "I've coached a lot of wonderful kids," Coach said, "but I've never experienced such a thrill."

President Bush and Jason McElwain walk toward reporters a month after Jason's amazing performance.

Living the Dream

⁹Jason's amazing performance was caught on videotape by a fan. Soon the video was being shown on national news and sports shows. The phone at Jason's house rang and rang. Reporters wanted to talk to him about his amazing game. Other people wanted to make a movie about Jason's big game. When he went outside, people crowded around him. They asked for his autograph. "I feel like a celebrity," Jason said.

¹⁰Because Jason had played only one game, he wasn't allowed to participate in the state championship. But that didn't bother Jason. He preferred to **concentrate** on team goals. "I just want to win as a team, not individually," he said. Jason got his wish. The Trojans won the championship. At that game, Jason was back in his shirt and tie, handing out towels and water bottles.

¹¹"I'm not really that different," Jason said. "I don't really care about the autistic situation, really. It's just the way I am. The advice I'd give to autistic people is just keep working. Just keep dreaming. You'll get your chance, and you'll do it." Jason certainly did.

Jesse Owens competes at the 1936 Olympic Games in Berlin, Germany.

Getty

A Hero
On and Off the Track

[1]Jesse Owens never had it easy. He grew up very poor. On top of that, he was often sick. And when he wasn't sick, he had to work. His parents needed help paying for food and clothes. As a 7-year-old, Jesse picked 100 pounds of cotton a day. He did anything he could to bring in a little extra money.

[2]But one thing did come easy to Jesse—running. Jesse ran with great style and **grace**. With his smooth movements, Jesse made running look easy. One day in gym class, the students ran the 60-yard dash. Jesse

blew everyone away. He was asked to join the track team. After setting a lot of high school records, Jesse went to college. Again, he stood out on the track team. He won almost every event he entered. At one track meet, Jesse broke three records and tied another in just 45 minutes. His skills earned him a place on the 1936 United States Olympic team.

Jesse's Olympic Moment

[3]In 1936, the summer Olympic games were held in Germany. At that time, Adolf Hitler ruled Germany. Hitler believed that Germans were better than other people, especially black people like Jesse. Hitler was sure that Germans would dominate in all the big events. But Jesse proved him wrong.

[4]Jesse started out by easily winning the 100-meter dash. The next day, he competed in the long jump. That's where he ran into problems. Jesse had three chances to jump far enough to make the finals. He stepped on the starting line in his first two tries. Those jumps didn't count. Jesse's last jump was of **immense** importance. Everything was riding on it. If he stepped on the line again, he would not make the finals.

[5]Before Jesse's final jump, a tall man introduced himself. His name was Luz Long. He was Germany's best long jumper. Luz **advised** Owens to place a towel just before the takeoff line. Then he could jump from behind the towel. That way he would not step on the line again. Luz's suggestion worked. Jesse made the finals. And he was determined to win. "I decided I wasn't going to come down," he said. "I was going to fly. I was going to stay up in the air forever."

[6]Jesse's jump was good enough for first place. At the awards ceremony, he **clenched** his second gold medal tightly in his fist. And his winning didn't stop there. Before the Olympic Games were over, Jesse had won four gold medals. He also had a new friend in Luz Long. "It took a lot of courage for him to befriend me in front of Hitler," Jesse said.

Coming Home

[7]Jesse was received as a hero when he returned home. But he still faced problems. In the 1930s, black people often were not treated fairly. Once, a dinner was held in Jesse's honor at a big hotel. Black people were not allowed to use the regular elevator. Jesse had to ride the freight elevator.

56

[8]Discrimination also kept Jesse from making money. Everyone wanted to shake his hand or slap his back, "but no one was going to offer me a job," Jesse said. One way he made money was by racing people. He usually gave them a head start. Sometimes he even raced people on motorcycles. Jesse also worked as a band leader, though he couldn't play an instrument. "I'd just stand up front and announce the numbers," Jesse said. "They had me sing a little, but that was a horrible mistake." Later, he made money by delivering speeches. He also started a business that helped companies with their public image.

A Lasting Legacy

[9]The Olympics didn't make Jesse rich. They made him famous, though. Honors and awards came from all over the world. A street and a school in Germany were named after him. But Jesse never forgot where he came from. He used his fame to help poor kids. He started youth sports programs. Jesse also offered young people his **sincere** advice. "We all have dreams," Jesse would tell them.

"In order to make dreams come into reality, it takes an awful lot of **determination**, dedication, self-discipline, and effort." The kids knew Jesse meant what he said. All they had to do was look at the way he lived his life.

[10]Jesse Owens faced plenty of problems in his life. But he refused to let his problems prevent him from becoming a champion. And through it all, he kept a positive attitude. "Find the good," Jesse said. "It's all around you."

AFP/Getty

Olympic athletes Luz Long and Jesse Owens

57

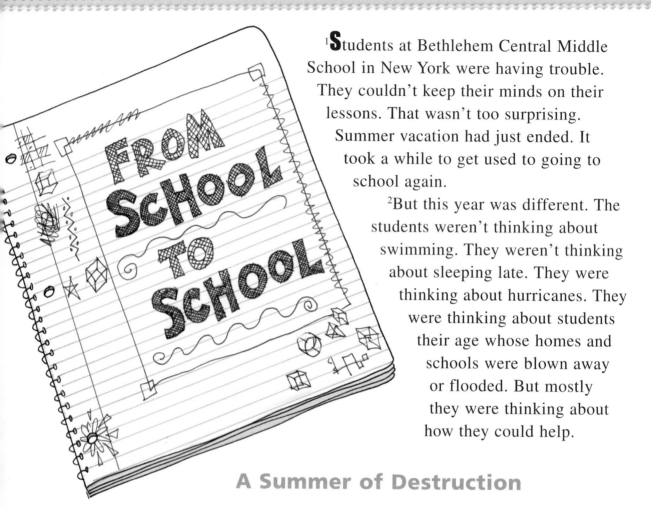

¹**S**tudents at Bethlehem Central Middle School in New York were having trouble. They couldn't keep their minds on their lessons. That wasn't too surprising. Summer vacation had just ended. It took a while to get used to going to school again.

²But this year was different. The students weren't thinking about swimming. They weren't thinking about sleeping late. They were thinking about hurricanes. They were thinking about students their age whose homes and schools were blown away or flooded. But mostly they were thinking about how they could help.

A Summer of Destruction

³That summer, Hurricane Katrina had hit the Gulf Coast. Many cities were badly damaged. Thousands of people left the area. Many could not return. Their homes had been destroyed. Some of them settled in new cities. These cities welcomed them. But there was a problem. Some schools in the new cities were short of money.

⁴Bethlehem students figured out how to help. They would raise money to help one school. Teacher Imran Abbasi helped plan the project. "Everybody wanted to do something after Katrina," he said. "Being a school, we wanted to help a school." They picked Robert Lewis Middle School in Natchez, Mississippi. "Robert Lewis was a school in need to begin with, even before taking in these extra kids," Abbasi said.

Raising the Money

[5]Each class came up with a way to raise money. Some of the students held a fun run. Students asked people to give money for each runner who finished. That helped the runners keep going when they got tired. Teachers raised money with a basketball game. But the students and teachers didn't just use their athletic skills. They also used their minds. They raised money with a read-a-thon. People gave money for each book a student read. Some students even gave their own money.

[6]Robert Lewis Middle School had asked for $2,000. But Bethlehem students raised more than $7,000. They used the extra money to buy school supplies. Bethlehem students stuffed the supplies into more than 70 backpacks. The backpacks and supplies would go to the new students in Natchez. They also collected boxes and boxes of books and teacher supplies.

Getting in on the Act

[7]Other Bethlehem schools helped, too. The high school raised more than $8,300. All five elementary schools did their share. More than 140 students and parents from one school raised money with their legs. They ran in either a ½-mile run or a 1-mile run. The runs raised more than $1,035.

[8]Another school held a "Dollar Dash." Students could enter the race by giving a dollar. Every student in the school raced. "The main goal was to raise money for hurricane relief," teacher Carol Walts said. "But it was great to have students and staff working together and supporting each other in a healthy, fun activity." One school raised money with a coin drive. Another gave

more than 2,000 books. Students at one school collected toys. Then they sold the toys to raise money.

Delivering the Goods

[9]On December 1, two vans were loaded with supplies. Six teachers drove for 24 hours from New York to Mississippi. When they arrived, they delivered the money and supplies. Then they took 32 of the new students shopping. They used the extra money they had raised. "Some of these kids arrived in Natchez with nothing," Abbasi said. "The state provided them with school uniforms because they are required. But we're hoping to get them jackets, hats, and whatever else they need down there for the winter." One Natchez teacher said that her students were thrilled with the shopping trip.

[10]The students who were forced from their homes and schools still have a lot to overcome. But help from people like those in Bethlehem will make the students' lives better now.

Bethlehem Middle School Contributions

Amount Robert Lewis Middle School asked for	Amount Bethlehem Middle School raised	Amount left over for extra help
$2,000	$7,000	$5,000

FACT OR FICTION?

- *How can you tell what is real?*
- *Why might someone spread false information?*
- *Why do some people want to change their appearance?*

Urban Legends:
Today's Tall Tales

[1]**W**ait! Don't flush that toilet—not at halftime during the Super Bowl. What if everyone watching the game on TV flushes at the same time? Your city's water system will break down. That wouldn't be a pretty sight. And if this happens in New York City, look out! Hundreds of huge alligators will crawl out of the sewers onto the streets. You think these 'gators are big? Ha! They're not nearly as **enormous** as the 21-foot-long crocodile found in New Orleans after the hurricane.

[2]Before you repeat this information, you should know one thing. None of it is true. It's all the stuff of **legend**—urban legend, that is.

What Are Urban Legends?

[3]Chances are you've heard an urban legend from a friend. Or you may have read one in an e-mail. An urban legend is a story passed from person to person as truth. It can also be stated as a fact. *Alligators live in the sewers below New York City. An 8-foot woman was discovered hiding in a house in Nebraska.*

[4]These stories or "facts" have many of the same features. They are often unusual. They can be shocking. They can be funny. Some are based on true events. But by the time they become urban legends, they're mostly or completely untrue.

Where Do They Start?

[5]What are the sources of urban legends? It's hard to know where they start. They're told and retold by millions of people. They often change with each retelling. Some stories come and go. Others reappear after a few years, maybe with a new twist.

[6]Some people have tried to locate the sources of some urban legends. What have they found? "Most of these stories seem to come from nowhere," says one researcher. "It's **possible** that many of them begin as a way for someone to play a joke on a friend."

How Do They Spread?

[7]Urban legends travel quickly. Certain types travel especially fast. This includes stories about things we fear. *A rat was found in a soda can. Part of a finger was found in a bowl of chili.* Are the foods we buy unsafe to eat? Yikes! That's scary.

[8]We pass along these stories by word of mouth. These days, we often spread them through the Internet. A friend might e-mail an amazing story to you and 20 other friends. You read the story and **instantly** e-mail it to 20 more people. These stories can even appear on TV news programs or in newspapers.

Why Do People Pass Them Along?

[9]People of all cultures have spread urban legends for many years. Why? If they think a story is true, they may want to warn others. *Don't buy cans of soda! Don't eat chili!* They may

pass along a story because it **contains** an important lesson. Or they may spread an urban legend just because it's interesting or funny. Urban legends are good stories. And that's the main reason we pass them along. We like to tell good stories.

[10]We also like to think that strange things might be true. "This really happened!" a friend might say. Or, "This happened to a friend of a friend." We seldom check to see if the story is true.

[11]Speaking of stories, did you hear about the woman who had a spider's nest in her hair? She hardly ever washed her hair. The spider laid hundreds of eggs in it. The eggs hatched. When the woman combed her hair, the baby spiders began biting her. She died from the bites. No, really! It's true. It happened to a friend of a friend.

Can You Believe It?!

National Intruder

LEARN THE TRUTH

[1]Lydia told herself not to panic. After all, she'd faced scarier things than having to write a paper for class. There was the day she accidentally dropped her silver bracelet in the cafeteria trash can and had to pick through mounds of smelly garbage to find it. And a few weeks ago, she'd been alone in her house when a storm caused the lights to go out. Last summer, she was picking grapes with Aunt Elsa and got stung on the face by angry bees. Her nose and lips were unbelievably large for three days. "You look like some kind of weird fish!" her brother had said. Mando could be very impolite at times.

[2]So, why get so upset over a class paper? It was Friday afternoon. The paper was due on Monday. Lydia still hadn't chosen a topic. She

looked at the assignment sheet once again: *"Write about a real person—perhaps someone you admire. Or, write about an event that actually happened to you or someone else."* Then an idea came to her.

[3]"Mami!" Lydia called to her mother. "I'm going to the store. I'll be right back." At the supermarket, Lydia gazed at the magazine racks. One magazine caught her eye. It had a picture of her favorite movie star on the cover. Below the picture were these words written in large, fat letters: ***LEARN THE TRUTH ABOUT JUSTIN CASE AND HIS STRANGE CHILDHOOD!!*** Lydia now had a topic for her paper. She paid for the magazine and rushed home.

[4]At home, Lydia paged through the magazine, working her way to the article about Justin. It took her awhile to get there. She had to read about the scientist who developed a pill that makes people invisible. And about the pig born with a dog's head. And about the **discovery** of a live rat in a soda can.

[5]Lydia finally reached the story about Justin. She began to scribble some notes as she read.

[6]*Found in a hollow log in a forest. Raised by gypsies. Original name was a 22-letter word meaning "Turtle Face." Traveled the countryside. Danced and sang for money when he was a year old. Caught a* **horrible** *virus at age 2. After the terrible illness passed, could suddenly speak five languages. Learned to play the violin at age 3. Was sold to a farmer's family. Correctly guessed Earth's exact size at age 10. Preferred to sleep on the roof. Ate nothing but turnips for a whole year.*

[7]*This is amazing*, thought Lydia as she continued to read. *Wait until people hear this!* She hadn't known these facts about Justin's life. She kept making notes until she had enough information. Then she used the notes to begin writing her paper.

[8]Lydia grew more and more pleased with the way her story was developing. She had feared that the writing would be a struggle. *But this paper is practically writing itself*, she thought with a sense of **relief** and delight.

[9]Lydia wanted to read her paper to Mando, even though it was incomplete. After all, he too was an admirer of Justin. She found Mando in the backyard. He was repairing his skateboard. "Mando, listen to my paper," she said to her brother. "It's not finished, but you've just got to hear this. You won't believe it!"

[10]Mando put down his skateboard

and sat on an overturned crate. Lydia sat on the grass in front of him and read what she'd written so far. Then she looked up at Mando. "The students are going to fall out of their chairs when I read this to them!" she said excitely.

[11]"Yes, they'll fall out of their chairs," agreed Mando with a smile, "—laughing." Lydia look puzzled. "Lydia," Mando said gently. "All those things are lies. None of that is true." He **regretted** having to tell her this hard truth.

[12]"But I read it in the *National Intruder*," Lydia protested.

[13]"That magazine fabricates stories and publishes them as truth," Mando said. "You can't believe something just because it's in print."

[14]Lydia was disappointed. But she was glad that Mando had saved her from public embarrassment. From now on, she'd be more careful about believing what she read.

[15]*But now what'll I write about?* Lydia wondered. She had even less time to write her paper. She told herself not to panic. Another idea came to her. Lydia got a notebook and a pen. Then she sat down at the kitchen table. She began to write:

[16]*I once had the face of a strange fish. This is a true story. I know because it happened to me last summer. My Aunt Elsa and I went to her friend's farm to pick wild grapes . . .*

Is Seeing Believing?

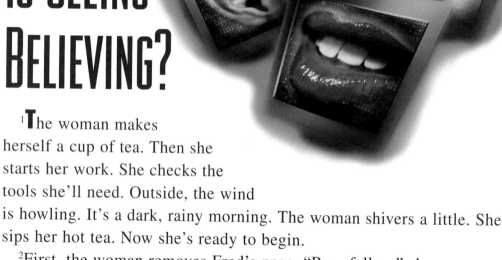

Mark Wiens/Getty

¹The woman makes herself a cup of tea. Then she starts her work. She checks the tools she'll need. Outside, the wind is howling. It's a dark, rainy morning. The woman shivers a little. She sips her hot tea. Now she's ready to begin.

²First, the woman removes Fred's nose. "Poor fellow," she says under her breath. The woman doesn't know the man's real name. But she thinks he looks like a Fred. She works for a minute. Then she goes to a certain place. It is where she has saved dozens of heads. She has collected both men's and women's heads. The woman studies some of the men's heads. "Aha!" she says finally. She has found just the right nose. It's smallish. It has a nice shape. She takes the nose from this face. She places it on Fred's face. "Much better!" she says. The woman is pleased with herself. Next, she **concentrates** on Fred's eyebrows. Too thick, she decides. She carefully shaves the brows. Now they are just the shape she wants.

Nobody's Perfect

³Is this a scene from a scary movie? Is the woman a mad killer? No, she's a type of artist. Her tools are in a computer program. She's using these tools to alter, or change, a picture of a man. His face looks too **ordinary**. The woman's job is to make the face look as perfect as possible. Today she will change Fred into a much more handsome man. Why? A company is paying her to do this. The company sells

68

men's hair products. The newer, more handsome Fred will show up in a magazine ad. The company hopes that "regular" men will buy its products so they can look as good as Fred.

⁴Most pictures that you see in magazines have been digitally edited. This means that someone has used a computer program to change the pictures. This is especially true in the world of fashion. Have you **admired** a model's perfectly shaped legs? Did you long to have her perfectly shaped lips? Did her perfect blue eyes take your breath away? An artist probably created most of this perfect beauty.

The Art of Artificial Photos

⁵Computers use a digital language of numbers. You easily can play with a picture when you change it into computer language. You can stretch it or twist it. You can add new parts to it. You can **arrange** parts in new ways. You can even take out parts you don't want.

⁶Artists can take the head of one person and put it on the body of another person. Are a model's ankles a little thick? Artists can make them look thinner. They can make a stomach look flatter or teeth look whiter. They can make lips thicker and hips narrower. They know how to make wrinkles **vanish** in seconds. Does the model in the photo have a zit on her forehead? Zap! It's gone.

Colin Hawkins/Getty

Fake Photos: What's the Harm?

⁷Is it wrong to change the pictures that appear in magazines? There's plenty wrong with it, say some researchers. They've studied the effects. These unreal pictures can affect the way people see themselves.

⁸Many of the people who look at popular magazines are teenagers. Some teens may not feel comfortable about their changing bodies. They see the perfect faces and bodies in the pictures. Then they compare these to their own faces and bodies. Some teens may feel pressure to look like the models. They think this will help them be accepted and liked

by their peers. Girls may try to make themselves too thin. Boys may overwork their muscles with weights. And, remember, the ads are to sell products. Many teens waste money on beauty products that don't deliver what they promise.

[9]A few companies are starting to use models that look more like real people in their ads. That's not what most people want, though. A magazine editor says, "People like to look at beautiful pictures of perfect people." She admits that her magazine changes most of the pictures it uses. Even the pictures of beautiful models? Especially those, she says. These pictures go through many changes. You wouldn't know many of the models if you saw them on the street, the editor says. Supermodel Cindy Crawford once said, "I wish I looked like Cindy Crawford." That should tell you a lot.

[10]We've been taught not to believe everything we read. We shouldn't believe everything we see either these days. That's especially true of the perfect faces and perfect bodies in magazine ads. The next time you see an ad that shows a handsome man, think about this. His amazing muscles, ideal nose, and neatly trimmed eyebrows were probably put together piece by piece like a beautiful puzzle.

Effects of Reading Fashion Magazines (Results of a Study of More Than 500 Girls)

	Read women's fashion magazines often	Read women's fashion magazines rarely
Girls who have dieted to lose weight, based on reading a magazine article	22%	13%
Girls who say that pictures in the magazines make them want to lose weight	57%	41%
Girls who say that pictures in magazines affect their idea of the perfect body shape	79%	59%

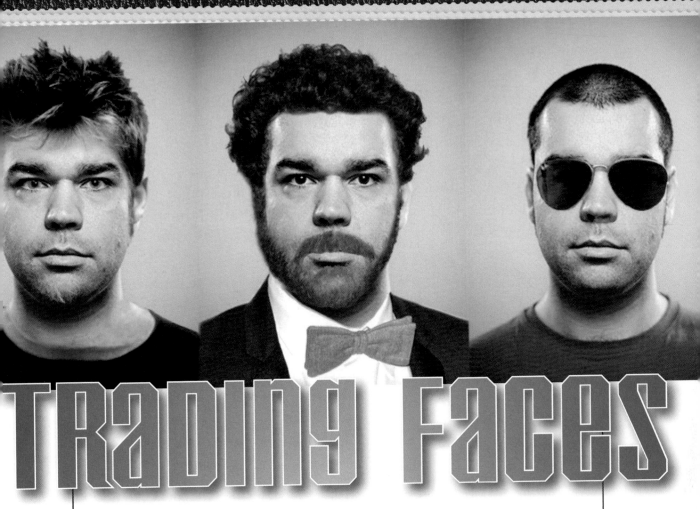

TRADING FACES

[1]**S**uppose you want to be very sneaky. You want to change your looks so that no one will recognize you—not even your mother. What changes would you make? Would you use makeup? How about a wig or a floppy hat? Would you add a bushy mustache maybe? How about a fake nose? You want to **avoid** drawing attention to yourself, though. The point is to keep from being noticed.

[2]Now, suppose that your life depends on how well you can change your appearance. This isn't a costume party or Halloween. It's your job. You're a spy for the United States government. You're changing your looks for a special **purpose**. It's to learn the secrets of another country. Spying is serious business. You could get in big trouble if people in the other country caught you spying on them.

Master Spy

[3]Tony Mendez was a master spy for 25 years. He worked for the CIA. The CIA helps keep the United States safe. Tony was hired because he was an artist. His first job at the CIA was to create false documents. These are special papers that give information about a person. They tell a person's name and address. It could be a driver's license or a birth certificate. Or, it might be a passport. These are **necessary** tools for spies who sneak into other countries.

Don Spiro/Getty

Might one of these people be in disguise?

[4]Tony began doing other jobs there after a few years. He used his skills as an artist to create **disguises** for himself and for other spies. He figured out ways to change a person's looks so that the person would not be recognized or even noticed. With a few tricks, he could change a spy into a college student or a house painter, for example.

[5]Tony was sent to other countries as a spy many times. He became a new person for each new job. He met people in these other countries. He learned secret information from them: *Was this country planning to attack another country? Was it making bombs?* The work was dangerous. Tony says he was often **nervous** about getting caught. Captured spies could be harmed or even killed.

[6]One important job Tony had was to sneak people out of other countries. These were often U.S. spies and their families. They were people who faced danger if they stayed in the country. Some were being held as prisoners. Tony had to plan a way to sneak them out. He once rescued a group of Americans by pretending to be a filmmaker.

Creating Disguises

[7]To change his looks, Tony used many of the same tricks used in the movies. He would put on a wig. He might add a mustache or a beard. He might put a fake skin mole on his face. The mole might even carry a

piece of spy equipment! He might put a gold cap on a tooth. He changed hairstyles. He made his hair color lighter or darker. Often a simple change could make a big difference. He might just put on a new pair of eyeglasses.

[8]These changes are only part of the art of fooling others, Tony says. A successful disguise uses "the whole body, not just the head." You need to be a good actor to fool people. You have to "imagine what you are and be that," he says. If you're trying to look like an old man, you have to *become* one.

[9]So, suppose Tony has used the tools of his trade to change your looks. Now you need to change other things. How about the way you talk? You must change your rate of speech. Slow it down or speed it up. You'll need to change the way you move, too. Do you have a certain way of walking that others—especially your mother—know well? Put a small rock in your shoe, Tony says. That will change your walk.

[10]Tony became the Chief of Disguise at the CIA during his years there. He married a woman who was also a spy, Jonna Mendez. Jonna was an expert at taking secret pictures.

Life After Spying

[11]Tony and Jonna no longer work for the CIA. They live on a large farm in Maryland. Tony is a full-time artist now. His paintings have won many awards. Jonna is also an artist. She's a photographer. The two have written books about their lives as spies. They give speeches. They also work with the International Spy Museum in Washington, D.C. It's a great place to learn more about spying. But we won't tell you about it here. You'll have to do a little investigating of your own to learn about it. But you won't need a disguise to do it.

¹**W**hich of these is not necessary if you want to run for president of the United States?
- You must be at least 35 years of age.
- You must be able to walk on your own.
- You must be a natural-born citizen of the United States.
- You must have lived in the United States for at least 14 years.

²Did you guess the second item on the list? You're right. No law says that you can't run for president if you cannot walk. It seems silly, in fact, to think that if you couldn't walk, you couldn't be president. What does that have to do with being a good leader? Why did one of our presidents try to hide the fact that he could not walk on his own?

Nothing to Hide

[3]Can you name the president? It might not be easy. Few pictures show him as he really was. He did not like to draw attention to his condition. He didn't want people to feel sorry for him. And he didn't want them to think that weakness in his legs meant that he would be a weak leader.

[4]Today, most people would not judge a person in this way. Many famous people have disabilities. They do not try to hide their conditions. These people include:

Adam Pretty/Getty

- Bob Dole, a U.S. senator who lost the use of his arm in battle
- Louise Sauvage, a wheelchair athlete who was born without the use of her legs
- Stephen Hawking, a scientist who is paralyzed by a disease
- Marlee Matlin, an actor who is deaf

Louise Sauvage of Australia in action

- Doug Heir, a wheelchair athlete and attorney who was paralyzed in a diving accident
- Itzhak Perlman, a violinist whose legs are paralyzed from polio

No Pictures, Please

[5]So who was the president? It's Franklin Delano Roosevelt. He was also known as FDR. He became the 32nd president of the United States in 1933. Twelve years earlier, he had developed polio. This disease affects the muscles. It caused Roosevelt to lose the use of his legs. He often used a wheelchair. He stood with the help of steel leg braces. Sometimes he used a cane. He tried many different ways of treating the disease. But he never again was able to walk on his own.

[6]Newspaper reporters did not take pictures of Roosevelt in a wheelchair. They did not show him being helped out of cars. Roosevelt developed his upper body so that it became very strong. He used his arms to balance on crutches. He held tightly onto the arms of people when he stood. This made it seem as though Roosevelt was able to stand and walk on his own. He did not want people to see how much he depended on others for help. Can you imagine a president doing this today?

The FDR Memorial in Washington, D.C.

Getty

[7]Roosevelt died in 1945. The fact that he could not walk did not keep him from leading the country for 12 years. In fact, he is remembered as a great president. He gave Americans hope during hard times.

The FDR Memorial

[8]In this country, we have honored our greatest presidents with monuments. Americans wanted to honor Roosevelt in some way. But this presented a problem. How would Roosevelt be shown in the monument? Would he be shown in a wheelchair? Many people who use wheelchairs said, "He must be shown as he really was. There's nothing wrong with that." Other people said, "Let's honor his wishes as they were when he was president. Don't show him in a wheelchair."

[9]The FDR Memorial opened in 1997. It tells the story of Roosevelt's 12 years as president. The memorial has four outdoor rooms. The path from room to room takes visitors past gentle waterfalls and huge stones. Roosevelt's words are carved on the stones. They include this famous statement: "The only thing we have to fear is fear itself." There are 10 sculptures of Roosevelt. Only one of them shows him sitting in a wheelchair. His monument is the first one designed so that people in wheelchairs can easily move through it.

BELOW THE SURFACE

- *Why is the ocean important to us?*
- *What can we learn from undersea exploration?*
- *Why might we live underwater?*

The Heart of the Sea

© Jeff Divine

Born to Surf

[1]**W**ould you like to spend your days riding the Hawaiian surf? That is exactly how Rell Sunn spent her whole life. All her time in the ocean paid off, too. She became one of the top woman surfers in the world.

[2]Shortly after Rell was born, she was given a middle name that means "Heart of the Sea" in Hawaiian. It was a good name for a girl who was diving and surfing before she even started kindergarten. She spent all day in the ocean. Instead of feeling **secure** by hugging a teddy bear at night, Rell slept snuggled up to her surfboard! It wasn't

1950	1954	1966	1975
Born on the island of Oahu	Began surfing and spear fishing	Won her first surfing competition	Founded the Women's Professional Surfing Association

long before she could fish well enough to bring dinner home for her family. First, she would **descend** deep into the water. Then, while she held her breath, she would spear fish and octopuses. She fished with a three-pronged spear. When she had enough fish, she would pile her catch onto her surfboard. Finally, she would paddle her load to shore.

[3]Young Rell showed no fear of sharks or powerful waves. The ocean was her playground. Rell believed that family members who had passed away all lived in the ocean. They would not let her drown or be hurt. It was no wonder she felt happy and secure in the sea. She was surrounded by her guardian angels!

© Jeff Divine

Teen Dreams

[4]During her teen years, Rell worked hard on her surfing skills. At age 14, she began competing. Two years later, she won her first surfing contest. Often, the competitions didn't have a division for women. That didn't stop Rell. She just competed against the men. She always made a good showing, too.

[5]Many of the world's best surfers competed at Makaha Beach near Rell's home. She listened to their stories of surfing big waves all around the world. The stories were **thrilling** to her. Her dream was to become a world-class surfer. There was one big problem though. The dream Rell had chosen was only for men. Women were not allowed in international contests.

Changing the World

[6]Rell realized there was no place for women on the world surf scene. But she didn't accept the way things were. Rell decided to change the

1976	1977	1982	1996	1998
Organized the first annual children's surfing contest	Became Hawaii's first woman lifeguard	Ranked number 1 woman on longboard	Inducted into Surfing Walk of Fame	Died of cancer; ashes scattered on the ocean

world. In the 1970s, she worked with other female surfers to **establish** the Women's Professional Surfing Association. Then she started a professional surfing tour for women. Soon women were competing all over the world. Surfers everywhere knew Rell's name. They admired

Caroline Schiff/Getty

her as a great competitor. They respected her for fighting for change.

[7]These successes meant a lot to Rell, but she wanted to do more to **benefit** others. Hawaiians call that "the spirit of aloha." That spirit led Rell to start a surfing contest for children. The event was held on her beloved Makaha Beach. Rell kept the contest going year after year. She wanted to get children involved in surfing. She hoped that surfing would help them stay out of trouble. It was her way of fighting drugs and other **social** problems in her community. People on the island loved what Rell did for children. They loved her warm smile and the way she made everyone feel like her friend. They named her the Queen of Makaha.

Rell's efforts led many Hawaiian children to take up the sport of surfing.

Aloha to the Queen

[8]Even after Rell became a mother, she kept surfing. She competed at the highest level. Time and again, she was ranked in the top 10 female surfers. Her dream had come true! She even had her own stone on the Surfing Walk of Fame.

[9]In 1998, the world said good-bye to the Queen of Makaha. Though she died young, Rell lived her life in a big way. She was fearless in the water and graceful on her board. She broke down barriers and changed surfing forever. She loved people and helped hundreds of children. Rell Sunn truly lived with the spirit of aloha!

Living Underwater

¹**T**he ocean has always **tempted** people to dive in and explore. But surviving in the ocean is a big challenge. To meet that challenge, people have invented many different **devices**.

²Leonardo da Vinci's underwater inventions were ahead of their time. In the early 1500s, he drew plans for submarines. He also sketched designs for diving suits. The suits had hoses for breathing air from the surface. Da Vinci never built his submarine. He never made suits for divers to use. But divers in those days did get to use an invention

Some scientists use diving saucers like this one designed by Jacques Cousteau.

called the diving bell. It was a large, open jar of air. Divers carried the jar upside down in the water. Water pressure held the air inside. When divers needed to breathe, they stuck their head into the bell. A jar of air may not seem very high-tech now, but it was a big breakthrough back then.

³Over the years, diving equipment changed. Divers tried leather suits. They tried metal helmets. Some carried air down with them in barrels. Others pumped air from the surface through long hoses. These things helped divers stay down longer. But the equipment was heavy and clumsy.

⁴In 1943, Jacques Cousteau changed that. He invented equipment that was light and easy to carry. It was called scuba **gear**. Scuba divers wore tanks that contained compressed air. Hoses carried the air from the tanks to the diver's mouthpiece. The gear also had a new part called a regulator. It kept air at the right pressure for the diver to breathe. At last, divers could move around easily. They could stay underwater longer than ever before.

⁵Today, deep-sea technology makes many different activities possible. Now scientists can work underwater for days. Between dives, they stay in cabins on the ocean floor. The cabins are called underwater habitats. Each cabin has living space for six people. Scientists can also work in submersibles. Submersibles are part submarine and part robot. They can go much deeper in the ocean than a diver can. On the outside of the sub, there are cameras and robotic arms. Scientists control the equipment from inside the sub. They can take pictures without scaring away the fish. They can do underwater experiments without even getting wet.

⁶Nowadays, underwater life is more fun, too. You can even vacation underwater! The place to go is Jules'

82

Undersea Lodge. It is a deep-sea hotel in Florida. To get there, you'll need to dive 21 feet down. Next, find the opening in the bottom of the hotel. Then pop your head through. You're in a pool in the central room of the lodge. Now you can climb out of the pool and go check out your room. There, you'll be greeted by schools of fish. They swim right past your window. If you get tired of fish-watching, you can watch TV. If you're hungry, order a nice meal. You can even phone your friends. And, of course, you can do all the diving you want. Thanks to technology, you can film your dive, too. An underwater camera will let you make a video all your friends will want to see.

⁷So what changes will we see in the future? Many say that we'll build cities underwater. A floating city of submarines may not be far off. **Recently**, the Navy has been designing subs that could be part of the city. Some will carry labs and businesses. Others will house apartments. Tourists will stay at submarine hotels. There will even be mall subs for shopping.

⁸Some subs in the floating city will help solve problems. Police subs will patrol for **illegal** activity. Towing subs will help with breakdowns. Several submarines can attach to a sub that won't run. Then they can tow it to the surface for repairs.

⁹All of these submarines will move together. Some will be locked together in groups. As they travel, one sub will lead the way. It will be a super sensor sub. The lead sub will sense anything **irregular**. It will steer the city away from strong currents or other trouble.

¹⁰Engineers will learn a lot from the floating city. Maybe then they can build a city on the ocean floor. Buildings for the city may be built on land. Then they can be lowered into the ocean. Strong cables will attach the buildings to the ocean floor. They'll keep the buildings from floating away.

¹¹People in the undersea city may drive tiny submarines like cars. When they get to school or work, people will lock their sub into a parking dock. The dock will connect an air-filled passage to the sub. Then passengers can step out of their sub and go right into the building.

¹²Building an undersea city will take a lot of planning. It will cost a lot, too. It's a big job for one country. Maybe someday, countries will work together to build the city. Then the city at the bottom of the sea will belong to the whole world.

Peter Pinnock/Getty

A diver explores a coral reef in the South Pacific Ocean.

[1]**S**cuba diving is more than a hobby or sport. It's an adventure! As a diver, you get to explore a world filled with **aquatic** life. You can see plants and animals you would never see on dry land. To explore underwater, you must learn to move, breathe, and communicate in special ways. That is just what you will learn in a good scuba class. If you complete the three-part training, you can become a certified scuba diver.

How to Get Certified

[2]The first part of scuba training takes place in a classroom. Spending your free time in school may not be your idea of fun. But the things you study in class will keep you safe later. You need to learn scuba terms. They will help you understand your teacher's

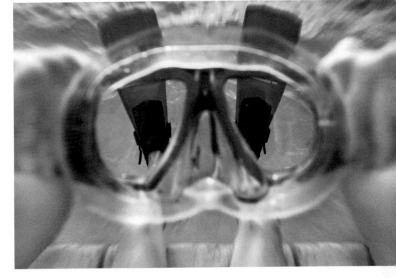

instructions when you're in the water. You must learn about your scuba equipment before you try to use it, too. Everything you learn will give you confidence later when you dive.

[3]Next, it's time to get into a swimming pool. The purpose of this second part of the training is getting to know your equipment. The most important thing you will learn is how to suit up. The first step is getting into your wetsuit. Then put on your vest and tank. Make sure that the air supply is turned on and the tank is full. After that, fasten your weight belt around your waist. Next, put on your mask and check the fit. It should fit snugly against your face. Finally, put on your fins. Before hopping in the pool, make a final check to be sure everything is in order.

[4]While you're in the pool, you'll work with a buddy. Your instructor will have you practice the things you will do on a real dive. You'll

learn to breathe through your mouthpiece. You and your buddy will work on communicating underwater. You'll also go through emergency procedures. Pay close attention to any **advice** your instructor offers. Tips about techniques or equipment could save your life someday.

[5]The last part of your training is the open-water dive. It can take place in a deep lake or in the ocean. You won't do much that is new during this dive. You'll use the same skills you practiced in the pool. The feeling, however, will be very different. This is the real thing. You'll dive much deeper than the bottom of a pool. There will be fish and plants in the water with you. You'll feel excited and maybe a bit nervous. Just remind yourself that you've practiced all the skills you need. If you stay calm, you'll remember what you've learned. Then the dive will be a great experience.

Stephen Frink/Getty

[6]During your open-water dive, you'll take a skills test. It shows whether you can dive safely. If you pass, you'll receive your diver's license. At last, you'll be a certified scuba diver! Your license allows you to buy diving equipment. You'll also get a logbook. Be sure to record all of your dives in it. Before you can go on any dive trip, you'll need to show the book to your guide. It is proof of your diving experience.

Fighting the Fear Factor

[7]When you start diving without an instructor, new fears may arise. Don't think your concerns are silly. Safety questions can shake a

diver's confidence. Get answers to your questions before you dive. Here are some things many new divers wonder about.

- *Will I be eaten by a shark?* Shark attacks are rare. Humans are not part of a shark's normal diet. If you do see a shark, don't **panic**. Sharks are attracted to injured or startled fish. Make sure you don't move like one! Stay calm and move away slowly. Then the shark is likely to swim right past you.

- *Will I get trapped?* The only things likely to trap you are seaweed or fishing line. That's why you should always carry a knife when you dive. If you get tangled, carefully cut yourself loose. The worst that will happen is you'll lose some good dive time.

- *What if I get lost?* This fear is easy to avoid. Carry a compass and know how to use it. Be **aware** of the direction you go when you leave the boat. Then reverse direction to find your way back. When in doubt, surface and look for the boat.

- *What if I can't breathe?* Your breathing regulator isn't likely to fail. But just in case, you should keep an "octopus" with you. It is like a double regulator. It allows you and your buddy to **cooperate** and breathe from the same tank. If your tank is running low on air, use the sign language you learned in class. To say "low on air," make a fist at your belly, then move it up to your chest. This should get a **prompt** response from your buddy who will surface with you right away.

[8]Once you understand what to do in tense situations, you're ready to dive. You've studied. You've practiced. You've passed your test. Now the whole ocean is waiting. Let the adventure begin!

Searching for Sunken Treasure

[1]Did you know that many people have become rich just by diving in the right place? They found treasures from ships that sank long ago. Today, there are still many undiscovered shipwrecks on the ocean floor. Their treasures may one day be found.

Fortunes Lost

[2]It was September 4, 1622. Twenty-eight Spanish ships set sail from Cuba. One ship, the *Atocha*, carried silver, gold, emeralds, and pearls. But the *Atocha* never reached Spain. It was caught in a hurricane one day after leaving port. The **desperate** sailors tried to save their ship. But the *Atocha* sank, along with seven other ships from the fleet.

[3]Many ships have suffered the same fate. In 1755, a hurricane destroyed a French ship called the *Deliverance*. It was carrying silver and gold to Spain. The ship and its treasure sank near Florida. More than a hundred years later, the SS *Republic* left New York headed for

New Orleans. The Civil War had just ended. The SS *Republic* was to deliver money to help rebuild the South. It carried a fortune in gold and silver coins. The ship disappeared when a hurricane struck the coast of Georgia.

[4]For centuries these ships, like many others, were lost at the bottom of the ocean. But the memory of the ships did not die. Many years later, people still dreamed of finding the lost treasures. A few people's dreams came true.

Fortunes Found

[5]In 1969, Mel Fisher and his family began searching for the *Atocha*. They **sacrificed** all their time and money to the effort. They bought ships and instruments. Then they hired search crews. They even lost two family members and a diver during the search. Still, the family didn't give up. Finally, in 1985, the search ended. Mel Fisher's son Kane found the *Atocha* near Key West, Florida. The first thing Kane saw was a stack of 1,000 bars of silver. Later, he found the rest of the treasure buried beneath it. The Fisher family was rich!

[6]Greg Brooks and John Hardy own a search company. They spend their time looking for sunken treasure. In 1998, their underwater instruments picked up some interesting signals. The searchers got excited. Then they got to work. First, they researched all the shipwrecks in that area. They learned that several treasure ships had sunk there. After that, the two men did a full survey of the area. They used remote control sensors and vehicles. The instruments pinpointed a sunken ship. They recorded the size and shape of it. The data was clear at last. This was the *Deliverance*! Brooks and Hardy couldn't believe their luck. This treasure wasn't worth millions. It was worth BILLIONS! Its cargo included chests of gold bars, thousands of gold coins, boxes of gems and jewelry, and 1 million pieces of silver. The discovery started a big argument. Spain and France both claimed the treasure. Brooks and Hardy found out that it's hard to settle an international argument. They ended up in a long court battle. It is still going on today.

[7]In 2003, a large search company called Odyssey **revealed** a secret. After a 12-year search, the company had located the SS *Republic*. During the search, workers kept their activity secret. They even had a code name for the SS *Republic*. This was to keep looters from getting to the ship first. The coins Odyssey recovered are worth $150 million. The best part

is that the ship is in open waters. No government has any claim to it. That means it is truly a "finders keepers" treasure!

Coins found near sunken ships help searchers date shipwrecks.

How to Search for Sunken Treasure

[8]Sunken ships are all over the ocean. Could you claim the treasure from one of them? If you want to try, you should follow a few steps.

- First, figure out where to look. Read about when and where ships disappeared. Learn which ones carried treasures. Remember, **antiques** are highly valuable, too.
- Next, find out if the treasure is available to claim. Sometimes the rule is "finders keepers," but not always. The ship may be in an area claimed by a government. Or there may be a living **heir** to the company that owned the ship. You can hire a researcher to find out for you. If you **neglect** to do this step, you may end up in court.
- After you decide on a site, plan the search. If you just work with a team of divers, your chances of finding treasure aren't very good. It's best to hire a search company to explore the area with high-tech equipment. They will use sonar and underwater robots, sensors, and cameras. This kind of study can cost millions. Be prepared to find investors to put up money for the project.
- When you find a sunken ship, the next step is to recover the treasures. Robots and trained divers are best for this job. They will work their way slowly through the ship, packing the valuables from each section as they go.
- Finally, conserve each object you find. Everything must be specially treated, cleaned, and photographed. Historic objects should go to museums. Once you have published a paper about your finds, your work is done. Now relax and spend your new fortune!

90

Yngve Rakke/Getty

Undersea remains of a 1600 shipwreck

Pirates of Old

¹Ever since people took to the seas, pirates have been trying to rob them. Early pirates started raiding ships in the Mediterranean Sea around 4,000 years ago. Finally, about 2,000 years later, the Roman army cracked down on the outlaws. All the pirates were captured or killed.

²Later, during the Middle Ages, religious pirates took over the Mediterranean. Muslim pirates robbed Christian boats. Christian pirates robbed Muslim boats. These pirates also took ship passengers as slaves. Rich passengers were exchanged later for money. This period lasted for about 1,000 years, ending in the early 1500s.

91

The Bridgeman Art Library/Getty

Long ago, pirates sometimes killed enemies by having them "walk the plank," as shown in this picture. More often, though, pirates simply threw their victims off the ship.

The Golden Age of Piracy

[3]When Columbus found his way to the New World, pirates were not far behind. Spanish treasure ships sailed from ports in South America and the Caribbean. This area was called the Spanish Main. Rulers who were not lucky enough to get riches from the Americas were jealous. They hired pirates and gave them permission to take Spanish goods. The pirates shared the loot with their employers. These "legal" pirates were called privateers. One of the most famous was Sir Francis Drake. He brought back fortunes in stolen goods for Queen Elizabeth I of England. That country held him up as a hero. Spain thought he was an outlaw.

[4]In the 1600s, a new kind of pirate appeared—the buccaneer. Buccaneers didn't start out as pirates. At first, they were just settlers who lived on the island of Hispaniola. They hunted the wild pigs that lived there. Then Spanish soldiers killed all the pigs. The settlers had no food. To survive, they turned to a life of crime. Buccaneers were known for sneak attacks. They used small boats that were easy to hide. Before the crew of a ship even noticed them, the buccaneers had slipped on board. After that, they quickly took control.

[5]Pirates had a lot of respect for one another. After all, most were just sailors who were out of work. True, some were heartless murderers. But many were fair, at least to one another. On some boats, crew members made decisions together. They planned their route and chose their captain. They decided how the loot would be split, too. Any pirate who tried to take more than his share was beaten or killed.

[6]Not all pirates were mean. But they liked people to spread scary stories about them. If victims were scared enough, they would give up without a fight. One man who inspired scary stories was Blackbeard. His murderous raids started around 1713. Blackbeard was a big man with a cruel scowl. In his hair, he wore pieces of burning rope. He walked in a cloud of black smoke. It was easy to believe he was a demon! Blackbeard met his end in 1718. In a battle with British sailors, he was beheaded. As a warning to other pirates, his head was hung from the bow of his ship. The British began doing the same to

other captured pirates. This harsh treatment got results. Around 1725, the Golden Age of Piracy came to an end.

Today's Pirates

[7]Pirates are not a thing of the past. They are a big problem today. There are pirate gangs in every ocean. Each year, they raid hundreds of boats. They rob everything from tiny fishing boats to cruise ships to huge tankers. No boat is safe from pirates.

[8]Today's pirates are like pirates of old. They will steal anything they can sell on the black market. They still kidnap the rich and hold them for ransom. They are as ruthless as any pirates who ever lived. But now pirates have new tools. Their speedboats can outrun victims. They carry automatic weapons. They communicate by cell phone. These tools make pirates more deadly than ever.

Today, pirates can be found in every ocean.

Pirate Protection

[9]It's hard for police to save you from pirates in open waters. If you take a boat trip, following the steps below could save your life.

- Before your trip, plan your route to avoid dangerous areas.
- After boarding the boat, put a few items in the boat's safe. Then hide the rest. If pirates attack, they may not look further than the safe.
- During the trip, travel with other boats. Stay in radio contact with them, too.
- Finally, if pirates come near, let them know you have ways to protect yourself. If they keep coming, ram their boat. Remember, pirates will do anything to get what they want. Do anything you have to do to get away.

Expedition 7

IS THIS ART?

- What *is* art to you?
- Where can art be found?
- How can you wear art?

What Is Art?

AP Images

Many people complained when the city of Las Cruces, New Mexico, planned to pay artist Olin Calk $10,000 for this large sculpture made of recycled trash.

¹Picture in your mind a heap of gray rocks. Wait. That's too boring. Let's start over. Picture in your mind a bunch of trash. That's better. This is like the trash you might see in a vacant lot or on the sidewalk. Imagine food wrappers, paper cups, and broken bottle pieces. Maybe there are some leaves and some animal hair. This trash is different, though. Somebody has carefully arranged it in an interesting way. Pieces of it are glued onto a board. It's a work of art.

²Did I hear someone say, "That can't be art"? Why not? An artist had a **brilliant** idea about how to arrange the bits of trash. The artwork shows the artist's ideas and feelings. Looking at it makes you think about the whole idea of what we throw away. This is what makes it art. Do you like your grandmother's colorful quilts? These are art. What about a **preschool** child's drawing of a horse? That's art, too. So is a cartoon character on a skateboard. Art is all around you. Once you begin to notice it, you can't **ignore** it.

"Inside the Lines"

[3]Some people think a painting that shows, for example, a vase of beautiful flowers is "real art" or "true art." The realistic painting is the kind of art you might expect to see in most museums and galleries. This type of art has been made for hundreds of years. It often shows people or scenes from nature. It might also show scenes from history. Flowers usually look like real flowers, and people usually look like real people in these artworks.

[4]About 200 years ago, artists and art teachers developed some rules. These rules told how to make art and how to look at it. They decided that certain colors and subjects made up beautiful art. "This is how to judge the **quality** of a work of art," they said. "Any artist who does not follow these rules does not produce true art."

Juan Gris, *Guitar and Newspaper*, oil on canvas, 1925

It was as if they were saying, "Good art is when you color inside the lines. Bad art is when you color outside the lines."

"Outside the Lines"

[5]Now let's examine another kind of art. Unlike the art described before, this art is not bound by rules or special conditions. A painting made with splatters of color is one example of this art. A comic book illustration is another example. It also can be a house made of hubcaps. It can be a huge blob of glass. It can even be part of an ad. This art is often surprising. It's fresh and **unexpected**. It is sometimes found in museums and galleries. Some of it is found outdoors. You can see this kind of art in a wheat field in Texas.

Boyer, *Double Bass, Score Sheet and a Sword*, oil on canvas, 1693

97

Stanley Marsh III and The Ant Farm (a San Francisco art collective), *Cadillac Ranch*, 1974

There, 10 Cadillacs are planted in the ground with their ends pointing toward the sky.

[6]The artists who create artworks like these want people to think about art in new ways. They want to create art in new ways. In contrast to artists of earlier times, many of these artists are self-taught. They do not follow the old rules for creating art. A painting of a vase of flowers by one of these artists might look like a bunch of rectangles and squares. A portrait of a child might look like a collection of busy lines.

Art All Around

[7]There's plenty of room for both types of art. In fact, both types of art can enrich the lives of the people who experience them. Does it really matter whether an artist colors inside the lines or outside the lines? All art has the power to excite us or calm us. It can bore us or disturb us. It can make us think. It can remind us of things in our own lives. There are many **marvels** in the world of art.

[8]An old saying is: "One person's trash is another person's treasure." Someone might look at bits of trash on a board and call it trash. On the other hand, you might call it treasure. What matters about art is *looking*. You don't even have to define or understand art. Just look. Look around you. Where do you see art right now?

98

Art that Celebrates: Holiday Costumes

A.J. Sisco/Corbis

A Mardi Gras Indian sings while wearing his colorful, handmade costume.

Costumes of the Mardi Gras Indians

[1]Like many celebrations, Mardi Gras brings art to life. New Orleans has one of the most famous celebrations leading up to Mardi Gras. The two-week celebration is known for colorful floats and lively music. It also is known for the costumes people wear. Among those who create and wear **fabulous** costumes are the Mardi Gras Indians. This group's name can be **misleading**. The "Indians" are really African American

99

men. On the other hand, the name fits the costumes the men wear. The costumes honor **native** people of long ago.

²Years ago, some Native Americans helped people escape from slavery. Often, those who escaped joined the tribe. The tribes helped people who came from West Africa. There, everyone believed in showing respect for their hosts. The freed slaves did that by dressing as their hosts did. They made costumes with feathers and beads just as their Native American friends did.

³The Mardi Gras Indians continue that show of respect today. Their costumes blend the Native American and West African styles. Each year, the Indians make new costumes. This takes a lot of time and **patience**. The costumes are works of art. The men spend hundreds of hours making each one. First, they cut a vest, apron, and headdress from canvas. Then they sketch every **detail** of their design. Next, they cover each piece with beads and jewels. Last, they sew on hundreds of feathers. Huge ostrich plumes spread out from the costume like a sunburst. They make the wearer look large and powerful.

⁴Each Indian group is eager to show off its creations. When two groups meet in the street, they compete in a dance. Pairs of dancers face off. They size each other up. One calls out a challenge. Then they dance and chant. In contrast to other contests, this one offers no trophy. Dancers compete for the cheers of the crowd.

The Chinese New Year Dragon

⁵The Chinese New Year's celebration lasts 15 days. Like Mardi Gras, the Chinese New Year is known for parades and costumes. The parades always include a huge dancing dragon. Chinese artists in country shops make the beautiful dragons. They ship them all over the world. The dragons appear in Chinese New Year's celebrations everywhere.

⁶The dragon is a symbol of good luck. Long ago, people in China believed the dragon dance kept away evil. It protected against drought. It stopped the spread of sickness. These beliefs led to the tradition of the New Year's dragon dance. The dance is thought to bring joy and good fortune for the coming year.

Actors perform a dragon dance to celebrate the Chinese New Year.

101

[7]The New Year's dragon is actually a giant costume. The head is made of paper glued over a frame of wire and bamboo. Artists paint colorful details and designs on the dragon's face. The body is made in sections. Each one has a frame of bamboo. Silk is stretched over the frames. Then, the sections are fastened together. The finished costume may be more than 200 feet long!

[8]During the big parade, the dragon winds through the streets. Unlike most costumes, the dragon is carried by as many as 50 people. They are the dragon dancers. The dancers must be in top shape. Most people don't have the strength necessary to move the heavy dragon. Each dancer holds a wooden pole that is fastened to the dragon's body. The lead dancer moves the head to make the dragon seem alive. The head looks from side to side. It bobs up and down. Sometimes it even breathes out smoke! The other dancers make the body slither and twist. Just as Mardi Gras Indians do, dragon dancers hope their costume and dance will make the crowd cheer.

AP Images

A woman competes in a Day of the Dead costume contest in Mexico City.

Mexico's Walking Dead

[9]The Day of the Dead is a time for remembering loved ones. It is not a sad time. It is a joyous **festival**! For three days, people welcome the spirits of the dead into their homes. They decorate graves in the cemetery. They also have a parade to make fun of death. The costumes in the parade show that the dead are happy and fun-loving!

¹⁰In contrast to some people from other cultures, most Mexicans do not believe the dead are scary. They are just loved ones who have died. People hope their loved ones will return to visit them. Families fill their homes with things the dead enjoyed in life. They cook special foods. They arrange flowers on altars. They want the dead to feast and have a good time. Then they hold a parade for the dead. Parading as happy skeletons, the people show they are not afraid of death.

A man and girl dressed in costumes dance during a Day of the Dead celebration in Mexico City.

AFP/Getty

¹¹Anyone dressed like the dead can join the parade. Compared to a costume like the Chinese dragon, these costumes seem simple, but they are quite dramatic. People wear masks or paint their faces to look like a skeleton's face. They dress in party clothes. Some men wear tuxedos and top hats. Others wear white clothes and big sombreros. Women often wear ball gowns with veils or big hats. A few people wear extra long costumes. Then they walk on stilts!

¹²The parade follows a band through town. People stop to dance and have fun along the way. They watch performers who put on plays or do stunts. The parade ends with a party at the cemetery.

Art with a Message

¹³The costumes for these three celebrations look different. But in some ways they're alike. Not only are they all forms of art, but each has a message of courage. Mardi Gras Indian costumes honor those who stood against slavery. The dragon reminds us we can overcome bad luck. It promises a bright future. Day of the Dead costumes show that not even death should scare us. Through color and art, all these costumes express a spirit of daring and fun.

One Picture Is Worth a Billion Dollars

[1]"**O**ne picture is worth a thousand words." You may have heard this saying before. It means that a picture can say a lot on its own. That's what logos are meant to do. A logo is a printed design or symbol. A symbol is something that stands for something else. A logo can be a simple drawing. It might include a few words. It is not a **decoration**. It's much more than this. But, like a decoration, it has to look good. After all, it "speaks" for a company.

[2]A company uses a logo as a special sign. The logo tells people about the company's product or service. It can tell what a company thinks about itself. It can also tell what a company thinks about its customers. The company wants you to see its logo and make an immediate connection. It wants you to want to *buy* something!

[3]Where have you seen logos? You've seen them on television. They are in magazine ads. They're **visible** on billboards and signs along the nation's highways. Which of these logos do you recognize?

- A red and white target
- A yellow seashell
- The number 7 with the word *ELEVEN* through it

You see logos on products you wear or use. They're on wrappers of foods you eat and cans of soda you drink.

AP Images

Justin Sullivan/Getty

AP Images

This McDonald's museum was built to look just like the first McDonald's, which opened in 1955.

The Arches and the Swoosh

[4]What do you think of when you see double yellow arches that form an *m*? Hamburgers. What does a swoosh mark make you think of? Shoes. That's exactly what McDonald's and Nike want you to think when you see their logos. In fact, these companies don't just want you to *think* of hamburgers and shoes. They want you to *buy* a lot of them.

[5]McDonald's Golden Arches had their beginning nearly 50 years ago. The owners of the **original** McDonald's sold hamburgers in a small building. The building had an arch on each side. In 1962, a designer named Jim Schindler drew a picture of the two arches together. They formed an *m*. "Aha!" said the McDonald's owners. "We have a logo!" The McDonald's company called its logo the "Golden Arches." Today, this logo is known all over the world. Even children who haven't yet learned to read recognize it.

[6]Raise your hand if you've never heard of Nike sports shoes. On second thought, don't. People might give you a funny look. Unlike the Golden Arches, the Nike logo orginated long ago. The name Nike comes from Greek mythology.

Elsa/Getty

The Greeks of long ago told stories of Nike. She was the goddess of victory. She watched over ancient battles.

⁷Like McDonald's, the Nike company was already in business before it created a logo. The owner of Nike asked a college student to design a logo in 1971. Her name was Carolyn Davidson. She was studying advertising. Davidson drew a design in the shape of a check mark. She wanted to create something that looked like the wing of the goddess Nike. Her design became known as the Nike "Swoosh." The company paid Davidson $35 for her work!

The Power of Pictures and Words

⁸The McDonald's and Nike logos are easy to recognize on their own. Even so, both companies have added words to go with them. This makes their messages even more powerful. These short, catchy messages are called slogans. McDonald's has had many slogans over the years. Their current one is "I'm lovin' it." It's aimed at people between the ages of 15 and 24. This message seems to say, "I love McDonald's food, and so will you."

⁹In contrast to McDonald's, Nike is mainly known for one slogan, "Just do it." The slogan is like a battle cry. It seems to be urging, "Get up! Don't make excuses! Get fit!"

¹⁰When you think about it, these companies' messages are very different. McDonald's tells us, "Eat more burgers and fries!" Some people think this is unhealthy. Meanwhile, Nike tells us, "Move your body! Get healthy!" What do these logos and slogans say to you? Perhaps together they say, "Put on your Nikes and run to McDonald's for a Big Mac!"

What Difference Do Logos Make?

[11]A good logo plus a good product can lead to big success. McDonald's is the largest fast-food restaurant chain in the world. The company has more than 30,000 restaurants in the United States and in most **foreign** countries. It has **exported** a part of American culture to almost every corner of the world.

[12]This is also true of Nike. The company has earned billions of dollars from selling shoes and other athletic wear. Nike is more than a symbol for running fast. It's a symbol of being cool.

Dollar Signs

[13]The Golden Arches and the Swoosh are simple but powerful signs of success for both McDonald's and Nike. They're also symbols of hard work and the willingness to change with the times. Sometimes this even means changing a logo. This can be tricky though. Changing a logo can change the way people see a company. McDonald's and Nike haven't **altered** their logos much over the years. Why mess with success? And they know that a picture is worth more than a thousand words. It can be worth millions or even *billions* of dollars.

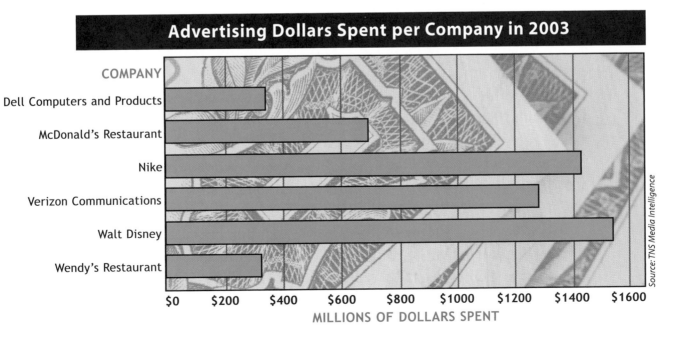

Advertising Dollars Spent per Company in 2003

Source: TNS Media Intelligence

107

Rhapsody in Tile

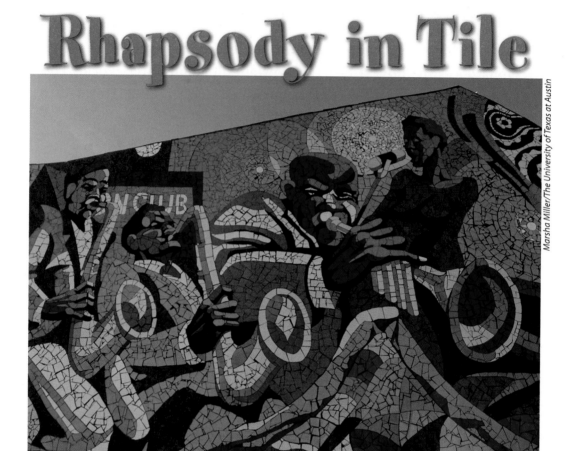

Marsha Miller/The University of Texas at Austin

¹**R**hapsody. RAP. Suh. Dee. What do you love? Shout it out! What do you celebrate? Sing its praises. Make a rhapsody. *Yeah!* A rhapsody can be a song or a poem. It can even be a work of art. *Rhapsody* is a work of art. It's a mural created by John Yancey, an African American artist and professor. His mural stands in a park on the east side of Austin, Texas.

²A mural is public art that's made on a wall. Most murals are painted, but *Rhapsody* is different. It was made from thousands of pieces of brightly colored tile.

³When Yancey began his *Rhapsody*, he was thinking of a famous mural in his hometown of Chicago called *Wall of Respect*. The mural honors black heroes. Yancey wanted his mural to **reflect** an important part of Austin's past. He wanted to honor African American life in the

east part of the city long ago. He wanted to make a rhapsody. *RAP. Suh. Dee.*

[4]Seventy years ago, the main street in this neighborhood was buzzing with activity. People greeted one another. *Glad to see you, friend!* They discussed the latest news. *Did you hear about the game?* Children played on the sidewalks. Jazz musicians made lively music in neighborhood parks. *Man, listen to that trumpet!*

[5]These days, more white people are moving into the neighborhood. Its flavor is changing. Yancey thought about these changes and talked to people in the community. *How can we make way for change and yet honor the past?* he wondered.

[6]Yancey went to the Austin History Center. He read about African American life in Austin and studied old pictures. Yancey wanted to show these scenes in the mural.

[7]The 50-foot mural took three years to finish. Yancey began with a design and hundreds of squares of tile. He used a hammer to break the tiles. *Bam!* Then, he used another tool to cut the tile pieces into the shapes he needed. *Snap!* Yancey and two helpers put the pieces together to form the scenes in the mural.

[8]As Yancey and his helpers prepared the concrete wall for the mural, they **attracted** attention in the neighborhood. *Whatcha doing?* People stopped to talk. Some shared what they remembered of old East Austin.

[9]One scene flows into another on the mural. You see patterns from the costume of an African dancer, shapes from a colorful quilt, and a bright yellow sun. You see a church and a school. The tiles show three boys changing a bicycle tire, and jazz musicians and a singer making music. *Sweet!*

[10]The mural flows out of a neighborhood's past to touch its present. Yancey has created many murals in his life, but this one is special. It's the one he's proudest of. It's his rhapsody. *RAP. Suh. Dee. Yeah!*

Marsha Miller/The University of Texas at Austin

Artist John Yancey sits in front of a section of *Rhapsody.*

The Great Wall of Los Angeles

FOREBEARERS OF CIVIL RIGHTS

©SPARC

The Great Wall includes many different themes. It features historical figures, such as these civil rights heroes from the 1950s.

¹It was once a long, blank wall of concrete. It was built to protect against flooding in a part of Los Angeles, California. The wall was useful, but it was boring. Today, it is a grand and colorful painted mural that tells an exciting story. It's the story of how people of many cultures made California great. The mural stretches for 2,754 feet along the wall. It is near a park and bicycle trail.

²*The Great Wall* began when officials in the city government took a good look at the blank wall. They decided it needed something to add life to it. So they got in touch with Latina artist Judith Baca. They wanted her to make something interesting on the wall. Baca liked the idea. She made a **decision** to create a mural that showed California's history.

³She began working on the mural in 1974. Baca and others interviewed young people between the ages of 14 and 21. They were

110

seeking people mainly from poorer families. They trained the mural makers in art. They taught them about the history of the state.

[4]It took Baca's crews five summers to complete the mural. Each year, the artists added several hundred more feet to the mural. In all, more than 400 young people and their families helped make the mural. They were from backgrounds as different as those they were showing on the wall. Some of them were even gang members who had fought each other on the streets of L.A. Some workers were nervous about this at first. "While our sense of our individual families' places in history took form, we became family to one another," says Baca. The workers began to better **appreciate** their history. They began to understand one another. And they began to understand themselves.

[5]The mural was called *The History of California* at first. But, in 1980, when people saw what was being created, they began calling it *The Great Wall*. Each section took a year

Judy Baca holds plans for *The Great Wall* as the artists paint a section titled *Jewish Family Under the Shadow of Hitler*.

to research, **organize**, and paint. Workers prepared the wall surface. Then they marked grid lines on the wall. These matched grids on the plan drawings. They drew on the wall. Then they used these drawings as guides for painting.

[6]Thousands of people visit the mural each year. The story told on the mural begins with the dinosaurs and continues through the 1950s. Work on the wall continues today. Baca is raising money to repair parts of the wall. And she wants to make it even longer.

[7]*The Great Wall* celebrates the different groups who shaped the history of California. It celebrates courage and the will to succeed. And, especially, it celebrates working together. It's a great wall indeed. It unites, rather than divides.

111

Two women from a village in Madagascar, a large island east of Africa, wear traditional face paint.

Two Faces of Art

[1]**A**rt is everywhere. It's in museums, of course. It's also in our gardens and parks. It's on the sides of buildings and on concrete walls. It's on fast-food restaurants and on running shoes. It's even on our faces.

[2]Human beings, past and present, have decorated their faces. They've dotted their cheeks with yellow sap from trees. They've put wooden disks inside their lips and bones through their noses. They've carved patterns of lines into their faces. They've put metal rings through their eyebrows and ears. They've powdered their eyelids and tinted their lips. Look around. Do you see art on the faces around you?

[3]The human face is a wonderful canvas. It comes in many colors. It moves. It can be decorated to show off its beauty. It can be marked in ways that say, "This is where I come from. This is who I am. This is what I care about." Let's take a look at two kinds of face art. Each of these carries a powerful message.

Fan Face

[4]For some sports fans, it's not enough to sit in the stands and cheer the team to victory. Something extra is needed. Something more than a huge "Number 1" hand or a yellow cheese hat. What's needed? Face paint! Are your team colors red and white? Paint one side of your face red and the other white. *Now* you're talking. Add a rainbow-colored wig and oversized sunglasses. How can your team help but win?

[5]Fans who paint their faces do it to show team support. They're proud of their sports team and want everyone to know it. Face painting is also a way to have fun at a game and be part of a special group of fans. It's a way to make instant friends with fellow face painters. It's a way to fit in and stand out at the same time. A camera at a sports event will always find a painted face.

[6]Finding the right kind of paint is easy. Sports fans can buy face-painting kits at some sporting goods stores, in costume shops, and in party shops. They can order face paints in team colors online. The directions are not hard to follow. Some of the paints are creamy, like finger paints. They're put on the face with a sponge, a brush, or the fingers.

Some face paints come in the form of markers or crayons. These can be used to add details such as stars or letters. Most face paints are easy to remove. They wash off with soap and water. In some cases, they're washed away by tears shed when the sports team loses.

Andy Lyons/Getty

A Tennessee Titans fan hopes her team will win the football game.

Maori Moko

[7]Just as some sports fans decorate their faces, the Maori people of New Zealand have decorated their faces for many years. But these decorations can't be washed off with soap and water. That's because they're tattoos. The Maori call these tattoos *moko*.

[8]Ancient Maori used moko patterns to show tribe membership. These tattoos were a sign of pride. In this way, they are similar to team colors used by sports fans. A moko was also a sign of social class. A Maori chief's moko was different from those of his tribe members. Sometimes the pattern told the type of work a person did. Detailed tattoos often completely covered a man's face. Many of the Maori women wore tattoos on their lips and chins.

[9]The art of moko is still practiced. Today, many young Maori men and women wear these tattoos. They're a way for modern Maori people to connect to their past. "We're still proud of who we are," the moko says. These Maori use some of the same patterns their ancestors used. This is a way to keep their culture alive. It's also a way to wear fine art.

[10]Long ago, Maori moko artists used sharp pieces of bone to carve swirling designs into the face. This

The moko on this Maori warrior's face is similar to the tattoos worn by his ancestors.

made ridges and grooves in the skin. Then they rubbed ink into the cut areas. Sometimes they used a type of pen to ink a design. Unlike face painting, this was a painful way to decorate the face. In contrast to earlier ways of making a design, today's moko artists use modern tattoo tools. People who want to experiment with moko can have a design painted on their faces, rather than tattooed.

[11]Each person's face tells a story on its own. A sports fan who paints her face or a Maori who wears a moko adds to the story. It's a story of pride. It's a story of belonging. It's part of the rich and never-ending story of art.

114

MAKE IT RIGHT!

- *What is the connection between you and your environment?*
- *What can you do to make the environment safer?*
- *How does the way you get to school affect the environment?*

Let's E-Cycle!

¹Join us for a visit to our city dump. Now that we're here, take a deep breath. Ahhhhh. There's nothing like the ripe smell of rotting garbage. Watch out for that rat near your foot! Don't step in those dirty diapers! Now come over here and look at this heap of garbage. It's called e-waste. (The *e* stands for "electronic.") Can you see the old cell phones and computers? See the mound of printers and the snarl of cables? There must be a hundred broken TVs, VCRs, and stereos here! Look at this fax machine. Are you thinking what we're thinking?

Maybe this isn't garbage after all. Maybe we need to recycle this stuff. We think our city should develop an electronic equipment recycling center—an *e*-cycling center. We shouldn't let e-waste go to waste!

²There are two good reasons to start an e-cycling center. The first has to do with safety. Throwing away this e-waste is dangerous to health. It doesn't matter whether you toss it in a field or cart it to the dump. It's still harmful. Parts of these items are toxic, or poisonous. They can include materials such as lead and mercury. If these get into the groundwater, they can harm or kill wildlife. They can affect our drinking water. If e-wastes are burned, harmful gases can form in the air and make us sick. We can protect our water and air by recycling electronic equipment. By doing so, we'll protect our health.

³The second reason for starting an e-cycling center has to do with new opportunities. We will give people opportunities to learn new skills. The people at a city e-cycling center would repair the equipment. The center would hire and train people in need of work. These people could learn to sort and repair items. They would gain knowledge in repairing and using the equipment. Some could help sell the items in a city shop. Others could work with schools to supply them with needed equipment. Students could even help repair old computers. Many students could probably be coaxed into taking them apart and putting them back together. What a great way to learn about computers!

⁴There are some **objections** to starting an e-cycling center. First, there's the matter of cost. Some people say that there's too much **expense** involved in e-cycling.

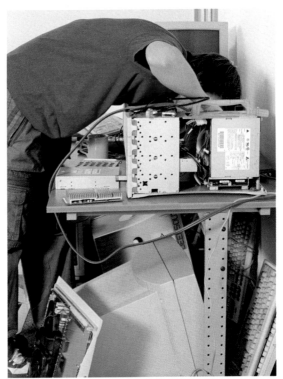
A worker looks inside a computer.

This 21-foot robot man was built to show the amount of electronic waste an average person in England creates in a lifetime.

With volunteer help though, we can **accomplish** the task at a low cost. Another **argument** is that no one wants to use "old" equipment. But once these items are refurbished, they're as good as new! There are also those who say that recycling is just too much trouble. They don't want to be bothered with taking items to the curb or hauling them to a recycling center. We could have teams pick up items for free. Or, we could hold community e-cycling fairs during the year. People could bring their unwanted equipment to the fair. The city then would take these items to the e-cycle center. We realize that some items just can't be repaired and reused. They don't have to go to the dump, though. We can recycle them in our art classes. The parts can be turned into artwork!

[5]We hope you'll **conclude**, as we have, that e-cycling makes good sense. We've watched our dump fill with old computers, TVs, and stereos. The National Safety Council reports that more than 130 million cell phones are thrown away each year. Should all of these go in our city dumps? We don't think so! Instead, most of the e-waste should be reused. Every time you reuse an old item, you're helping to **conserve** our resources. So let's start a city e-cycling center. It's bound to have a good e-ffect!

From Kitchens to Cars:
A New Kind of Fuel

TISD School Board
413 Rydale Road
Terrence, OH 98432

October 17, 2008

Dear School Board Members:

[1]You have been working to keep junk food out of our schools. This is because you want students to be healthy. That's great. But, I want to **propose** a new way to use junk food. It will help everyone in our town. French fries and doughnuts are part of the plan. Don't worry. I don't want our students to eat these unwholesome foods. Instead, I have a better plan. Let's put our school buses on a fast-food diet! Does that sound strange? Well, listen to this. Scientists have found a way to recycle fast-food cooking oil. They burn it as fuel. What a great idea! I think our school district should start using this oil to fuel its buses.

[2]Keeping the environment clean is a good reason to use cooking-oil fuel. Cooking oil is a clean fuel. Burning gas gives off carbon dioxide. That is not good at all. Carbon dioxide can cause global warming. Nobody wants

to overheat the planet! Using cooking oil is a smarter choice. It produces 90% less carbon dioxide than gas does. My plan leads to cleaner air. It cuts down on global warming. What more could you want?

[3]Well, there is more. Running buses on cooking oil saves money. My dad and I checked it out. We learned a surprising fact. The district spent more than $100,000 on fuel last year! Wouldn't you like to save that money? Well, I've got good news. You can. Used cooking oil is free. You've got to like that! Just think of what you could do with the money you'll save. You could buy books and computers. You could build new schools. And don't forget about your "Healthy Foods" **campaign**! You could provide students more choices of healthful foods in our cafeteria. Of course, there is some cost for switching fuels. Fortunately, you won't need to buy new buses. You won't even have to change the engines in any way. But, each bus will need a special tank. The tank has a filter that cleans the oil. It also has a warmer that keeps the oil from getting thick. Don't be anxious about how well the fuel works. The buses will have just as much power as they do now. Soon the tanks and filters will be paid for. Then the savings begin. You can get cooking oil from any place that serves fried foods. It can be stored in barrels until it is needed. When the supply runs low, just call for more.

[4]Many people like this idea. They think it's smart. Others aren't so sure. They don't like the plan. They think it will be hard to get oil to run our buses. I **disagree**. There are a lot of fast-food restaurants in town. Every one of them uses cooking oil. All we have to do is ask for it. Owners will want to help us. Believe me. They'll be glad to get rid of the oil for

free! Right now, that's not the case. They pay to have waste oil taken away. We'll save them money. Some people have **complaints** about the fumes. They don't like the smell. I think that's **nonsense**. Most people like the smell of French fries. That's what cooking-oil fumes smell like.

[5]The choice is easy. Let's change to cooking oil. We'll do the world a favor. We'll make the air cleaner. We'll reduce global warming. The district will save money. The savings can pay for things we need. On top of that, traffic jams will smell like French fries! It all makes sense. So please take my **request** seriously. Implement the change from gas to cooking oil.

Sincerely,

Jacob Rivera

A woman fills the tank of her converted car with cooking oil.

A converter like this one makes it possible to fuel a car with vegetable cooking oil instead of gasoline.

The City Press

MAY 8, 2008   EDITORIAL PAGE

Pollution from construction sites flows into our groundwater.

BATTLE OF THE BIG BOX:
A FIGHT WE MUST WIN

[1]Imagine turning on your faucet to get a drink. What trickles out is muddy and foul smelling. No one would want to drink it. Or, picture your family driving to Miller's Lake to fish or swim. You climb out of the car only to find a smelly swamp choked with algae. The only fish you see are dead ones floating in the water. Do you think it can't happen here? It can if owners of those huge stores build over our groundwater supply. It won't happen tomorrow or even next year. But slowly, it will happen. It's disturbing to think about it. But we have to stop this while we still can. We have to boycott big-box stores—those stores that sell everything under one roof. If not, they are sure to ruin our water.

[2]The main reason for keeping businesses from building in certain areas is to protect our water supply. When we let construction crews work over our groundwater supply, we are asking for pollution. The crews start

Trees and ground cover are cleared to make way for new construction.

by clearing the site. That wipes out the trees and grasses that help rain **filter** into the ground. Without that ground cover, heavy rain just runs off into the creeks. It carries with it all the dirt and chemicals from the work site. This is a major **biohazard**. After construction ends, the problem gets worse. Now the rain hits concrete buildings and paved parking lots. Again, it can't filter down into the groundwater. It runs off as dirty storm water. The water contains oil and grease from the parking lot. So, construction and the finished business sites create the same result. Instead of filling our groundwater with pure, filtered rain water, we get toxic runoff in our creeks. Some of that toxic runoff filters down into our water supply. The rest washes into our beautiful lake. And all of this

gets worse. The stores will attract more building activity. Developers will build a lot of new homes near the stores. That means more construction runoff. New roads will be built for those neighborhoods. There will be more traffic. The runoff from roads will increase. That all adds up to more oil and grease in our creeks. Day by day, our underground water supply will grow more polluted. The only **solution** is to stop the problem before it starts. If we refuse to buy from big-box stores, they won't move in. We will keep the clean water we have today.

[3]Here's another good reason to protect our water—money! If the lake is polluted, the animals that live in or near it die or leave. If the animals go, we lose more than wildlife. We lose visitors and the money they spend. People come from all over to fish, hike, and camp here. It's an **ideal** place to enjoy nature's beauty. But if the water is dirty, visitors will find other places to go. We know how many businesses here depend on out-of-towners. Owners of boat rentals, motels, restaurants, and many more would suffer. A lot of those businesses

could be forced to close. Plenty of workers could find themselves out of work. Do you really think those workers want to trade their jobs for a big-box store?

⁴But the most important reason for not building over our water supply is to protect the health of our citizens. Did you know that our bodies are made up largely of water? Because of that, the water we drink should be as pure as possible. What if our water becomes polluted? We can expect a lot of bad health effects. Some of these effects will be short term. For example, a person who drinks dirty water might get a sick stomach. He or she might break out in a rash. No

Fish cannot live in polluted water.

one wants to experience either of those conditions. Long-term effects will be more serious though. People who drink polluted water over a long period of time can become very ill. They might develop problems with their livers. Their kidneys might not work as they should. Some people will even develop cancer. So you can see that protecting our water is really important. We must fight for clean water.

⁵The **opposition** says we can't afford to lose these big-box businesses. We'll fall behind the times. We'll lose jobs. We'll lose tax money. Sure, big-box stores bring in jobs. However, many of those jobs offer poor benefits. As big boxes drive our smaller stores out of business, we will lose good jobs. We'll lose employers who know us and care about our families. Those who want big-box stores say our city needs the taxes the businesses would pay. There's just one thing wrong with that thinking. These big-box owners want reduced taxes. They asked our leaders to give them a sweet deal. Big-box owners will pay much lower taxes than those who have served our community for years! It doesn't matter what big-box stores might do for our economy. It's all short term. Look down the road. How will we feel if we have

Most big-box jobs do not pay as well as jobs at smaller, local stores.

lost our health? And how good will our economy be when our water supply is ruined? We'll have to pay some other community to supply us. We'll watch our tourist money go to places with clean lakes. Simply put, if we allow big boxes to build over our

water supply, we lose a lot more than we gain.

6There's just one way to sum it up: Protecting our water is a matter of life or death. Clean water is a **necessity** for life in our community. We need clean water to be here for our children and our grandchildren. Without a clean source of water, people will become ill. Plants and animals will die. Our city will slowly die, too. Let big business know the score. This is our community, and we intend to keep it alive and well. We won't sell out to the highest bidder. We won't buy from those who build over our groundwater. Let's send that message loud and clear. Boycott the big boxes!

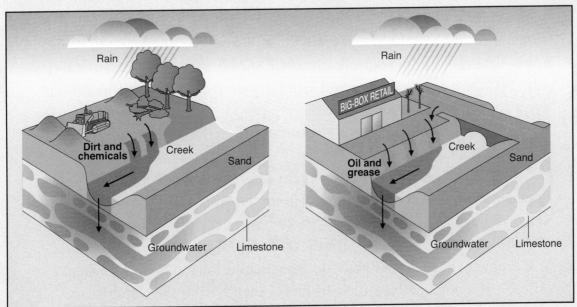

Water from construction sites and paved areas filters down through sand and limestone. This dirty water pollutes our groundwater.

125

Robert Y. Ono/CORBIS

Buy a Bus Pass:
Your Ticket to a Green Tomorrow

The following speech was given before students of Salina High School. The speaker was Teisha Simms, president of Students for a Green Tomorrow.

¹**Y**ou've heard it all. *It takes too long. There isn't a stop nearby. It's confusing. It smells bad. It's crowded.* These excuses that people give for not using the city bus line are lame. Those problems are all in the past. The city has purchased a fleet of SuperBuses. It has expanded the service area, too. Once you know about the new SuperBus service, you'll see that it's a great way to get around. Besides, riding the bus is good for the environment. I **recommend** that every student get, and *use*, a bus pass.

²We all need to use the bus to help the environment. I could **devote** a whole afternoon to describing ways that the SuperBus is environmentally friendly. First, these new buses run cleaner. They burn biodiesel instead of diesel. Biodiesel is a fuel that is made mostly of oil from soybeans. This new fuel produces a lot less pollution than diesel. It's not smelly, either. In fact, exhaust from the SuperBus leaves only a faint smell of vegetable oil. Just think—when we ride the SuperBus, we actually help make the air *smell* better! We also help

farmers who grow soybeans by creating a market for their crops. We can do all this for the price of a bus pass. What a bargain! In addition, riding the bus reduces the number of cars on the road. Fewer cars burn less fuel. That means less air pollution. When you think of all these benefits, you can see that the SuperBus deserves its name!

[3]Convenience is another reason you should be a regular rider on the SuperBus. The city **advertises** that this bus is "going places," and it's true. New routes reach all parts of the city. Some of the routes even serve areas outside the city limits. Do you want to go to the Riverwalk? Take Bus 24 heading south. Are you in the mood for a swim? Take Bus 87 out to Lake Park. Are you looking for bargains? Hop on Bus 311 to the flea market north of town. You can get anywhere on the SuperBus! The city also added new and **frequent** bus stops. You're sure to find a stop close to where you live and close to where you are going. To **promote** the new bus lines, the city is offering a special deal on SuperPasses, too. The bus passes are easy to buy and very affordable. A SuperPass costs only $10. That's just a few cents a day. The pass is good for one month and can be used on any bus any time. You can buy one at grocery stores, gas stations, and city offices. Could it be any simpler?

Monthly Pass
Adult
Public Transport Board
SuperPass 2008
No 8745
This pass is valid until 12/31/08

[4]We all need to get on board the SuperBus. After all, it's for our own good. We don't want to spend our adult lives in a polluted world. Let's set an example for the older generation. Show them how to quit clogging our roads with cars and pollution. Tell them that big, polluting buses are ancient history. There's a better way to get around. We can make use of the great bus system our city has created. It's convenient, it's cheap, and it's good for our world. I **applaud** the city for investing in our future. I challenge all of you to do the same. Make a small investment for a huge payoff. Buy a bus pass and *use* it!

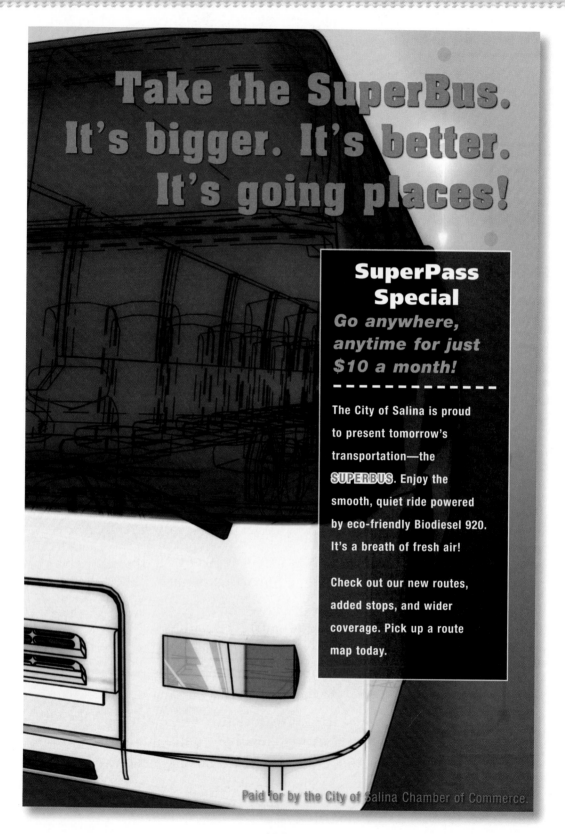

Jeff Greenberg/Alamy

| TO: | The National EnviroSchools Program |
| FROM: | The Students and Teachers of Robert L. Anton Middle School |

[1]Our school is writing to ask for your help. We need money for a special program. The name of our program is "Growing Strong." We want to start a garden at our school. We have a plan. We have a place. (A large vacant lot sits next to the school. The owner of the lot will let us use it for free!) And we have people. What do we need? We need money. We need money for tools and soil. We need money for plants

Gardening lets students apply math and science skills they learn in the classroom.

and seeds. We think our goals are the same as yours. We want to help the environment. And we want to educate students at the same time.

[2]How will having a school garden help the environment? It will teach students how to reduce waste. A study shows that our landfills are overflowing. Any plan that cuts down on garbage must be good for the environment. About one-third of the waste in our country is made up of food and yard waste. Two hundred pounds of food waste are thrown away each week in our school alone! Students who work in a school garden will use this "green" waste. They will add it to a compost pile. Students also can collect leaves and other "brown" yard waste from school grounds. They will add this to the compost as well. Over time, these wastes will turn into a rich, soil-like mixture. Then it can be worked into the garden soil. It will help fruits and vegetables grow.

We think that students who learn to recycle wastes like these at school will recycle them at home.

[3]How will having a school garden help educate students? Students will learn about nature, plants, and the outdoors. They will learn by planting, caring for, harvesting, and cooking food. A California study found that six of every 10 students thought that cotton comes from sheep. The same students thought that vegetables come from the store. This is shocking! Students who grow their own food will understand the link between the food they eat and its source. They will learn about fresh, healthful ways to eat. We hope to have a classroom kitchen. Students can learn to cook the foods they grow. Students will also learn about history, science, and math through the program. They will learn how early Americans grew their crops. They will learn how insects can help or harm a garden. They will learn about the effects of sunlight and water on plants. And, they will use math to plan garden plots. Research shows that students who work in school gardens score higher on certain science tests. So, one thing is clear. Our program will grow better students as well as fresh foods!

Chris Whitehead/Getty

131

[4]We have thought carefully about this program. Some people in the community have told us that it can't be done. They say a school garden will cost too much. But we have figured out just how much money we need for the program. We think we can find it. Parents and area businesses have already promised us money. They have offered their time, too. And, we hope to raise money through groups such as yours. Others say a school garden will take students away from "real" subjects. What could be more real than hands-on learning? Some people say there won't be enough interest in the program. That's not true. Students, teachers, parents, and neighbors already have shown interest.

Vegetables grown in the school garden can be cooked in a classroom kitchen.

[5]All of us at Anton Middle School are excited about this program. We are already planning our first food fair. This will be at the end of the growing season. Students will cook different recipes with the foods they have grown. It will be a time for students, teachers, and the whole community to create something together. And what happens once we do this? We will begin to care more about taking care of our planet. It's not just about growing food. It's about growing healthy. It's about growing smart. We hope you will help us grow.

THINKING BIG

- How can one person make an impact on the world?
- How can something positive come from a negative experience?
- How can one of your interests help others?

A GUY WHO FIXES THINGS

[1]Eddie Maldonado was a good kid from a good family, but something went wrong. Because of some bad decisions in his early twenties, Eddie went to prison. It was there that he found a way to make the world a better place. But how does a man behind bars change the world for the better? Eddie did it with a few simple tools and some broken bikes.

Off to a Good Start

[2]Eddie had a natural talent for fixing bicycles. He loved bikes from the day that he got his first one. It was a black five-speed that his mother bought for $25. That was a lot of money to a mother who had five sons to raise! At 14, Eddie decided to use his bike-repair skills to help his mom with expenses. He got a job in a New York City bike shop. Working kept him away from gangs and drugs. A year later, Eddie's family moved to Dallas. Since he was experienced at repairing bikes, he had no trouble getting a good job in a bike shop. He quickly became a bike expert and a valuable employee. Customers loved Eddie's outgoing personality. He made a lot of new friends.

Getting Off-Track

[3]Eddie's ability to make friends was a gift. But it also got him into trouble. He let a so-called friend talk him into doing something illegal. Eddie agreed to take guns from Texas to New York. He thought he was doing his friend a favor. It turned out to be a bad choice. The guns were for criminals in a drug ring. As a result, Eddie became wanted by the FBI. His story aired on the TV show *America's Most Wanted*. When police busted the ring, Eddie was arrested. He was sentenced to

18 years in prison. Eddie was ashamed of the way he had let down his family. He wished he could go back and do things right. But it was too late for that.

Eddie's Dream

[4]Being **confined** in jail gave Eddie time to think about what he wanted to do with his life. Eddie knew two things. He wanted to help people, and he loved bikes. One day, he found a way to put the two together. He asked the warden if he could teach other inmates how to run a bike shop. He explained that his workshop would teach inmates a trade. The warden liked the idea. It would help prisoners make an honest living when they were released. Therefore, the warden gave Eddie permission to **conduct** his workshop. Three days later, Eddie and his crew of inmates were building a bike shop. Eddie showed his students the best way to set up a shop. He made them think about opening their own shop someday. Police departments, churches, and other groups gave the inmates old bikes to repair. Eddie showed his students how to make the bikes look like new. The inmates repaired hundreds of bicycles and gave them to needy children. Fixing bikes to make things better became Eddie's passion.

Amy Conn-Gutierrez

Eddie's experience teaching inmates to repair bikes led to his successful workshops with students of all ages.

135

Bicycles Most Wanted

[5]After his release from prison, Eddie's passion for helping others stayed with him. He wanted to keep teens from getting into trouble the way he had. He wanted to offer them a way to make their lives better—by fixing bikes. He thought the best way to make his help **accessible** to kids was to go right into the schools. So Eddie made calls to school officials. At first, no one was interested. But Eddie didn't give up. His luck changed when he met Officer Mork. Mork worked in a middle school. He was **impressed** by

Eddie's idea. He liked Eddie's **enthusiasm** for helping teens. Officer Mork invited Eddie to try out his idea at Bussey Middle School. Consequently, Eddie was able to start the first Bicycles Most Wanted class. His determination had paid off!

Changing for Good

[6]Eddie worked hard to reach his new students. To **engage** their interest, Eddie started the class with a video. It was the *America's Most Wanted* show that told his story. Eddie described how a few bad choices had sent him to prison. He told the students that repairing bikes could help them stay out of trouble. They would be good at something. It would make their lives better. The students trusted Eddie. They knew he was sincere about helping them. As a result of Eddie's program, many students learned a trade instead of sitting in detention. They repaired bikes and gave them to charity. They learned how to be good at something and do good for others—just like Eddie.

[7]Eddie Maldonado's decision to help others turned his life around. One school official summed up Eddie's life this way: "This is a guy who was broken. He fixed himself, and now he wants to fix the rest of us." That's Eddie, all right. He's a guy who fixes things.

The Paper Clip Project

[1]In the small town of Whitwell, Tennessee, some eighth-grade students signed up for an after-school class. The topic of the class was the German Holocaust. The students read about this terrible time in the history of **humanity**. They learned that millions of Jews were imprisoned by the German government. The prisoners **endured** starvation and torture. The Whitwell students were saddened by the suffering they read about. They were also **inspired** by the prisoners' bravery. Students were horrified when they learned that 6 million Jews died in the prisons. They wanted to find a way to understand this number—to make it real somehow. They learned that people had worn paper clips on their collars to protest what the German government did. That gave them an idea. The students decided they would attempt to collect 6 million paper clips. Each clip would stand for a victim of the Holocaust. Students got right to work. They sent letters to famous people asking them to send paper clips. They also set up a Web site telling about their project. The students were excited. But they had no idea how amazing the results of their project would be.

Piles of Paper Clips

[2]In response to the students' letters and the Web site, paper clips poured into Whitwell. They came from all 50 states. Along with the paper clips came letters with stories of Holocaust victims and survivors. Within a few months, there were

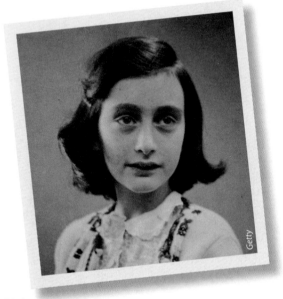

Holocaust victim Anne Frank provided through her diary a first-hand description of the horrors many endured.

100,000 paper clips in the collection. One hundred thousand paper clips is a lot, but it is far from 6 million. The students and their teachers began wondering if their goal was too **ambitious**. Then two German reporters, the Schroeders, discovered the Whitwell Web site. They published articles about the project in German newspapers. When people overseas read the articles, they responded. Whitwell Middle School was flooded with paper clips from Europe. The students had to spend hours before and after school opening the mail. They counted every paper clip and filed every letter. One class in Germany sent a leather suitcase. Students were surprised by its **contents**. It was filled with letters to Anne Frank, a young Jewish girl who died in the Holocaust. German students had written the letters to honor the brave girl. They apologized for the terrible way she and millions of others had been treated. Of course, the case also contained paper clips. Paper clips were piling up in barrels around the school. The students had a hard time believing that so many people around the world had heard about their Paper Clip Project.

Whitwell's Special Visitors

[3]The project brought more than paper clips to Whitwell. It brought the Schroeders, too. They were the German reporters who had written about the project. The couple traveled to Whitwell because they wanted to meet the students who were honoring victims of the Holocaust. The

Schroeders spent time talking with the students. They read some of the letters people had sent. They even helped students count paper clips. The reporters promised to do all they could to help the students meet their goal. In fact, the Schroeders were so impressed by the project that they wrote a book about it!

[4]The Paper Clip Project brought Holocaust survivors to Whitwell, too. A group of survivors in New York read about the project on the Internet. They were amazed. They couldn't believe these young people cared about them. They were even more surprised at where the students lived. Whitwell was a small town with no Jews at all! Four of the survivors wanted to meet the students, so they contacted the school principal. They made plans to speak at the school. The whole town turned out to welcome them. People listened in horror to the survivors' stories. They heard how families were separated forever. They heard how children worked as slaves. They wept when they heard stories of loved ones beaten or burned to death. At the end of the meeting, students crowded around the visitors. They hugged and cried. They thanked the visitors for sharing their stories. The survivors thanked the students, too. They told them it was important to remind people about the Holocaust. "That is the only way to prevent it from happening again," they said.

A Paper Clip Memorial

[5]Because people had sent them millions of paper clips, Whitwell students wanted to do something special with them. One teacher

Prisoners ride inside a nailed-up railcar on their way to a concentration camp.

suggested putting the paper clips in a German railcar. Railcars had been used to carry victims to the death camps. But where would they find one? Their friends the Schroeders came to the rescue. The couple traveled all over Germany to find a railcar used during the Holocaust. When they finally found one, they shipped it to America.

⁶In Whitwell, a crane lifted the railcar onto a set of railroad tracks. Students displayed the 6 million paper clips inside to honor the Jewish victims of the Holocaust. They displayed 5 million more for Holocaust victims who were not Jewish. Volunteers landscaped the grounds around the railcar. They planted gardens and built a pond. Then the town held a ceremony to **dedicate** the memorial. It was named the Children's Holocaust Memorial.

A Message for the World

⁷Because of the Paper Clip Project, an important message reached thousands of people. Many read about it in newspaper articles. Others heard about it on television news reports. Some read about it in the Schroeders' book. Thousands came to visit the railcar memorial. Many more found out about the project when a film company made a movie about it. But no matter how people learned about the project, the message was always the same: "All people—even those with different beliefs—must be treated fairly." The students didn't care that the victims had beliefs different from their own. They were sad for all the Jews who had suffered. They honored the victims' bravery. They asked the world to remember them.

More Than Paper Clips

⁸Some middle school students stayed after school to learn about the Holocaust. That was all they planned to do. Instead, the students changed the way they looked at others. Then they changed their community. And finally, with millions of paper clips, the students of Whitwell reached out to change the world.

Former Whitwell Middle School students show a Holocaust survivor around the Children's Holocaust Memorial.

140

SHOWDOWN IN TIANANMEN SQUARE

Turnley/CORBIS

[1]The 1980s were years of unrest in China. The country was divided by a powerful clash of ideas. Some people were ready for change. They wanted their government to allow them more freedom. This group staged protests for freedom of speech and freedom of the press. They also wanted to end dishonesty in the government. But others in China thought these were dangerous ideas. They wanted to silence protesters and preserve order. This group was determined to keep things as they were. Both groups felt strongly about their ideas. But no one predicted the brutal showdown in their future.

A Leader for Change

²Because there was such a conflict of ideas in the country, tension built in China's government. Most of China's leaders were against new freedoms. They opposed any form of protest. They thought people should be patriotic and never criticize the government. But one leader, Hu Yaobang, thought new ideas could make the country better. Hu was one of the top officials in the Communist Party, which ran the country. He was a popular leader because he listened to protesters' complaints. He thought the government should change and adapt to the needs of its people. For years, he argued for democratic reforms. Powerful leaders were angered by Hu's ideas. They took away his title of secretary general and gave him a low-level job in the government. Still, many people in China were loyal to Hu. They thought of him as the voice of change and democracy.

Beijing students gather in Tiananmen Square to honor the memory of Hu Yaobang.

Grief Turns to Protest

³As a result of Hu's loss of power, reformers came together like never before. When Hu died in 1989, they organized memorials to honor him. Many supporters wanted to honor his memory with social action. So students from 40 universities planned a **major** protest. They decided to gather in Beijing and call for the changes that Hu had supported. Informers sent word to officials that a protest was in the works. But the government was not able to derail plans for the demonstrations. Within days of Hu's death, 100,000 students and workers arrived in Beijing's Tiananmen Square. They brought flowers to honor Hu.

142

[4]Then they stayed to protest. They chanted and carried signs. They called for government leaders to meet with them and hear their demands. Days stretched into weeks. The number of protesters swelled to more than 1 million. Still, no government leaders came to talk with them. The demonstrators grew frustrated. Since their demonstrations had gotten no response, 3,000 of them went on a hunger strike. They stopped eating in hopes of drawing more attention to their cause. Two days later, officials agreed to meet with protest leaders. But talks broke down quickly. Neither side would give in.

In Tiananmen Square, a student leader calls for a citywide protest march.

A Tough Reaction

[5]Officials could see that the protest was not going to end on its own, so they tried another strategy. They sent soldiers into the square to impose the law. But thousands of citizens blocked the troops. Angered by the military action, 10,000 people joined the hunger strike. Reporters from all over the world snapped pictures of determined students starving for their cause. Protesters **assumed** that all the news coverage would force leaders to back down. But officials saw things differently. The protest was an embarrassment to them. It had become too much to **tolerate**, and it had to be stopped. Consequently, Chinese leaders sent military troops to take control. Their orders were to take back Tiananmen Square at any cost.

The Massacre

[6]Because of the decision to send in troops, horrific events took place. Late on the night of June 3, 1989, the army approached the site of the protest. As they moved through the city, soldiers opened fire on unarmed people in the streets. Shocked citizens ran from the bullets.

Some threw rocks or bottles at the troops. Others tried to set army vehicles on fire. But they were no match for tanks and automatic weapons. The shooting went on for hours. Protesters, reporters, and innocent bystanders were shot, attacked, and beaten. Slowly, thousands of troops made their way to the square. They surrounded the protesters. The students stood together and sang a Chinese anthem. As they sang, shots rang out, and victims dropped to the ground. In the early hours of June 4, the lights in the area went out. Thousands of protesters huddled together in the dark. They had no idea what was happening. When the lights came back on, the tanks rolled into the square. They crushed tents that protesters had put up for sleeping. Some student leaders shouted that protesters should fight to the death. But others negotiated. Soldiers gave them until sunrise to clear the square.

Reuters/CORBIS

A group of journalists supports the pro-Democracy protest in Tiananmen Square.

Stunned protesters lined up and filed out of the square with guns pointed at them. The conflict had ended. The wounded and the dead covered the streets. Hundreds, perhaps thousands, of people had been killed.

[7]The next day, the tanks returned. That is when one young man took a dramatic stand. He had seen the bloodshed in Tiananmen Square. He wanted the soldiers to stop killing innocent citizens. Therefore, with unbelievable courage, he stepped in front of the line of tanks. The tanks came to a halt. Amazed photographers snapped pictures. Nervous crowds watched in **suspense**. The soldiers received orders to ignore the man and move ahead. The lead tank tried to drive around the man. Each time, the man moved to block its way. Then he crawled up onto the tank to talk to the driver.

Jeff Widener/AP Images

A brave, lone protester stands in the way of tanks as they try to enter Tiananmen Square.

Worried onlookers rushed to pull the man back into the crowd. The tanks continued on their way. But their brief encounter with a rebel was a moment the world would not forget.

The Unknown Rebel

[8]The man who stood up to the tanks is called the Unknown Rebel. No one knows his name for sure. But the photograph of his **incredible** act of bravery was published around the world. People everywhere were awed by his courage in the face of impossible odds. The Unknown Rebel will forever be a powerful symbol of what an **individual** can do.

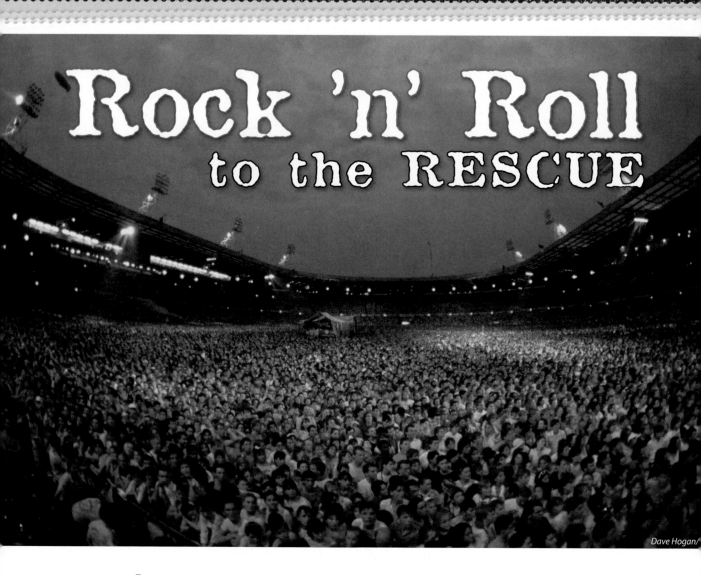

Rock 'n' Roll
to the RESCUE

Dave Hogan/

¹It was an October day in 1984. A man was relaxing and watching TV. Suddenly, a news report grabbed his attention. It moved him so deeply that it changed the course of his life. The man was Irish rock star Bob Geldof. What changed his life was a report on starvation in Ethiopia. It described how a 10-year drought had dried up crops and fields in this African country. Millions of people were struggling to survive. The program showed an American Red Cross nurse surrounded by 85,000 starving people. Many were children. They were sick and desperate for food. The sight was heartbreaking. Geldof couldn't get the images out of his mind. Within days, he bought a plane ticket and flew to Ethiopia.

Band Aid for Africa

[2]On his trip, Geldof saw for himself the grim conditions in Africa. Because of what he saw, he resolved to raise money for aid. His friend Midge Ure wanted to help, too, so they wrote a song for the victims. The song was "Do They Know It's Christmas?" Geldof and Ure called on some big stars to help them. They got 36 rock-music **idols** to come together to record the song. Among the artists were Sting, Paul McCartney, and Phil Collins. Everyone worked on the project for free. Geldof worked hard to promote his cause. He reached a lot of people

In Africa, Bob Geldof meets with the victims of famine.

through radio shows. On the shows, he told about the **famine** in Africa. He explained that some big-name rock stars had formed a group called Band Aid. They would soon release a song to raise money for aid. He asked listeners to buy the recording. Geldof

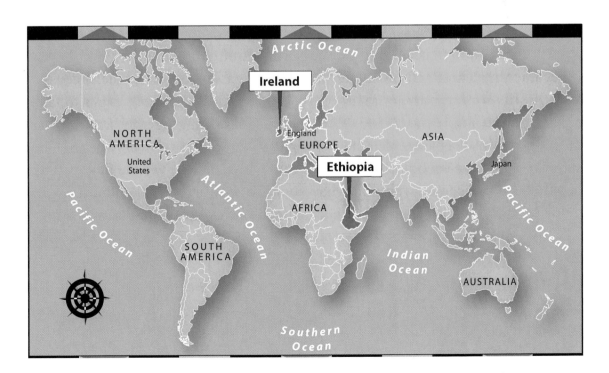

147

David Mcgough/DMI/Time Life Pictures/Getty

Singer Mick Jagger of the rock group The Rolling Stones performs at the Live Aid concert.

hoped to raise $100,000. The money would then be used to send food to Africa.

[3]The recording went on sale on December 7, just in time for the holiday season. As a result of good timing and good promotion, the recording was a big success. In fact, it became the fastest selling single ever. Profits were far higher than expected. The single raised $13 million. Geldof was amazed. One song was going to feed millions of people! The project showed him what a powerful tool rock music could be.

Live Aid Rocks the World

[4]Since Band Aid was such a success, Geldof took on an even larger project. He planned the biggest concert in history! It was a worldwide TV concert called Live Aid. Geldof wanted the concert to reach around the globe, so he arranged for one stage in England and another in America. The concert also would include shows from Japan, Australia, and other **remote** locations. Making all that happen was a challenge. It called for real broadcasting genius. A 16-hour live broadcast to the whole world had never been tried. The Live Aid crew members worked on details of the broadcast for months. They arranged to use almost every TV satellite in orbit. Lining up talent for the show was an easier job. After the success of Band Aid, stars were eager to take part. Geldof put together a show that got the attention of every rock-music fan on the planet. On the day of the concert, people in 150 countries tuned in to watch. They saw

October 1984	December 1984	July 1985	1986
World's first report on Ethiopia's famine airs on TV.	Band Aid raises $13 million for Africa.	Live Aid raises $140 million for Africa.	Geldof is nominated for Nobel Peace Prize.

performances by hundreds of artists, including 60 of the biggest stars in the business. Between acts, Geldof asked the audience to donate money. Money for Africa poured in. Phone banks around the world received millions of calls and pledges.

[5]Nearly 2 billion people watched the Live Aid concert. Because of the great music and Geldof's **constant** pleas for donations, the event raised $140 million. All of the money was spent on aid for Africa. Half was used for food. The other half paid for long-term projects that improved living conditions. Live Aid brought Geldof a lot of honors. He was nominated for the Nobel Peace Prize. Queen Elizabeth even made him an honorary knight! But for Geldof, Live Aid was never about fame or awards. It was a way to help people who were dying in poor nations. Live Aid was only a start. The concert had been huge, but Africa's problems were much bigger. Geldof knew he had to **maintain** people's interest in the cause. If the world forgot about

CORBIS

David Bowie performs in Wembley Stadium in London during Live Aid.

Africa, its problems would only get worse.

Live 8 Rocks World Leaders

[6]Money from Live Aid saved many lives. But it didn't end starvation in Africa. Therefore, Geldof stayed on the job. He planned more concerts to reach even more people. This

1986	July 2005	July 2005	2006
Geldof receives honorary knighthood.	Live 8 pressures world leaders to aid poor nations.	Leaders of G8 nations budget $50 billion for aid to Africa.	Geldof is nominated for Nobel Peace Prize again.

Destiny's Child performs during the Live 8 concert in Philadelphia.

U2 performs during the opening of the Live 8 concert in London.

time, he had a different goal. He wanted to raise awareness rather than money. The concerts would take place just before a meeting of world leaders. They were the heads of the G8 nations, the world's most powerful countries. These countries had money and resources. Geldof wanted the leaders to do more to end world poverty. During the concert, he planned to ask people to help send that message. Together, they could get world leaders to act. Since the idea was to pressure G8 leaders, Geldof called his project Live 8. On July 2, 2005, there were 10 Live 8 concerts around the world. It was an even bigger event than Live Aid. More than a thousand artists performed. This time, 3 billion people watched!

[7]As a result of Live 8, Geldof presented a written request to G8 leaders. It was signed by 30 million people. They were people who wanted action. They wanted more aid for poor nations. The paper also asked **prosperous** nations to forgive the debts that poor nations owed. The plan worked. A few days after Live 8, the leaders took a vote. They increased aid to Africa. They canceled the debt owed by the poorest countries. In all, they committed $50 billion to African relief.

[8]Bob Geldof demonstrated the power of taking action. He saw a bad situation and did more than just shake his head. He stepped up and challenged other people and artists to get involved. To help others, he figured out how to do things that no one had ever done before. By thinking big, Bob Geldof changed millions of lives.

Teens Who DREAM BIG

[1]Most teens dream of great things they'd like to do as adults. But not all teens can wait that long. Some begin amazing careers while they're still in school. How do they get such an early start on success? Every story is different.

Esteban Cortazar: Fashion Designer

[2]Esteban Cortazar came to Miami from Colombia. He was only 10 years old, but he was already moving toward a great career. In his family, being creative was a way of life. His mother was a jazz singer. His father was an artist. Because of their example, Esteban wasn't afraid to be creative. He studied acting, dancing, and singing. He starred in musicals, and he loved costumes. When his mother got ready for a show, Esteban was fascinated. Her costumes transformed her into a star! He began to sketch

Esteban Cortazar shows his collection during New York's Fashion Week in February 2006.

151

fashion designs. Then he would create his fashions by cutting up old clothes and stapling the pieces together. That interest in clothing never left him.

[3]In 1997, fashion designer Todd Oldham opened a shop near Esteban's home. The 13-year-old boy couldn't believe his luck. He rushed to the shop and showed Oldham his sketches. Oldham was so impressed that he invited the boy to his next New York fashion show. As a result of that trip, Esteban fell in love with fashion. He went home and designed a new collection. When his school held a talent show, Esteban had his friends model his designs. A fashion expert saw his collection. She invited him to be part of a professional show in Miami. Esteban's collection was a hit. Consequently, he became an overnight success. He was the youngest designer ever to show his fashions at New York's Fashion Week. Now he designs gowns for many celebrities. His client list includes Eva Longoria, Beyonce Knowles, Paris Hilton, and Cindy Crawford. Esteban Cortazar is definitely living his teen dream!

Akiane Kramarik: Artist and Poet

[4]Like many 4-year-olds, Akiane Kramarik drew pictures of animals and family members. But her drawings weren't like other children's. They were so good, they were lifelike! Her mother began buying canvasses so Akiane could use oil paints. Each day, the young girl woke up before dawn. She painted for hours. The faces she painted were full of feeling and life. As Akiane grew, so did her talent. As a result, her artwork received more attention. People said Akiane was a genius. By the time she was 10 years old, she was appearing in magazines and on national talk shows. Her paintings sold for thousands of dollars.

[5]Art is not Akiane's only talent. She also has written two books of poetry. Her books and paintings bring in big money. She has big ideas about how to use it, too. Akiane believes she must use her talent to help others. Since that is her goal, she gives much of her money to

Akiane Kramarik adds finishing touches to one of her paintings.

Photo courtesy Art Akiane LLC/Digital Color/Sean Watson

charity. One group she helps is a group of needy children in Lithuania. They are called "the garbage children" because they live in garbage dumps. Akiane wants to send them food and build a hospital for their care. She also plans to go on a world tour to raise money to fight AIDS in Africa. Clearly, this teen has what it takes to do great things. Big dreams, big talent, and a big heart are the secrets to her success.

Ryan Patterson: Inventor

[6]The next time you do a science project, choose one that will make you famous. That's what Ryan Patterson did. Because he wanted his project to be meaningful, he tried to think of an invention that would make life better. As he sat in a fast-food restaurant, he remembered something he had seen there once. Some customers who were deaf had to ask an interpreter to order their food. Then he thought about a deaf student at his school. The student had an adult interpreter with him

all day long. Ryan thought he would not like to have an adult tag along with him all day. Then he got the idea. Why not have a tool for translating sign language? He decided to invent a glove for translating sign language into text. That would be too ambitious for most students, but not for Ryan.

[7]Ryan was an engineering whiz. By third grade, his questions were too hard for his parents to answer. So Ryan found a retired scientist to guide him in his studies. They built and experimented together every Saturday for 7 years. Due to this training, Ryan knew more about engineering than most college graduates. It took months to work out a plan for his invention. It took even more time to build it. Ryan worked right up to the deadline. He finished his project the day before the science fair.

[8]Ryan called his invention the Handy Glove. He made it by wiring sensors into the fingers of the glove. When the wearer formed a letter, the glove sent information to a small wireless receiver. The receiver then displayed the letters, and the "listener" could read the words the person was signing. After the science fair, Ryan entered the glove in national contests. His whole life changed as a result. He received awards and scholarships. He was invited to Sweden to meet with Nobel Prize winners. He even won $300,000 in prize money. Ryan saved most of the money for college. He did use some of it to buy a red Mustang with a state-of-the-art sound system, though. He may be an engineering genius, but he's a teenager, too!

Photo courtesy National Institute on Deafness and Other Communication Disorders (NIDCD)

Ryan Patterson demonstrates how his Handy Glove works.

[9]Not everyone can become a teen tycoon like Esteban, Akiane, or Ryan. But some people do. Could you be one of them? Remember, it's never too early to think big!

E-WORLD

- How does technology affect your daily life?
- Is technology good for us?
- How can technology make you safer?

MP3 Players:
They're Breaking All the Records

¹**C**ome with us to a long-ago time. Let's visit the days before MP3 players. Let's go back before CD players or even tape players. Here's how you would have listened to a mix of your favorite recorded songs 40 years ago. You slid a long-playing record out of its cardboard holder. The record was as big as a dinner plate. A thin, shiny black band marked the beginning of each song. You looked on the printed record holder to see the order in which the songs appeared. Let's say you wanted to hear the third song. You counted to the third thin band on the record. This is how you knew where to place the needle. The needle was attached to the arm of the record player. You turned on the record player. Such a player could be as large as a suitcase. The record began to spin on the turntable. Then you carefully placed the needle on the record and listened to your song. After that, you put this record away. Then you got another one and repeated the steps.

²Instead of a long-playing record, you may have gathered a stack of smaller records called "45s." These records had one song on each side. You put several of your favorite 45s on the player. You turned the player on. You heard clattering

Turntables like this one played both long-playing records and 45s.

and clicking sounds. The first record dropped and began to spin. The player arm moved over the record, and the needle settled onto it. You listened to a song. Then the arm moved off the record, and the next one dropped. Listening to 20 of your favorite songs **involved** a lot of work. It could take a whole afternoon!

Traveling Tunes

[3]Now we live in an age of MP3 players. The **development** of these pocket-sized devices has changed the way we collect and play music. MP3 players have taken us far beyond records, tapes, and CDs. These players are much easier to handle. You can easily take one wherever you go. Forty years ago, taking your favorite music with you to a friend's house was a problem. There was no easy way to carry a large record player and a **cumbersome** stack of records. Also, record players had to be plugged into an electric outlet. This meant you had to listen to music indoors mainly. MP3 players make it easy to take your music with you. A portable MP3—the kind you can carry around—is **capable** of storing a lot of tunes.

Portable players make it easy to listen to music wherever you go.

That's because the music is compressed into a small space on a digital file. You can buy armbands and belt clips to carry a player. MP3 players are powered by batteries. You don't need to plug them into an outlet. An MP3 player is so light and compact you can even listen to music while jogging.

Be Your Own DJ

[4]Another problem with listening to records was that you couldn't easily pick and choose your songs. One choice was to listen to an entire record of 10 or more songs. Otherwise, you had to move the arm

of the record player from place to place to listen to certain songs. In addition, you had to buy all the songs on a record. What if you didn't like one or more of them? An MP3 player allows you to create your own mix of music from CDs, Web sites, or even FM radio. Some of this music is free or inexpensive. The music can be played in any order you choose. It can be grouped according to music type or by artist. An MP3 player will even **display** information about the songs as you're listening to them. You can be your own DJ.

No More Jumping

[5]A third problem with records and even with CDs is that the music can "jump" or "skip" when it's playing. This is because record players and CD players have moving parts. Also, you can scratch or wear out records and CDs if you play them over and over. An MP3 player solves these problems. It has no moving parts to interrupt the music.

You can't wear out or scratch the record or CD by playing the same song again and again. This is because the music is stored as code rather than recorded onto a surface.

With a click of the mouse, listeners can download music from a variety of Web sites.

Music Made Easy

[6]Music is the soundtrack to our lives. Listening to recorded music is an **essential** part of each day for many of us. Makers of MP3 players know this. That's why they keep working to make it easier to collect, store, and listen to music. What will the future bring? It will likely bring smaller players that can hold more music. We're beginning to see everyday objects such as cameras and cell phones that include built-in MP3 players. You can even buy sunglasses with MP3 players in them! The future of music players looks bright. It seems so bright you just might need those sunglasses.

USING HIGH TECH TO CONNECT

[1]**A**re you ready for a pop quiz? Here it is:

1. Angelo forgot to bring his lunch money to school. He doesn't want to borrow money from his friends. But, he needs to eat lunch. What can he do?

2. Celia left an important school paper at home. The paper is due today. She knows that if she turns in the paper a day late, her grade will be much lower. What can she do?

3. Max was running alone on the track after school. He has hurt his ankle and can't walk home. He wants to call his dad to come pick him up. The school office is closed, though. What can he do?

4. EXTRA CREDIT. What do the following mean?
   a. HRU
   b. SLAP
   c. G2G

Did your answers to the first three questions have to do with cell phones? Most young people these days would have answered the same way. "Angelo can use his cell

In emergencies, cell phones provide a quick connection to help.

phone to ask someone to bring lunch money." "Celia can send someone at home a text message to ask him or her to bring the paper." "Max can use his cell phone to call someone to pick him up." (The answers to the fourth question will come later.)

[2]Cell phones were created so that people could solve problems such as these. Parents use cell phones to stay in close touch with their children before and after school. "Don't forget your doctor's appointment." "I'll pick you up at 4:00." Children use them to

reach their parents in case they need something or their plans change. "Forgot my lunch money." "Going to Ryan's house after school."

[3]Cell phones are also useful in real emergencies. For example, two students walked through the halls of Columbine High School in Colorado several years ago. They began shooting other students. Some students used cell phones to call their parents. Others called the police to ask for help. Perhaps it's a good thing that nearly half of Americans between the ages of 12 and 19 have cell phones. These phones offer families more peace of mind. They solve the problem of staying in touch. However, the use of cell phones by teens has created some problems too.

Deadly Distraction

[4]A *distraction* is something that takes your attention away from what you're doing. Everyone knows that drinking and driving don't mix. Neither do talking on a cell phone and driving. Talking on a cell phone can be a deadly distraction—especially for teen drivers. Teens have little driving experience. They

need to focus all their attention on what's in front of them and what's behind them. They need to know what other drivers are doing. Even a small **lapse** in concentration can cause them to run a stop sign or crash into the back of another car. A car company did a study on this recently. The study showed that teen drivers are four times more likely to be distracted by cell phone use than adult drivers. Several states have banned teen cell phone use while driving.

Reading, Writing, and Ringing Cell Phones

[5]Another problem has been the use of cell phones during class periods. There has been much discussion by school officials and parents over this. School officials say that the calls distract students from learning. But many parents want their children to carry a phone. Some schools have established rules against using cell phones during school hours. They require students to leave the phones in their lockers. Others allow students to bring phones to class. But they must keep them turned off.

[6]The newer cell phones are more than telephones. They can be used as writing instruments. Students now use text messaging to stay in touch with one another. Some students sneak their phones into class. They **compose** text messages to friends instead of listening to the teacher. Some students **conceal** the phones under their desks. They thumb their messages without even looking at the key pad. And many cell phones come equipped with video games. Students who concentrate on winning a game are not paying attention to the teacher. "Cell phones are a nuisance," says one principal. "They don't belong in school."

Tools for Cheating

[7]A third problem is the use of cell phones to cheat on tests at school. Students have used camera phones to take a picture of a test. They share the photo of the test with other students who have not yet taken it. Some students sneak their phones into the classroom and send text messages during tests. "ANS #3?" they might text to a fellow student. The other student will send the answer back in a text message. Teachers in China have found a solution to this problem. They use modern tools to solve a **technological** problem. They use

cell phone jammers. The jammers send a signal that blocks the use of the cell phones during tests.

Some students use cell phones to play games during class or to cheat on tests.

Cool School Tools

[8]Cell phones are a quick and simple way to communicate. Should they be used while driving? No. Should they be banned from schools just because they can be misused? Not necessarily, some may argue. Pencils and scissors can be misused, too, but we don't need to ban these tools. The solution is to set reasonable limits—no driving while talking on a cell phone and no cell phone use in class. It's not cell phones that are the problem. It's the way they are used. In fact, some schools are even looking at how to use cell phones for educational purposes. They can be used as calculators, say some teachers. School officials can use them as a way to **notify** students of school information. Students can use them to store information about class **assignments**. Some cell phones can be used to connect to the Internet. They can be used as dictionaries. Clearly, cell phones can be helpful school tools, if used wisely.

[9]Now, back to the pop quiz at the beginning of this passage. How did you do on question number 4? If you are a regular text messenger, you probably got them all right.

   a. HRU is "How are you?"
   b. SLAP is "Sounds like a plan."
   c. G2G is "Got to go."

Tech Tools for

FIGHTING CRIME

David Young-Wolff/Getty

¹It's a sunny afternoon. Girls and boys swarm out of the double doors of Elmwood Elementary School. Suddenly a car comes speeding down the street. The principal yells angrily at the driver as the car flies past the school. "SLOW DOWN!" The driver keeps going. Across town, at the same moment, a girl stands in an aisle of a department store. She looks around to see if anyone is watching. Then she picks up a pair of sunglasses and slips them into her backpack. She walks toward the store's exit. In a building in another part of town, a man walks into the lobby of a company. He pretends to be a new employee at the company. He plans to steal an important file from the office.

²What do all of these scenes have in common? In each one, a crime is being committed. A crime happens when someone breaks a law. The driver is breaking a traffic law by speeding through a school zone. The girl in the store is breaking a law against shoplifting. The man in the office is also breaking a law against stealing. Laws are put in place to protect us and keep us safe. Most people obey laws. But some people don't. When people break the law, all of us are a little less safe. That's why governments, police, and others work hard to stop crimes

Surveillance cameras help police catch criminals, like this man who was photographed while breaking into a car.

from happening. They also work hard to catch the people who commit crimes. Today's technology helps them do this work. Here's a look at three ways in which technology is used in the fight against crime.

Private Eye

[3]When is a street lamp *not* a street lamp? When it's a camera. Cities in many countries now are using cameras to catch lawbreakers. Some cameras are disguised as street lamps. Others are in plain sight. Both kinds of cameras are called *surveillance* cameras. This means that they are used to **monitor** people's activities. Some cameras catch people breaking traffic laws. Some keep watch over neighborhoods that have had shootings and other crimes. Others catch people selling drugs on city streets or in parks. Some cameras film thieves in the act of stealing. Many stores and all banks use these cameras to prevent robberies. ATM machines have cameras. So do many subway stops. Cameras are found in parking lots and airports. They are used

in government buildings. The photographs and films help officials **investigate** crimes and bring criminals to justice.

[4]Cameras are also used in some schools. School shootings and other problems have led school officials to install surveillance cameras. The officials say that they want students to be secure and safe from harm. They also want to protect school property. A group of students may think twice about making mischief if they think a camera is pointed at them. Cameras in schools can be placed in central hallways. They can be in lunchrooms. They can be in school parking lots and stadiums. Some schools have even placed cameras in school restrooms. The cameras **assist** school staff in keeping students and staff safe.

ID Badges

[5]Another high-tech tool for fighting crime is the ID badge. This type of badge is used to check a person's **identity**. An ID badge makes it harder for a person to pretend to be someone else. Many workers wear ID badges. They must show or scan the badge to enter a building or an office. This includes people who work in laboratories. It includes people who work in government offices. It includes doctors and nurses. Not all ID badges are alike, though. Some have bar codes like the ones on products at grocery stores. Some badges have photographs. Some have magnetic strips. And some may have a **microscopic** radio tag. The radio tag sends out a signal. The signal can be "read" by a receiver. A **typical** ID badge is about the size of a playing card. It has a person's name and other information. The person moves the badge through an object that reads the information on it. If the information checks out, the person is allowed to enter.

ID badges make it hard for a person to pretend to be someone else.

[6]Today, many schools are using ID badges. Some schools' badges have radio tags. This allows a student's movements to be tracked

by a radio signal. In other schools, students insert the badges into a "reader." This helps school officials keep track of which students are in school each day. It also helps them make sure that strangers cannot enter the school without permission. Students in some schools must use their ID badges to buy school lunches. They must use them to check out books from the library. Some students must use them to enter or exit classrooms. In most schools that use badges, everyone—including teachers and school visitors—must wear ID badges while on school property.

Getty

ID chips like this one are often placed under the skin of pets and farm animals.

ID Chips

[7]An ID chip is like an ID badge, but an ID chip is placed under the skin. The chip is a small electronic object. It's about the size of a grain of rice. It gives off a radio signal. The signal can be picked up by a scanner. A person's ID number and other information is sent to the scanner. These ID chips are like those that people have been using for their pets for several years. When lost or kidnapped pets with ID chips are found, they can easily be returned to their owners. Other ID chip users include farmers. The chips help some farmers keep track of livestock. But human ID chips are not yet in wide use. Not everyone likes the idea of having an ID chip in his or her body.

Technology in Action

[8]The speeding driver you read about earlier was caught. A camera near the school recorded his license plate number and speed. The girl who tried to steal the sunglasses also was caught. A person watching the pictures on the store's security camera saw her put the glasses in her backpack. What about the man who pretended to be a new employee? He never got into the office. That's because he didn't have an ID badge.

ARE VIDEO GAMES HARMLESS?

¹**Y**ou're a huge monster with one bulging eye in the middle of your face. You're as tall as a three-story building. You're mad. You're *really* mad. You're stomping through the downtown streets, crushing cars with your feet. Another monster has thrown a radio tower at you as if it were a spear. The blow has weakened some of your powers. You want **revenge**. You have a fist full of thunderbolts. When you find the monster, you'll throw the thunderbolts at him. You'll show *him* who's boss!

²Welcome to the action-packed world of a video game. Chances are this is a world you've visited before. Maybe it wasn't a fighting game. It could have been a game in which you were the mayor of an imaginary town. Or perhaps you were a race-car driver or a football player. Video games are like the one-eyed monster you read about earlier. They're huge. They're powerful. But, are they good for us? Are they bad for us? No one yet knows for sure. Let's look at some of the problems these games are said to create.

Friends have fun playing video games together.

Violent Games Make Violent Teens

[3]*Violence* is the use of force in a way that harms a person or property. Many popular video games have fighting, killing, and blowing up objects as part of the action. Players solve problems in these games by injuring or killing other characters. Some people think that these video games make children and teens violent in real life.

Some scientists see a connection between violent games and violence in real life.

[4]"Kids who see violence are more likely to act it out," says a scientist who studies teen behavior. Players in some video games can take on the roles of "bad guys." What's wrong with this? Many people think that pretending to be a bad guy in a game encourages bad behavior in everyday life. They think teens who play violent games are more likely to get into fights with parents, teachers, and peers. One of the killers in a school shooting liked to play violent video games. Some people blamed these games for the shooting.

Some Games Are Not for Children

[5]Video games are beginning to **resemble** films. The movements of video game characters today are much like those of film characters. More games have story plots, just as movies do. What's the problem with this? It's the same problem as with some movies. The subjects are better suited for adults than for children. Some subjects can be too disturbing for children or teens. They can be too confusing. "Video games **expose** kids to adult subjects that kids aren't ready for," says one parent. The games are marketed to children and teens, though. Senator Hillary Clinton says these types of games are "stealing the innocence of our children." She says that they're making the hard job of being a parent even harder. Games that show characters using adult language or in adult situations are for **mature** players. Children and teens should not be able to buy or rent them.

168

Video Games Are a Waste of Time

⁶Some people think that video games are a waste of time. It's true that some of these **critics** have never played a video game. They think these games are worse than films and music. They say that at least movies and music can make you think. Some argue that playing video games is a mindless activity. "Who wants to waste a day roaming around a make-believe world killing monsters?" People who say this may not know that there are hundreds of different kinds of video games. "Kids are role-playing when they should be involved in real life," adds another critic. Some parents think their teens should be playing sports or reading books instead of playing video games. Here's how another U.S. senator feels about the subject: "Little Johnny should be learning how to read, not how to kill cops."

Hooked on Video Games

⁷Another problem with video games is that they can become an addiction. An *addiction* is the state of being dependent on something. People can be addicted to drugs. They can be addicted to alcohol. And they can be addicted to video games. For teens hooked on video games, playing the games is not just a **leisure** activity. They spend all of their time playing

Some children and teens would rather be playing video games than doing anything else.

games. They neglect their studies and other activities. They quit seeing friends. Playing video games isn't a part of their lives. It *is* their lives. This description doesn't fit most children or teens who play video games, though. Gaming doesn't take the place of their social activities. They can stop playing when they

Addiction to video games has become a problem for some teens.

need to. One teen counselor says that students who are hooked on video games are experiencing several problems. She says these students need to work with counselors. They need to "figure out why video games are so much more fun, relaxing, or interesting than school, friends, or family." Signs of video game addiction can include the following:

- not being able to stop playing
- wanting more and more time for playing
- avoiding family and friends
- feeling empty or angry when not playing games
- lying about how much time they spend playing
- having problems in school
- playing for 10 or more hours straight

Gaming Isn't Cheap

[8]The final problem with video games is that they're expensive. Game systems now cost hundreds of dollars. New game titles can cost $50 or more. That's a lot for most teens to pay. Each new system is more expensive than the last. Why? Players can expect new and amazing effects. They want movements, sounds, and pictures that are increasingly more lifelike. Game systems are like many computers. They have a short life. They are made to last about 5 years. Then it's time to buy a "new, improved" one. The add-ons are expensive, too. You need speakers to improve the sound. You need special control sticks. You need special TVs that make the pictures look even sharper. When you think about all of these costs and all of the problems, it's enough to make you mad. *Really* mad. Somebody hand me a thunderbolt!

The Sound of Music

[1]Recorded music has been around forever. That is, if by *forever* you mean "for the past 150 years." What did home entertainment technology look like before then? It was pretty simple, says writer Rick Karr. The "hardware" was "a piano and a daughter to play it," he says. The "software" was "a piece of sheet music." Look around your home. How many ways can you listen to music today? Do you have a radio? A stereo? A computer? A CD player? An MP3 player? How did things change so fast in 150 years? The change began the way all progress begins—with a problem.

"Mary Had a Little Lamb"

[2]How can we record the human voice? This was the problem that inventors were trying to solve in the late 1800s. Inventor Thomas Edison didn't have music in mind when he worked on a solution to the problem. No one was demanding recorded music during his time. After all, there were marching bands. There were music halls and opera houses, and of course, there were pianos in parlors. Edison wanted to record voices for other reasons. He wanted to improve telegraph machines. He was also thinking about how to record telephone messages. And he was looking for a new way to record business letters and contracts. This could be useful, he thought. When people made

171

business agreements, they could rely on the actual spoken words. A voice recording wouldn't lie.

[3]In 1877, Edison spoke the words *Mary had a little lamb.* into his machine. The machine played back his words. It was the first recording of a human voice. This first successful model of a phonograph contained no new parts. It was put together with materials that other inventors had worked with for years. The phonograph used a cylinder, which is a long, rounded object, similar to a soda can. Edison wrapped tinfoil around the cylinder. The machine had two sharp needles. One needle recorded sound by making grooves in the foil. The other needle played back the sound. Edison worked in his lab until he found the right way to combine all these parts. His invention inspired other inventors. They began to improve on Edison's machine. Edison kept a close eye on them and saw that they were creating new uses for the technology he had helped develop. The phonograph could be used to play recorded music. Edison went back to work in his lab.

Making Music Available for All

[4]The next problem, then, was how to make the technology available to everyone. Early phonographs were expensive. Most people could not afford to have a phonograph in their home. Those who could afford

Music Players Throughout the Years

1877	1800s	1906	1929	1934	1948
Thomas Edison invents the phonograph.	Nikolai Tesla invents radio.	First radio program of voice and music is broadcast.	FM radio is introduced.	Joseph Begun builds first tape recorder for broadcasting.	Columbia Records introduces long-playing (LP) records.

the machines still had a problem. They were not easy to operate. Maybe there was a way to create a machine for public places. People might pay a few cents to listen to songs on this machine. Thomas Edison helped solve this problem.

[5]Edison and others developed early models of what we now know as jukeboxes. Edison figured out a way to produce inexpensive wax cylinders. Then he recorded music on them. Finally, he placed them in a music-playing machine. People put coins into the machine, and the sounds of music came out! Before long, people wanted their own music machines. Inventors developed discs on which sounds could be recorded. The discs were one-sided records at first, but two-sided records soon followed. Phonograph manufacturers kept figuring out ways to improve the quality of sound on the recordings. By the early 1900s, many people were able to afford their own record players. Electrical recordings made voices and music much clearer. Many people stopped gathering on porches or in backyards to make their own music and instead gathered around the record players. A world of new music opened to them. The music industry was born.

Homemade Music

[6]Recorded music soon became available to everyone. As the time line shows, new technology began appearing every few years. Audiotapes followed records. Then there were CDs, and MP3 players followed

1949	1965	1969	1979	1983	1989	1998
RCA introduces 45 RPM records.	Eight-track magnetic tape is introduced.	The Internet is created.	The Sony Walkman cassette player is introduced.	Sony and Philips introduce compact disc (CD) technology.	The Fraunhofer Institute in Germany patents the MP3 format.	The first MP3 players are introduced.

CDs. By the 21st century, a new problem had arisen. People wanted to record their own music to sell or to share with a wide audience. How could they do this cheaply?

[7]Elizabeth Sharp has a tiny space in her apartment. She has padded the space so that the walls are soundproof. A drum kit, a stack of guitar amps, and a computer fill the space. This is a home recording studio. Sharp records and mixes music in her space. A decade ago, the equipment would have cost around $50,000. How can Sharp afford her own studio? The technology has become affordable. And it is powerful. Today, you can turn a laptop computer into a recording studio. You can do this for less than a thousand dollars. Musicians all over the world can use this technology to record music. Even non-musicians can record music.

Technology helps people compose and record their own music.

What's Next in Recorded Music?

[8]What does the future hold for recorded music? What new problems will arise, and how will they be solved? People are already able to record music made with computers instead of with real instruments. They are putting together and recording slices of human-made and machine-made music. They are able to share the music, and even sell it, on the Internet. Will we no longer need record companies? How will people store and play recorded music in the future? Here's an idea. Perhaps scientists will figure out how to make music directly from thoughts in our brains. Maybe we'll be able to store this music inside our heads. We could even play back the music in our heads. We could call it "biomusic." Perhaps 150 years from now, your great-great-grandchildren might say, "Biomusic? That's been around *forever*!"

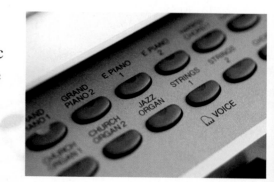

Expedition 11

MOTION AND EMOTION

- Why do people dance?
- How is movement used to show emotion?
- What kinds of dance appeal to you?

175

n/Getty

Mika/zefa/Corbis

In a SPIN:

B-boying and B-girling

[1]The air feels electric. That's because everyone knows what's coming. They don't know *exactly* what's coming, though. "B-boys, are you ready?" the disk jockey shouts. "B-girls, are you ready?" The DJ has two turntables, a mixer, and two copies of the same record. He's coming to a break in the music. That's when you'll hear only the beats, the pounding rhythm. Now it's time! A dancer is on the floor. The others form a circle around him. The dancer is upright, moving his upper body like a jerky robot. Now he's gliding across the floor, as if he has no bones. He's riding the rhythm. And now he's dropped to the floor. He did that so smoothly! He's shuffling his legs. Next, he's spinning on his back. His legs make a *V* in the air as he spins. His moves are **thrilling** to watch. People around him are nodding and smiling. Some are saying "YEAH!"

[2]Can you tell what the dancer is doing? He's b-boying, or break dancing. The *B* stands for "breaking." This refers to dancing to breaks in music. The **activity** is part athletics and part dance. It's an art form. The best dancers, or "breakers," show amazing style and strength. Their bodies are very flexible. B-boying began in the early 1970s in the South Bronx part of New York City. Street gangs would meet to set a time for a rumble, or fight. At these meetings, gang leaders would

Highlights of B-boying/ B-girling History

▶ **1970**
Break dancing originates in the streets of the South Bronx in New York City. B-boys experiment with new moves.

▶ **1980**
Break dancing reaches a larger audience through film, TV, and other media.

▶ **1990**
Break dancing goes out of the media spotlight. But, it becomes popular in Europe and Asia.

▶ **2000**
Break dancing continues to be popular around the world. Older dancers are passing on their knowledge to new generations of b-boys and b-girls.

Denis Felix/Getty

177

have dance contests. The leader who could "bust out" moves that the other couldn't match was the winner. That meant that he could decide where the rumble would be held. As a result of these dance-offs, b-boying gained attention. Soon it moved from the streets to discos, parties, and talent shows.

Breaking Out

James Brown, a spirited performer, inspired many b-boy/b-girl moves.

[3]During the 1970s, b-boys on the streets began improving their style and inventing new moves. They studied singer James Brown. Known as the "Godfather of Soul," Brown would spin and drop to the floor while performing. Groups such as the Rock Steady Crew and the New York City Breakers imitated these moves. They spun on their back, head, and hands. They added moves that **resembled** those in kung fu movies. B-boys even borrowed moves from cartoons and comics. Because this new dance style was so exciting, many young people wanted to try b-boying.

[4]B-boys and b-girls gave names to their moves—*toprock, swipes, flares, freezes*. DJs were experimenting, too. They wanted to find ways to extend break beats in music. That way, dancers could have more than a few seconds in which to do their moves. Dancers were breaking to different kinds of music—hip-hop, jazz, soul. People outside the b-boy culture were beginning to notice this exciting new style of dance.

Break Dancing Gets Discovered

[5]In the 1980s, a brief scene from the movie *Flashdance* showed b-boying. As a result of this, breaking reached a wider audience. The media also discovered b-boying/b-girling during this time. It began to show up on television channels such as MTV. B-boying movies were produced. Now that it was in the spotlight, this art form became well

known as "break dancing." The attention from the public gave new life to the form.

[6]Break-dancers were encouraged by the public's interest to invent new moves, such as the windmill. This is one of the most famous moves in b-boying. A dancer spins on his back. His legs are in the air in the *V* position and are twisting around during the backspin. During the 1980s, b-boys and b-girls also added more acrobatics and gymnastics to the dances. Break-dancers **altered** some of the basic moves by adding their own special flavor to them.

[7]Fashion became important in b-boy culture in the 1980s. Many break-dance groups, or crews, wore matching hats, shirts, and shoes. B-boys and b-girls often wore nylon tracksuits. The slick nylon made it easy to slide and spin on the floor. Pants and shirts in the 1980s were usually baggy. Certain clothing brands began to be linked to this culture.

Out of the Spotlight

[8]By the 1990s, breaking was beginning to fade from public view. It wasn't shown on television or in movies as much as it had been in the 1980s. Therefore, the public thought that the art had died. But, people were still b-boying and b-girling, even if the public wasn't watching. Breaking became popular in Europe and in Asia in the 1990s. Young people there learned moves from images on television or on the Internet.

Getty

A dancer in Mongolia practices the windmill, a popular move in break dancing.

[9]Break dancing still is developing today. Breaking events and contests occur all over the world. Some dance schools now teach breaking. And many of the "pioneers"—the b-boys who began the form in the 1970s—are still active in breaking. They're passing on their art to new generations of b-boys and b-girls. You may not see as much break dancing as in earlier years. But it's still very much alive and kicking—and spinning and toprocking and windmilling.

Jutta Klee/Getty

DANCeSPORT:
GeT iN STeP!

[1]It's Friday night. Twenty-five teens have gathered at a mall. Which one of these activities will the teens most likely do tonight?

    a. hang out

    b. play video games

    c. dance the tango and the waltz

Tonight, they'll be dancing—partner dancing. They're not only dancing the tango and the waltz. They might be practicing the foxtrot, too—and maybe the rumba and samba, as well. Two instructors will be moving around the dance floor with the teens. They'll help the kids improve their dance steps. *"One-two-three, one-two-three! Remember to lead with your hip! Move from the balls of your feet! Get those elbows up!"* The young dancers are smiling. Some of the teens are better dancers than others. But all of them are having fun. Some are amazed at themselves. A month ago, they were tripping over their feet. Now they're actually dancing! Not only that, they're dancing with another person. And the training is working. These teens have discovered ballroom dance. Yes—*ballroom*. If you're thinking that

teens, *ballroom*, and *fun* are words that don't belong together, think again. If you're thinking this kind of dancing is only for grandparents, take a closer look at the dancers. Ballroom dancing is back. It's hot. It's cool. It has shaken off its stuffy image. It even has a new name: dancesport. If you're a teen and you haven't yet discovered ballroom dancing, take our **advice**. Put on your dancing shoes. Get in step! Ballroom dancing has a lot to offer you.

Lisa Maree Williams/Getty

A couple prepares to compete in a ballroom dancing contest.

[2]Why should you try ballroom dancing? This form of dance is a **fabulous** way to get fit and stay fit. That's why some people now call it *dancesport*. People all over the globe are entering dancesport contests. Dancers train for the contests as they would for other athletic events. Being a good ballroom dancer requires strength and stamina, which is the ability to keep going without tiring

too quickly. It's like sports such as soccer and swimming. Ballroom dancing—especially the Latin dances such as rumba, samba, and mambo—develops strong leg muscles and strong abs. Don't believe it? Try one of these dances, or even the waltz, for 20 minutes. You and your partner will know that you've had a workout! Your muscles will be tired. You'll be out of breath. And you'll be smiling. Dancing is more fun than jogging or lifting weights, too. "Dancesport feels powerful and comfortable," says one teen dancer. "I play basketball for my school team. And dancing helps me stay quick on my feet for moving around the basketball court." Ballroom dancing is a great way to stay active and build strength.

Antonio Banderas sweeps his partner across the floor in *Take the Lead*.

Kerry Hayes/New Line Productions/Bureau L.A. Collection/Corbis

[3]Another reason to try ballroom dancing is that it helps you develop useful social skills. Teens can sometimes be timid or shy. The teenage years can be a time when you might feel a little unsure of yourself. Learning ballroom dancing can help build your self-confidence. It can give you a sense of pride in your newfound abilities. "Some teens have never done anything like this," says a ballroom dance teacher. "So, the whole experience might be hard for them at first. But once they get it, they *really* get it, and they just blossom!" In ballroom dancing, you can ask someone to dance without feeling embarrassed or awkward. And even if you're not a shy teen, you can develop other social skills through ballroom dancing. You can sharpen your teamwork skills by learning to lead or follow while dancing. Ballroom dancing **promotes** trust and respect for others. It helps teach politeness and good manners. This form of dancing gives you a sense of dignity. And it's a good way to express yourself: *Look at me—I'm a mambo king!*

[4]Some people **assume** that ballroom dancing is old-fashioned and boring. They think that all female ballroom dancers wear long, fancy dresses and that all male ballroom dancers wear

182

stuffy suits. They even go so far as to call partner dancing geeky. They haven't seen recent movies such as *Take the Lead*, *Mad Hot Ballroom*, and *Strictly Ballroom*. Or, they didn't watch television programs such as *Dancing with the Stars*. These movies and programs show that ballroom dancing is back in style. They show the excitement of ballroom dancing. They show the challenges and rewards of learning to dance with a partner. The outfits—especially for teens—are not old-fashioned at all. In fact, these days you can wear whatever clothes you want, as long as they allow you to move freely across the dance floor. Some people are ballroom dancing to newer kinds of music. They're even adding hip-hop moves to the older dances. Ballroom dancing is as hot as hip-hop. Young people all over the world are discovering this form of dance. Students from grade school to high school are trying it.

⁵So if you're a teen who wants to get fit and strengthen your social skills, ballroom dancing is for you. Are you still not convinced? You should at least give ballroom dancing a try, taking one step at a time. First, watch one of the ballroom dancing movies. You won't be able to sit still—especially during the Latin dances. The movie *Mad Hot Ballroom* will show you that anyone can learn how to ballroom dance. It just takes the willingness to try something new, and it takes practice. The students who look so polished at the end of the movie practiced for months in order to look that good on the dance floor. When you see how much fun the dancers are having, you'll want to sign up for lessons as soon as the movie is over. What's the next step? Look for ballroom dancing classes in your area. Check with your community center. Call a local dance school to ask about lessons. Then, put your best foot forward. Ballroom dancing is about grace. It's about showing your style. It's about fun. And it's about time you tried ballroom dancing. Come on! Give it a whirl.

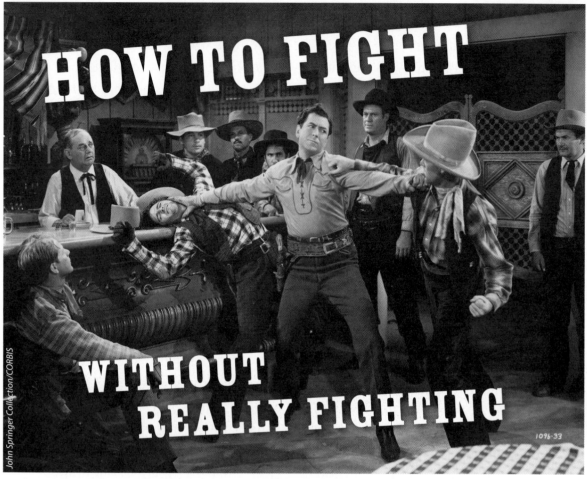

HOW TO FIGHT
WITHOUT REALLY FIGHTING

John Springer Collection/CORBIS

1096-33

Fight scenes like this one were common in old-fashioned Western movies.

[1]The phone rings and you pick it up. Your acting agent is on the line. "Hiya, kid," she says. "Guess what? You got the part in the movie!" *What?* You can hardly believe your ears. This is a dream come true! This could be your big break! You will play the role of an action hero. A famous director will make the movie. Millions of people will see this film. Millions of people will see *you* in this film. "Okay, you have a lot of work to do," says your agent. "You will have hundreds of lines to learn. But first, you will **devote** 3 months to learning how to fight."

[2]Westerns, action adventures, and martial arts films—what do these types of movies have in common? They all have good guys and bad guys. When you have good guys against bad guys in movies, what else do you have? Fights. Not real fights, of course, but stunt fights. Fake fights. From silent movies to today's blockbusters, fighting

has been an **essential** part of the action. And most of the time, the punching and kicking in a fight look real. That's because someone has choreographed, or planned, every **detail** of the fight. Stunt fighting is a lot harder than it looks. All the moves have to be designed with the camera in mind. That's why you have to train for 3 months. Here's a sample of what you will learn during the training.

Some Basics of Stunt Fighting

[3]Before we get started, you need to know three important terms: *sender*, *receiver*, and *impact line*.

- The sender is the person who delivers a punch, kick, or other type of blow.
- The receiver is the person being struck.
- The impact line is an imaginary line between the camera and the receiver. The sender and receiver work closely together around the impact line when they are having a stunt fight. This way, the fight looks real, but no one gets hurt.

MGM/Corbis

In a scene from the movie *Rocky IV,* Drago (Dolph Lundgren) and Apollo Creed (Carl Weathers) pretend to hit one another during a boxing match.

185

Oh, and here's another basic of stunt fighting: You have to be in top physical shape.

[4]Now, let's get started. The first thing you need to do is warm up. Make sure especially to warm up your neck muscles because you will be practicing *head snaps*. A head snap is when you jerk your head back as if someone has hit you in the face. Do some gentle stretching for a few minutes. You don't want to pull a neck muscle. Next, put pads on your elbows and knees. They will protect you during practice falls and rolls.

[5]Viewers can't tell how far a punch is from a receiver when the punch crosses the impact line. That's because film has only length and width. It doesn't have depth. This is good news for you if you are the receiver. It means that the sender can throw a punch that's a foot or more away from your face, but if your timing is right and if your response follows the direction of the punch, it will look as if you were hit.

Al Bello/Allsport Concepts/Getty

The Punch

[6]The person who plans the fight will tell you what kind of punch or kick to deliver. Let's say that you are throwing a punch at a receiver's nose. You will need to practice this move many times to **maintain** control over where your punch lands. You need to use an *air target*. Try hitting a piece of rope

Practicing in front of a mirror helps stunt fighters polish their style.

that's hanging from the ceiling at about face height. Hit the rope so that you barely touch it. The rope should not move at all. This exercise will help you learn to control a punch. It's good to practice in front of a mirror so you can see how this move looks.

[7]While you practice, be **aware** of the impact line. Try this: Extend your arm as if you have just thrown a punch. If your fist meets the imaginary impact line, you are right on target. Next, draw your arm back. Now, do it a second time, but faster. The punch will look real on the film.

The Reaction

[8]Now, you will learn how to receive a punch. Timing is very important here. The sender might throw a great punch, but if the receiver's timing is off, the effect will be spoiled. Another actor will deliver a punch aimed at your face. You will receive the punch. Watch for the moment the sender's arm fully extends and reaches the impact line. When you see this, quickly snap your head in the direction of the blow. Then make the rest of your body follow the head snap.

Stunt fighters must learn how to pretend they have received a punch.

[9]Here's a good way to get just the right snap of the head. Put on a hat. Then practice the head snap. Try to get the hat to fly off your head as you are doing the movement. No matter where you are receiving a blow, lead your reaction with that part of the body. Then let the rest of the body follow. Remember not to cross the impact line. If you do, you could receive a *real* punch! One way to prevent this is to draw a real line on the floor between you and the other fighter. If you are the receiver, make sure you never cross this line with your body. That will help you avoid painful mistakes.

Putting It All Together

[10]Over the weeks, a trainer will lead you through the fight scenes planned for the movie. You will follow the same routine for each scene. First, the trainer will show you and another actor a set of drawings of scenes in the movie. These drawings are called *storyboards*. The three of you will study the storyboards together. After that, you will practice all the moves in each fight scene. It will be like learning the steps of a dance. Then you will act out the fights while someone records them on a video camera. Finally, the trainer will play back the tape. Then, you can see where you need to make changes and correct mistakes.

[11]After months of rehearsing, it is time to start filming the movie. The fight scenes look perfect on videotape. You have learned all your speaking lines. Tomorrow, you will fly to another country to begin shooting the movie for several months. You are on your way to becoming a **major** star! Or, at least you have a fighting chance.

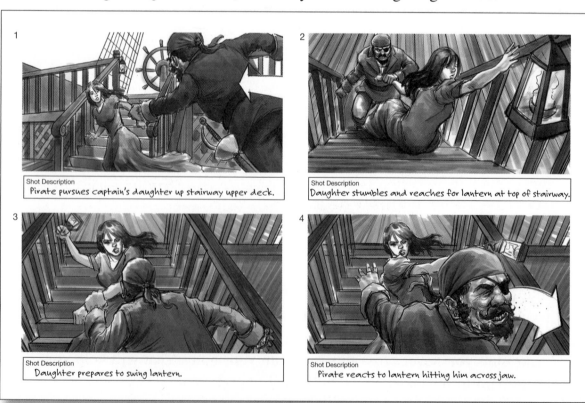

1 Shot Description
Pirate pursues captain's daughter up stairway upper deck.

2 Shot Description
Daughter stumbles and reaches for lantern at top of stairway.

3 Shot Description
Daughter prepares to swing lantern.

4 Shot Description
Pirate reacts to lantern hitting him across jaw.

Storyboards help actors learn the moves of each fight scene.

The Steelers vs. *Swan Lake*

Louie Psihoyos/Adastra/Getty

[1]Here's a match-up you're not likely to see on TV: a professional football team playing against professional ballet dancers. It's a *scary* thought, isn't it? Imagine a herd of 300-pound football players charging down the field toward a group of feather-light ballet dancers. Yikes! Football players and ballet dancers couldn't be more different. Or *could* they? Think about it. Both jobs demand a lot from the human body. And both groups perform in front of an audience. Let's compare a football player and a ballet dancer. They may be more alike than you thought.

The Professional Football Player

[2]Football is a sport in which two teams battle each other to score the most points. It's a highly physical game. It's mainly played by men. There are few women's football leagues. That's because most

women lack the body mass required to play football. Playing football is a high-pressure job. Fans expect a lot from players. They want to see exciting plays. They want to see their team win games. Size, strength, speed, and power are the four most important qualities in a football player. Are you big, strong, fast, and powerful? Your chances of getting picked to play pro ball are still slim. Are you in the top 1 percent of players? That's not good enough. You have to be in the top *half* of that 1 percent. How do you become that good? You practice. Professional football players usually start playing football in middle school. They don't begin their careers until their early 20s. By then, they've rolled up many years of experience.

Equipment, such as a sturdy helmet and pads, helps protect players from injuries.

Doug Pensinger/Getty

[3]A football player has to keep his body in top condition. He will spend long hours training on the field and in the gym. He'll practice plays with his teammates. He'll perform running drills. He'll lift weights and do other conditioning exercises. He's training his body for short bursts of activity during a game. He and his teammates will spend hours in the classroom with coaches. He will study football plays and watch videos of games. He'll eat a special diet that keeps him beefy but not fat. Players stay in shape year-round, even during the off-season.

[4]Football players wear a lot of **gear** to protect themselves from injuries. It's a rough game, after all. This equipment includes a padded plastic helmet, shoulder pads, hip pads, and kneepads. Injuries are common even with all this equipment. They can range from a sprained ankle to something much more serious. A hurt player often will **ignore** pain during a game. He will train himself to **endure** blow after blow to stay in the game. Why? A pro football player has a short career. He wants to get the most out of this brief career. The sport is too rough for an older body. Most players retire in their 30s.

The Professional Ballet Dancer

[5]Ballet, unlike football, is not a team sport. It's an art form that tells stories through movement. It's highly physical, though, like football. In the past, ballet was

190

mainly associated with women dancers. These days, however, there are many male dancers in ballet companies. Professional ballet is a high-pressure career, like professional football. Ballet dancers experience a lot of this pressure on days of a performance. Football players face the same pressure on game days. Audiences expect dancers to thrill them with dizzying twirls and high leaps. They expect dancers to have body shapes that are nearly perfect. Ballet dancers have less body mass in contrast to football players. Their art requires strength, gracefulness, and sometimes, speed. Are you tall, slender, graceful, and strong? Even if you are, your chances of being chosen for a ballet company are small. Professional ballet, like professional football, draws only from the best of the best. Many dancers begin training as children to be good enough to dance professionally. A professional career can begin between the ages of 16 and 20.

[6]The body of a ballet dancer must be in excellent shape, as with that of a football player. A dancer trains for many hours a week. The dancer might spend entire days in a studio, learning and practicing movements. The dancer will rehearse with other dancers until all her moves are perfect, and she will do stretches and special exercises. The dancer might also lift weights to build strength. Dancers, like football players, train for short bursts of activity. Their bodies cannot be heavy like those of football players though. After all, they spend a lot of time off the ground. They must eat plenty of the right kinds of food to stay healthy and strong. Dancers also train year-round.

[7]Ballet dancers, in contrast to football players, don't wear a lot of equipment to protect them from injuries. Still, professional ballet dancers become injured almost as often as do professional football players. Dancers' injuries can be just as serious as those of other athletes. They can develop everything from damaged foot joints to broken legs. Dancers sometimes push themselves to dance even when they are hurt. Their careers can be as brief as those of football players. They work hard through their 20s and 30s. They know that there are many other dancers

Dennis Degnan/CORBIS

Ballet dancers must be strong and graceful.

willing to take their places. They also know that as they get older, their bodies will be less **capable** of leaping and soaring across a stage.

Swan Lake

[8]So, what can you **conclude** about professional football players and ballet dancers? The two groups are more alike than you might have thought. Both are in physically demanding jobs. Both careers are short. Both undergo many hours of training. There *are* differences, though. You're not likely to see a 250-pound wide receiver dancing in the ballet *Swan Lake*. Or are you? In fact, more than one professional football player has studied ballet. The most famous example is Pro Football Hall of Famer Lynn Swann. He played for the Pittsburgh Steelers. He has said that the ballet training he began as a child improved his skills on the football field. One writer called Swann a "performing artist" on the field. "His leaping fingertip catches," said the writer, "were made with the grace of a ballet dancer."

Bettmann/CORBIS

Pro Football Hall of Famer Lynn Swann may have practiced leaps like this one while studying ballet as a child.

Getty

Tapmaster

[1] *RAT-a-tat-tat, RAT-a-tat-tat*. He was born in 1973. He loved rhythm from the start and began taking drum lessons at age 4. He was much better than the others in his class. So he entered a community school for the arts. He was the youngest student to receive a full scholarship to the school. This meant that all his classes were paid for by the school.

[2] At age 7, the child discovered tap dancing. It was a special kind of tap. Rhythm tap uses all the parts of the foot to make sounds. It was developed by African Americans from the old tap step-flap-step style.

Highlights in the Life of Savion Glover

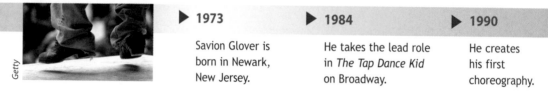

▶ **1973**

Savion Glover is born in Newark, New Jersey.

▶ **1984**

He takes the lead role in *The Tap Dance Kid* on Broadway.

▶ **1990**

He creates his first choreography.

TOCK-ticka-ticka-TOCK, *CLAP*, *shoopa-shoopa-TOCK*. He began taking tap lessons. He wore a pair of brown and beige cowboy boots because his mother couldn't afford tap shoes. The child was full of talent. He seemed born to tap. He danced with his head down. It was as if he wanted you to notice the music his feet were making rather than *him*. This was a child with rhythm in his soul. His name was Savion Glover.

Tap Dance Kid

[3]Glover's style of tap dancing was old and yet new in some ways. Consequently, Glover began to be noticed. His dancing caught the eye and ear of a choreographer for a Broadway musical. A choreographer plans the movement and steps for dances in a show. The musical was *The Tap Dance Kid*. In 1984, Glover got the lead role in the musical. He was 12. As a result of this, his career as a dancer was launched. Glover appeared in his first film about tap dancing a year later.

[4]Glover studied the old tap masters while he was gaining experience on stage and in front of a camera. He was hungry to learn all he could about rhythm tap. He learned from experts such as Sammy Davis Jr. and Gregory

Glover studied the movements of the experts, such as Sammy Davis Jr. shown here singing and dancing.

Hines. He learned technique—basic moves—so that he could go beyond technique to make his own kind of music with his feet.

▶ 1996	▶ 1997	▶ 2000	▶ 2005
Glover stars in *Bring In 'Da Noise, Bring In 'Da Funk*.	He creates his own dance company.	He stars in Spike Lee's film *Bamboozled*.	He keeps breaking new ground by performing with a string chamber orchestra.

Tapping into Success

[5]Audiences couldn't get enough of Glover's dancing. So Glover continued to earn roles in other musicals and in movies through his teen years and into his early 20s. He started teaching tap classes while continuing to perform.

Glover matches steps with tap legend Gregory Hines during the New York City Tap Festival in 2001.

[6]Glover kept pushing the boundaries of rhythm tap with his pounding style. He called his style "hitting." Picture a young man in baggy pants, a tank top, and size 12½ black tap shoes. He is drumming out beats on the stage. *Tocka-tick, tocka-tick, BAM! BAM! Tickita-tockita, tickita-tockita, BAM! BAM!* His beaded dreadlocks fly around his face as he dances. His back is to the audience. *Is he making this up as he goes?* you wonder. You have never seen such a sight. You have never heard such sounds.

[7]Glover created his first choreography in 1990. It was for a festival in New York City. He planned and starred in the show *Bring In 'Da Noise, Bring In 'Da Funk* in 1996. The musical uses song, tap dancing, photographs, and narration. It tells the story of African Americans and their dance. It was a huge success. Glover won a Tony Award for his choreography. The Tony is one of the highest awards given for work on the stage.

Tapping into Stardom

[8]Glover had become a star by his early 20s. This was due to his successes during his teen years. He appeared on the children's program

195

Sesame Street for five seasons. He continued to earn awards for his dance and choreography. He created his own dance company in 1997. He called it NYOTs. The name stood for "not your ordinary tappers." The company toured the United States and other countries. Glover has performed in programs as varied as "Monday Night Football," the Winter Olympics, and a Nike ad. He has appeared in other artists' music videos. He continues to appear in movies. In 2001, he formed a new dance company. He calls the company Ti Dii.

[9]It is rare for a tap dancer to become known outside the world of dance. Glover became famous because he's an original. He credits the lessons he learned from the old tap masters for his success. "You ask what they taught me—everything," says Glover. "It doesn't matter where I am, something one of them said will hit me. Mad things, like footnotes—'Make sure you put the right foot first, even if it's the left

one,' or 'If you can't flow with it, don't go with it'—and I'll have to ask myself: 'Are you talking about the dance or life?'" He appeals to audiences of all ages. He is amazing to watch. "I want to give the audience what they want, but also something unexpected," Glover has said. He does exactly that, time after time. Glover has changed the way people think about tap. He has brought about a new interest in tap, especially among young people and among

Glover rehearses with other dancers before the opening of his show *Improvography* in 2003.

African Americans. More than one dance writer has called Glover the best tap dancer on the planet. "The art is far more important than show business to me," says the man with rhythm in his soul. "I just try to have as much fun as possible." *Tippy-thunk, tippy-thunk SHOO SHOO, kah-chunka-chunka-chinka-chunka-BLAM!*

WATCH OUT!

- What scares you?
- Why do we like to be scared?
- What can we learn from a scary story?

THE BLOODY FANGS

**Retold by Arielle North Olson
and Howard Schwartz**

¹Long ago, there was a boy in Japan who wished he were as strong as his brothers. They could work alongside their father planting rice. They could jump and run and climb trees.

²The boy could not. He was small for his age and he tired easily. But he had a lively mind and filled his lonely hours drawing.

³The boy's family was poor and had no money for paper and ink, so he used whatever he could find. He sharpened sticks and scratched pictures in the dirt. He gathered pieces of charcoal and drew upon smooth stones.

⁴And what did he draw? Cats. Cats lashing their tails and cats washing their ears, cats stalking mice and cats leaping into the air.

⁵His brothers wanted him to draw goblins with **hideous** eyes and great sharp fangs, but the boy never drew anything but cats.

⁶The boy's parents realized he wasn't strong enough to become a farmer, so they decided he should become a priest. And why not? Even poor boys could hope to devote their lives to the service of Buddha.

⁷One morning, the mother and father walked down to the village temple with their small son. They stood before the door and listened to the prayers being chanted inside by the old priest. They waited until the chanting stopped. Then they knocked.

⁸The priest came to the door and asked what he could do for them. They told him they wanted the boy to become his student. The old man smiled. He would enjoy teaching such a bright and eager boy, so he invited him to live at the temple.

⁹The boy tried hard to think right and speak right and do right. He learned to recite important prayers, and he kept the temple free of dust— but he couldn't keep his mind on his studies.

¹⁰He had to draw cats.

¹¹When the sun set and crickets chirped in the grove around the temple, the boy would open the writing box, grind ink, mix it with water, and draw. He could hear the voice of the old priest reading scriptures on the other side of the temple, accompanied by the tinkling of bells. The boy knew he should be studying, but his hands could not be stilled. He drew cats everywhere, even on the walls and on the floor.

¹²The priest was not pleased.

¹³"You have an excellent mind," he told the boy. "You could learn everything a priest needs to know. But I cannot keep you as my student. Your heart is in your drawing. You must become an artist.

¹⁴"But take my advice," the man said. "Avoid the large at night, keep to the small."

¹⁵What did the priest mean? The boy was too upset to ask. Early the next morning he said good-bye and walked out the temple door.

¹⁶He wanted to go home to his family, but what would his parents think? They expected him to follow the ways of Buddha. How could he tell them he had failed?

¹⁷So he wandered down the road to the next village where there was

a larger temple and more priests. Perhaps they would welcome a young student.

[18]When he reached that temple, he was aware of a strange silence. No insects buzzed in the nearby bamboo grove. No temple bells rang. And there was no musical **droning** of voices from within.

[19]The boy knocked at the door, but no one answered. He knocked again and the door swung slowly inward, so he stepped inside. He was amazed to see that the temple was filled with cobwebs and dust. "The priests need my help," he thought to himself. "I'll wait until they come back."

[20]What he did not notice were the pawprints on the floor. Huge pawprints and the marks of sharp claws.

[21]All he noticed were large white screens, set here and there in the temple. He hurried to the writing box. Never before had he seen such magnificent places on which to draw cats.

[22]The hours flew past while he was drawing. Hundreds of cats now decorated the temple. Cats with every marking imaginable, contented cats and snarling cats, huge cats and newborn kittens.

[23]It began to grow dark, and still no priests returned. The boy decided to spend the night there, hoping the priests would come back in the morning. He peered around the dim temple. It was the largest place he had ever seen. Suddenly he felt his hair stand on end.

[24]"Avoid the large, keep to the small." That's what the old priest had said. What did the warning mean? The boy didn't know, but he hurried about looking for a small place—and safety.

[25]It was growing so dark he could hardly see, but finally he found a small cupboard. At first he thought he couldn't squeeze in, but he wiggled through the opening, pulled his knees up to his chin, and just barely managed to pull the cupboard door shut.

[26]There was a decorative **grating** in the cupboard door, a perfect peephole. He wanted to keep watch that night, but it was far too dark. Besides, he was tired, and before he knew it, he fell asleep.

[27]He had barely closed his eyes when something quietly pushed open the temple door and crept inside. Its claws clicked across the floor and its nose swung this way and that, sniffing, sniffing, sniffing. It smelled boy! And it wanted boy for dinner.

[28]It began to scratch at the cupboard door, hooking its claws in the

grating, trying to pull it free.

²⁹The boy woke up to the wildest, screechiest battle he had ever heard. The whole temple was awash with shrieks and howls, the **gnashing** of teeth, the slashing of claws.

³⁰The boy couldn't see a thing through the grating on the cupboard door. So he squeezed his eyes shut and curled up even more tightly than before.

³¹The terrible battle continued. Wetness splashed through the grating and onto his face. When the boy licked his lips, he thought he tasted *blood*.

³²It was almost more than he could stand. He now realized that his parents would have welcomed him home. They never would have wished such a terrifying night on their small son.

³³Just when he thought the howling and shrieking would never end, it stopped, just like that. And an **eerie** silence fell over the temple.

³⁴The boy didn't get another wink of sleep that entire night. When the sun finally rose, he peered through the grating in the cupboard door.

35He could scarcely believe what he saw. There were great clumps of hair on the floor and blood was spattered everywhere. Scarier still was the monstrous **carcass** lying against the far wall. It was bigger than a cow and had the most hideous face the boy had ever seen—the face of a goblin rat.

36Now the boy understood why the priests had fled from the temple.

37But what on earth could have torn the goblin rat apart? The boy pushed open the cupboard door and crawled out. He rubbed his aching arms and legs and looked around. Except for the gory mess, everything in the temple looked just as it had the evening before.

38Or did it?

39The boy looked at the cats he had painted on the great white screens, and he saw that every mouth of every cat was stained with blood—the blood of the goblin rat.

Connect to the Authors

Arielle North Olson

Arielle North Olson got an early start as a writer. Her inspiration was her father, writer and editor Sterling North. "He encouraged me to make up stories long before I entered school. Then he typed them and put them in a notebook, so I felt as if I were writing books, too."

Howard Schwartz, an English professor at the University of Missouri in St. Louis, has enjoyed a lifelong interest in folktales. This interest inspired his award-winning books and poems.

Howard Schwartz

For their book *Ask the Bones*, Olson and Schwartz collected scary stories from around the world. "The Bloody Fangs," a retold Japanese folktale, is one of the stories in that book.

Courtesy: Clarence E. Olson

202

Adapted from
The Legend of Sleepy Hollow
by Washington Irving

¹Long ago, a schoolmaster by the name of Ichabod Crane came to Sleepy Hollow. He was tall and lanky, with narrow shoulders, and long arms and legs. His hands dangled a mile out of his sleeves, and his feet might have served for shovels. His whole body seemed loosely hung together. His head was small and flat at the top, with huge ears on either side. With his clothes bagging and fluttering about him, he might have been mistaken for a scarecrow escaped from a cornfield.

²Ichabod also served as the local singing master and spent many evenings in front of crackling fireplaces, teaching the children to sing and then sharing stories with the farmers and their wives. Ichabod devoured the tales of ghosts and goblins, of haunted fields, brooks, bridges, and particularly of the Headless Horseman of Sleepy Hollow. The Horseman was said by some to be the ghost of a soldier

whose head had been carried away by a cannonball during the American Revolution. He searched the valley nightly for that missing head.

[3]Many of Ichabod's evenings were spent at the home of Farmer Van Tassel, a wealthy and hearty man whose daughter Katrina had caught Ichabod's eye. The schoolmaster had visions of himself married to the beautiful and wealthy young woman. Of course, Ichabod was not Katrina's only suitor. The most impressive of these was a burly, broad-shouldered man named Brom Van Brunt. Fun and arrogant, he had received the nickname Brom Bones for his skill as a fighter and horse racer. The neighbors looked upon him with a mixture of awe, admiration, and goodwill. When any silly prank or fight occurred in the area, they always shook their heads and decided Brom Bones was at the bottom of it.

[4]When Brom noticed the attention Ichabod paid to Katrina, he threatened to "double the schoolmaster up, and lay him on a shelf of his own schoolhouse." Ichabod wisely avoided Brom, and the fight that Brom wanted never took place. Brom instead decided to spend his time playing practical jokes on his rival. Brom and his gang broke into the schoolhouse and made a mess. They stopped up Ichabod's chimney and smoked him out. In general, they tormented the schoolmaster.

[5]One crisp fall evening, an invitation arrived for a party at the home of the Van Tassels. Ichabod dressed in his finest clothes, a worn black suit, and borrowed a horse to ride to the party. The horse was a broken-down old plow horse named Gunpowder. The skinny, shaggy horse and Ichabod the scarecrow made quite a pair as they jogged slowly on their way.

[6]A merry party and a feast of savory food greeted Ichabod on his arrival. After being served a sampling all of the treats laid on the tables, he joined in the dancing. What a sight he was! Who was his partner for many of the dances? The lovely Katrina Van Tassel. Ichabod did not notice Brom Bones watching sullenly from the corner of the room.

[7]When the dancing ended, talk turned to ghosts and goblins. The

Headless Horseman, it seemed, had appeared several times in recent days and was said to be patrolling the countryside. Brom Bones joined in the storytelling. He had seen the Horseman himself! In fact, he had bet the Horseman he could beat him in a race. Brom did win the race, he said, and crossed the bridge into town first. As the Horseman approached the bridge, he disappeared in a flash of fire.

[8]At long last the party ended, and Ichabod began the long ride home through the dark countryside. Stories of the Headless Horseman circled through his head. There was a certain tree everyone in town believed to be haunted, and as he approached that tree he spied something white hanging overhead. Could it be a ghost? Ah, it was just a white patch in the tree's bark. Then he heard a groan! Oh, it was the tree's branches rubbing together in the wind. He passed the tree safely, but other perils lay ahead.

[9]Just beyond the tree ran a stream where locals claimed to have seen ghosts as well. As Ichabod and Gunpowder approached the stream, Ichabod heard a sound. He looked ahead toward the stream and saw something huge, black, and towering. It did not stir. Rather, it seemed to wait in the darkness like some gigantic monster ready to spring upon the traveler.

[10]"Who . . . who are you?" Ichabod asked. He received no reply. Ichabod nudged Gunpowder into a trot, but to his horror, the shadowy object followed. Now Ichabod could see the form of the object. It appeared to be a giant horseman on a powerful black horse.

[11]Ichabod urged Gunpowder to go faster. The horseman increased his own pace. Ichabod slowed Gunpowder. The horseman slowed as well. As he reached the rise of a hill, Ichabod looked back and saw that the horseman was headless! His horror increased when he observed that the horseman's head, which should have rested on his shoulders, was carried in front of him on the saddle. Ichabod's terror rose to desperation. He **frantically** rained a shower of kicks and blows upon Gunpowder. Away they dashed, stones flying, and sparks flashing at every step.

[12]Ichabod remembered Brom's tale of the Headless Horseman

disappearing at the bridge. If I can reach the bridge, he thought, I will be safe. Just then he heard the black steed panting close behind him. He even imagined that he felt the horse's hot breath. Another kick in the ribs, and old Gunpowder sprang upon the bridge and thundered over. Now Ichabod looked behind to see if his pursuer would vanish in a flash of fire. Instead, he saw the horseman rising in his stirrups, in the very act of **heaving** his head toward him. Ichabod tried to dodge the dreadful missile, but he was too late. It hit his head with a tremendous crash. He tumbled headlong into the dust, while Gunpowder, the black steed, and the rider passed by like a whirlwind.

[13]The next morning, Gunpowder was found eating grass at his master's gate. When Ichabod did not appear at breakfast or at school, people began to search for him. Fresh horses' tracks marked the road, and near a broad part of the brook where the water ran deep, Ichabod's hat was discovered. Close beside it lay a shattered pumpkin. The unfortunate schoolmaster was nowhere to be found.

[14]The mysterious event caused much discussion. Some said the schoolmaster had left town in embarrassment and shame. Others came to the conclusion that he had been carried off by the Headless Horseman. Brom Bones, who did indeed marry Katrina, usually seemed a bit uncomfortable when the story of Ichabod was told, but he always burst into a hearty laugh at the mention of the pumpkin. This led some to suspect that he knew more about the matter than he chose to tell.

Connect to the Author

Washington Irving

Washington Irving was born in New York City at the end of the American Revolution on April 3, 1783. His parents were Scottish-English immigrants who named their son after George Washington. Irving had many interests, including architecture and traveling, but he is best known as a writer. In fact, he was the first American known to make a living solely from writing.

Irving traveled a great deal and often wrote about places he visited. For many of his stories, he used memories of his childhood in New York. "The Legend of Sleepy Hollow" is set in the lower Hudson River Valley area near Tarrytown, New York. "The Legend of Sleepy Hollow" and "Rip Van Winkle," both based on German folktales, are among Irving's best-known stories. Readers throughout the centuries have continued to read and enjoy these timeless and entertaining tales.

Irving never married. He shared his home in New York with his brother and his brother's daughters. Irving died on November 28, 1859. He is buried in the Tarrytown Cemetery, which was renamed Sleepy Hollow Cemetery following Irving's death.

The Scarecrow

¹It was supposed to be a harmless prank. We just wanted to scare him a little. Really.

²I guess I'll start at the beginning. In the middle of October, a new kid showed up in homeroom. His name was Alex, and right off, we decided we didn't like him. He was a tall, skinny guy with long arms and huge feet. His clothes hung on him like they were three sizes too big. Moose started it all by saying, "Hey, look! It's a scarecrow!" Everybody laughed, even Kayla.

³Alex kind of smiled and sat down in an empty desk. The mistake? The desk was next to Kayla, and Moose didn't like that at all. He frowned across the room for the next 15 minutes, and when the bell rang, he followed Alex into the hall.

⁴"Back off, Scarecrow Boy," he said and bumped Alex up against a wall. "Kayla's my girl."

⁵"Okay, whatever. I don't even know who you're talking about," Alex stammered.

⁶"He's talking about me," said a voice from behind us, "and I don't like it. He's totally **obsessed** with me, and it's gross. Nobody tells me who I can be friends with, and I've decided I want to be friends with you." It was Kayla, and her green eyes were narrowed at Moose like she couldn't stand him. When she said "you," she shifted her focus to Alex and smiled. Not just any smile. The full-power, millions of teeth, I'm-the-prettiest-girl-in-school smile that she uses when she wants something. Apparently she had decided she wanted to be friends with Alex.

⁷"Oh, hey, Nacho," she said when she saw me. My name is Ignacio, but everybody just calls me Nacho. It's kind of **annoying** having a name like a food, but I guess it's better than being called Moose or Scarecrow. "Are you coming to my party Saturday?"

[8]"Yeah," I said. "Moose and I are coming together. Thanks for the invite."

[9]She turned back to Alex. "Hey, you should come with them. You'll meet a lot of people. It'll be a good way to introduce you to everybody."

[10]You could almost see steam coming off Moose's head, but he didn't say anything. I think he figured it was better not to push it with Kayla just then.

[11]"Okay," Alex said. "Sure."

[12]Kayla smiled and took Alex by the arm. "Great! Now come on. Let's find your next class."

[13]That's how it started. Moose couldn't let it go, even though I tried to tell him to ignore her, that Kayla was just trying to make him mad. So he came up with The Plan. It was stupid. Really stupid. I still can't believe we did it.

[14]Friday, the day before the party, Moose and I waited until Alex sat down by himself at a lunchroom table. Then we sat down with him. I'm pretty sure he thought Moose would threaten him again, but Moose acted friendly. I laughed at all of Moose's jokes until Alex relaxed and started laughing, too. Then Moose said, "So, has anybody told you about Kayla's house? You know, where the party is?"

[15]Alex shook his head.

[16]"Seriously? Well, you should know about it before we go tomorrow. It's kind of creepy, and some of the other guys will probably try to scare you, so you should be prepared."

[17]Alex looked skeptical, but he nodded and put down his sandwich.

[18]Moose hunched closer to the table and lowered his voice like he was telling some really important secret. "There's this big field next to Kayla's house. Her dad grows corn, and right now cornstalks are covering the field. Everybody says that field's haunted."

[19]Alex stared at Moose for a second. Then he burst out laughing. "Right, haunted! I'm the new kid, but I'm not stupid."

[20]Moose kicked me under the table, so I chimed in. "No, really, we're not kidding. We thought it was some dumb story they tell little kids. Until a couple of years ago, that is. These two guys from the next town decided to check it out. They went in the field one night to prove it wasn't haunted, and nobody's ever seen them again. It really did happen. Nobody knows what happened to them."

[21]Alex laughed again. "Guys, really, you're not very good at this."

[22]Moose stood up. "Okay, Scarecrow Boy, we'll see who's right. We'll go out in the field tomorrow before the party. Then maybe you won't be so sure."

[23]This was part of The Plan. We just wanted to scare him a little.

[24]Saturday night was cold and dark. There was no moon and no wind. It was the perfect night. We picked Alex up and drove out toward Kayla's. We could see the lights of her house off in the distance, but we stopped at the edge of the road where her dad's fields started. The cornstalks were taller than me and dried out, so when we brushed through them, they made an eerie rustling sound. I'm pretty sure I heard something scurrying away a couple of times, but I never saw anything. Mice, probably.

²⁵We had set it up perfectly. Moose had even gotten a couple of the other guys in on it. When we got a few rows in, we came to a clearing. The guys were there with a couple of bales of hay and the perfect touch—a scarecrow. It looked like something my mom would get at a craft store to decorate for Thanksgiving, but it was as tall as a man. It did look kind of creepy with a weird painted smile and flat eyes. I didn't look at it too much.

²⁶Moose cracked up when he saw it. "Well, look here," he said. "A scarecrow and a scarecrow. You guys know each other?" He hooked his arm around Alex's neck, not tight, but not totally friendly either.

²⁷Alex tugged back a little, but Moose didn't let go.

²⁸"I think this real scarecrow here needs a little more filler, don't you guys think so? Maybe we should stuff him some. He's way too skinny." Moose grabbed some hay from a bale and shoved it down the collar of Alex's shirt. The other guys picked up handfuls.

²⁹Alex started struggling for real now. He pushed **furiously** against Moose's arm, but it didn't help. We all grabbed hay and started stuffing it into his clothes. I don't know how long it went on. Not all that long, I guess. Pretty soon his clothes were stuffed with hay, and the other guys were laughing like it was the funniest thing ever. I laughed some, too, but when I saw Alex's face, I stopped. Then everybody stopped.

³⁰Alex **lurched** to his feet. "Ha ha. Funny. You guys are a riot. Now get lost." He took off in a weird, stumbling run down one of the rows.

³¹"Should we go after him?" one of the guys asked.

³²"Nah, he'll find his way out," said Moose. "The house is just over that hill anyway."

³³So we left. We went to the party and told everybody about the scarecrow. We didn't really think anything about it when Alex didn't show up.

³⁴Monday morning Alex wasn't in homeroom. He wasn't there Tuesday either. People talked about it, but nobody knew for sure what happened to him. Some people said his dad's job transferred his family somewhere else. Some people said he had asthma, and the hay had made him stop breathing. Some said maybe that field really is haunted. I'm not going back to find out.

WHATIF

by Shel Silverstein

Last night, while I lay thinking here,
Some Whatifs crawled inside my ear
And pranced and partied all night long
And sang their same old Whatif song:
Whatif I'm dumb in school?
Whatif they've closed the swimming pool?
Whatif I get beat up?
Whatif there's poison in my cup?
Whatif I start to cry?
Whatif I get sick and die?
Whatif I flunk that test?
Whatif green hair grows on my chest?
Whatif nobody likes me?
Whatif a bolt of lightning strikes me?
Whatif I don't grow taller?
Whatif my head starts getting smaller?
Whatif the fish won't bite?
Whatif the wind tears up my kite?
Whatif they start a war?
Whatif my parents get divorced?
Whatif the bus is late?
Whatif my teeth don't grow in straight?
Whatif I tear my pants?
Whatif I never learn to dance?
Everything seems well, and then
The nighttime Whatifs strike again!

Jeff Albertson/Corbis

Shel Silverstein

Connect to the Author

   If Shel Silverstein had been more popular with the girls, he might never have become a writer. "When I was a kid . . . I would much rather have been a good baseball player or a hit with the girls. But I couldn't play ball, I couldn't dance. Luckily, the girls didn't want me; not much I could do about that. So, I started to draw and to write . . . . By the time I got to where I was attracting girls, I was already into work, and it was more important to me." Silverstein's work, which includes books, poems, plays, cartoons, and songs, is popular with people of all ages. His best-selling books *A Light in the Attic* and *The Giving Tree* are particularly popular with school-aged readers.

The Wendigo
by Ogden Nash

The Wendigo,
The Wendigo!
Its eyes are ice and **indigo**!
Its blood is **rank** and yellowish!
5 Its voice is hoarse and bellowish!
Its tentacles are slithery,
And scummy,
Slimy,
Leathery!
10 Its lips are hungry blubbery,
and smacky,
Sucky,
Rubbery!

The Wendigo,
15 The Wendigo!
I saw it just a friend ago!
Last night it **lurked** in Canada;
Tonight, on your veranada!
As you are **lolling** hammockwise
20 It **contemplates** you stomachwise.
You loll,
It contemplates,
It lollops.
The rest is merely gulps and gollops.

214

Connect to the Author

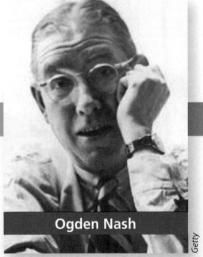

Ogden Nash

Ogden Nash admitted that he "intentionally maltreated and man-handled every known rule of grammar . . . and spelling." Despite that—or maybe because of that—Nash was one of America's best-loved poets. After leaving college in 1921, Nash held several jobs before becoming an editor. The poor quality of the stories and poems he read convinced Nash to try writing. Nash began writing humorous poems with clever and creatively spelled rhymes. This pun-filled poetry made him famous.

Along with writing poems, Nash was a frequent guest on game and comedy shows on the radio during the 1940s. Nash continued to write until his death in 1971.

How It Happened

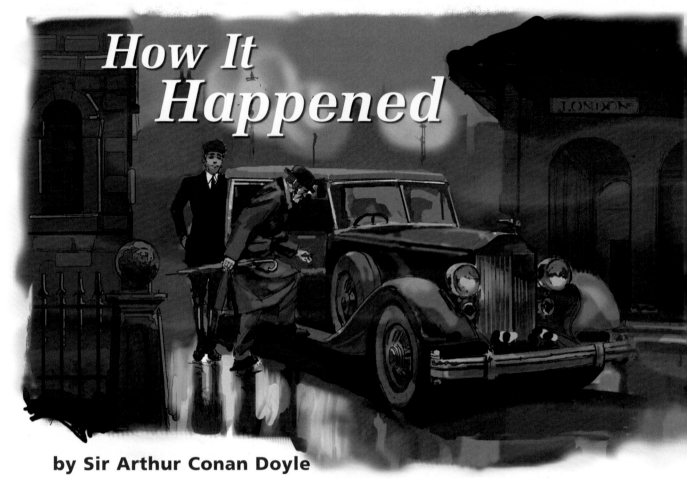

by Sir Arthur Conan Doyle

¹I can remember some things from that evening very distinctly, and others are like some vague, broken dreams. That is what makes it so difficult to tell a connected story. I have no idea now what it was that had taken me to London and brought me back so late. It just **merges** into all my other visits to London. But from the time that I got out at the little country station everything is **extraordinarily** clear. I can live it again—every instant of it.

²I remember so well walking down the platform and looking at the **illuminated** clock that told me that it was half-past eleven. I remember also wondering whether I could get home before midnight. Then I remember the big car, with its glaring headlights and polished brass detailing, waiting for me outside. It was my new 30-horsepower Robur, which had been delivered just that day. I remember also

216

asking Perkins, my chauffeur, how the car handled, and his saying that he thought its performance was excellent.

[3]"I'll try it myself," I said, and I climbed into the driver's seat.

[4]"The shifting lever is different from the one in the old car," he said. "Perhaps, sir, I had better drive."

[5]"No, I want to try it out," I said. And so we started on the 5-mile drive for home.

[6]My old car had the type of gear-shifting lever with notches on a bar. In this car you passed the gear lever through a gate to get to the higher gears. It was not difficult to master, and soon I thought that I understood it. It was foolish, no doubt, to begin to learn a new system in the dark, but one often does foolish things, with little consequence. I drove along very well until I came to Claystall Hill. It is one of the worst hills in England, a mile and a half long and very steep in places, with three fairly sharp curves. The gate to my property stands at the very foot of the hill, on the main London road.

[7]We were just over the brow of this hill, where the downward slope is steepest, when the trouble began. I had been driving at top speed, and wanted to slow down and coast along; but the car stuck between gears, and I had to shift into high gear again. By this time the car was going at a great speed, so I decided to use both brakes, but one after the other they gave way. I didn't mind so much when I felt my foot brake snap, but when I pulled hard on the emergency brake and the lever didn't catch, it brought a cold sweat out of me. By this time we were tearing down the slope. The headlights were brilliant, and I brought the car around the first curve all right. Then we rounded the second curve, though it was a close shave to keep from going into the ditch. There was a mile of straight road then with the third curve approaching, and after that the gate to my property. If I could steer into my driveway, all would be well, because the slope up to the house would bring the car to a standstill.

[8]Perkins behaved splendidly. I would like that to be known. He was perfectly cool and alert. I had thought at the very beginning of using the bank of the curve to help me slow the car, and he read my intention.

[9]"I wouldn't do it, sir," he said. "At this speed, the car will turn over, and we'll have it on top of us."

[10]Of course, he was right. He reached for the ignition switch and

turned it off, so we were no longer under power; but we were still running at a fearful pace. He grabbed the steering wheel.

[11]"I'll keep it steady," he said, "if you care to jump and chance it. We can never get around that curve. Better jump, sir."

[12]"No," I said. "I'll stick it out. You can jump if you like."

[13]"I'll stick it out with you, sir," he said.

[14]If it had been the old car, I could have jammed the gear lever into reverse to see what would happen. I expect that would have stripped the car's gears or smashed them up somehow, but it would have been a chance. As it was, I was helpless. Perkins tried to climb across and take control, but he couldn't do it going at that speed. The wheels were whirring like a high wind, and the car's big body was creaking and groaning with the strain. But the lights were so bright that I could steer **precisely**. I remember thinking what an awful and yet majestic sight we would be for anyone who met us. It was a narrow road, and we were just a great, roaring, golden death to anyone who came in our path.

[15]We rounded the corner with one wheel 3 feet up on the bank. I thought we were surely turning over, but after staggering for a moment, the car righted and darted onwards. That was the third corner and the last one. There was only the home gate now. It was facing us, but, as luck would have it, not facing us directly. It was about 20 yards to the left, up the main road we were approaching. Perhaps I could have done it, but I expect that the steering column had been jarred when we ran up on the bank. The steering wheel would not turn easily. We shot out of the lane and onto the main road. I saw the open gate on the left. I whirled the steering wheel around with all the strength of my wrist. Perkins and I threw our bodies across, and then the next instant, going at 50 miles an hour, my right wheel struck full on the right-hand pillar of my own gate. I heard the crash. I was conscious of flying through the air, and then—and then—!

[16]When I became aware of my own existence once more I was among some brushwood in the shadow of the oaks on the lodge side of the drive. A man was standing beside

me. I imagined at first that it was Perkins, but when I looked again I saw that it was Stanley, a man whom I had known at college some years before. There was always something peculiarly appealing to me about Stanley's personality; and I took pride in thinking I had some similar influence on him. At the present moment I was surprised to see him, but I was like a man in a dream, **giddy** and shaken and quite prepared to take things as I found them without questioning them.

[17]"What a smash!" I said. "What an awful smash!"

[18]He nodded his head, and even in the gloom I could see that he was smiling the gentle, **wistful** smile that I connected with him.

[19]I was quite unable to move. Indeed, I had not any desire to try to move. But my senses were exceedingly alert. I saw the wrecked car lit up by moving flashlights. I saw the little group of people and heard the hushed voices. There were the lodge keeper and his wife, and one or two more. They were taking no notice of me, but were very busy around the car. Then, suddenly, I heard a cry of pain.

[20]"The weight is on him. Lift it easy," cried a voice.

[21]"It's only my leg!" said another voice, which I recognized as Perkins'. "Where's master?" he cried.

[22]"Here I am," I answered, but they did not seem to hear me. They were all bending over something that lay in front of the car.

[23]Stanley laid his hand upon my shoulder, and his touch was inexpressibly soothing. I felt light and happy, in spite of all.

[24]"No pain, of course?" he said.

[25]"None," I said.

[26]"There never is," he said.

[27]And then, suddenly, a wave of amazement passed over me. Stanley! Stanley! Why, Stanley had died in the Boer War!

[28]"Stanley!" I cried, and the words seemed to choke my throat. "Stanley, you are dead."

[29]He looked at me with the same old gentle, wistful smile. "So are you," he answered.

Connect to the Author

You may never have heard of Sir Arthur Conan Doyle. But, chances are, you've heard of his most famous character, Sherlock Holmes. Although Doyle created Holmes more than 100 years ago, readers still enjoy following the great detective as he solves cases with his keen powers of observation. Holmes was so popular during the author's life that when Doyle killed him off in a book, readers were furious. They complained so much that Doyle brought him back to life in a new book.

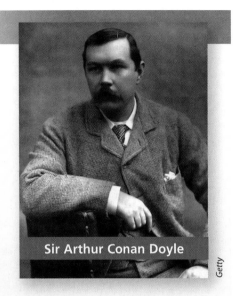

Sir Arthur Conan Doyle

Getty

Doyle was tall, athletic, and had a taste for adventure. Born in Scotland in 1859, Doyle studied medicine and practiced as a doctor while he wrote stories and books. His works included mysteries, horror stories, sports stories, and historical novels. His writing brought more success than his doctoring. By his early 30s, Doyle was able to support his family on his writing alone. By his 60s, Doyle was the highest paid writer in the world. When Doyle died in 1930, at the age of 71, more than 10,000 fans came to mourn his passing.

Dog Days

by Al Carusone

¹**P**olli Hartaway drove along the dirt road, glancing back now and then at the long trail of dust billowing behind her red sports car. She was driving way too fast for this stretch of country road, but Polli was lost.

²She thumbed through the dog-eared road map beside her. The thin line that had looked so promising as a shortcut had turned into the endless road on which Polli now sped.

[3]"The most important meeting on my schedule," said Polli, nervously drumming her fingers on the steering wheel, "and I'm going to be late."

[4]Then for just a moment Polli thought back to the time when her life was not a blur seen from a car window. Memories swirled through Polli's mind like snapshots tumbling in a dust storm, glimpsed only when at just the right angle.

[5]Polli itched in her prim suit. Sweat dripped from her short-cropped hair. She was still thinking about her childhood when the big dog ambled onto the roadway.

[6]Polli felt the thud. She swerved hard to miss the girl behind the dog. The car skidded off the road, struck a stump, and landed in a gully beside a field.

[7]Polli jumped out of the car. "Why don't you watch where you're going!" she screamed at the girl. "Look what you did to my car."

[8]"My dawg, you killed my dawg," sobbed the girl.

[9]"Your dog wrecked my car," said Polli. "Take me to your home so I can get someone to pull my car out of this ditch."

[10]The girl stared at her dog, then at Polli. Somewhere in the girl's maize-colored eyes, Polli saw dark feelings.

But a curtain was quickly drawn on whatever shadows danced in the girl's mind.

[11]The girl started across the field. "Just follow me," she said. "I'll take you where you're going."

[12]Polli followed, hot and thirsty, under the blazing sun. She cursed whenever her high heels snagged on a root or her skirt caught on a bramble.

[13]The girl moved effortlessly on her bare feet. Her slender legs danced through the brambles. Sometimes she glanced back at Polli, then picked up her pace. Polli struggled to keep up.

[14]At last they reached an old farmhouse that was falling apart under the weight of its rusted metal roof. Polli stumbled up the wooden steps into a doorway without a door. Inside, a thick-waisted woman turned from the table she was setting.

[15]Polli burst into the house. "I have to use your phone."

[16]"We got no phone to use," said the woman. She wiped her hands slowly on the faded apron she wore.

[17]The girl pointed at Polli. "She killed my dawg, Mama."

[18]"That's the last straw," said Polli. "I get dragged halfway across the state to a shack that doesn't even have a phone. Now I have to listen

to this brat whine about a dog that should have been on a leash."

[19]"She was speeding, Mama," said the girl.

[20]The older woman folded her thick arms over her waist. There was no hate in the woman's eyes. It was more like she was sizing Polli up.

[21]"I don't have to put up with this," Polli said. "But I'll replace the dog." She slipped her wallet out of her

pocket book. "What do I owe you?"

[22]"Don't fret about that now," said the woman, pushing Polli's money away. "There's plenty of time to replace the dog." There was a soothing catch to the woman's voice as she called into the back

room, "Granny, won't you please fetch some of your tonic? We have a guest."

[23]Soon a stooped old woman shuffled into the kitchen, holding out a glass of strange-looking liquid. "Here," she said to Polli. "Drink what Granny fetched you."

[24]Polli took the glass from the woman's wrinkled hand. She was so hot and miserable that she gulped the drink down. The tonic left a funny aftertaste in her mouth, a taste like a dog's breath.

[25]"What about my car?" asked Polli.

[26]"Pa and the boys can fetch it when they get home," said the girl's mother.

[27]Polli was no longer listening. Her head felt puffy, and a numbness was spreading through her limbs. She felt so, so drowsy. It wasn't seemly or ladylike, but she kicked off her high heels and loosened her collar. Polli felt relaxed for the first time in a long while. She felt so drowsy that she lay down right on the floor, curled up, and went to sleep.

[28]A commotion woke Polli from her sleep. Pa and the boys stomped into the house, brushing red dust from their jeans. "Well, the car's been moved," said Pa's powerful voice. He took a chewed corncob pipe from his

shirt pocket and walked over to Polli. "It's good that our girl got a new dog."

[29]Polli opened her mouth to protest, but could manage only a weak yelp.

[30]The girl wobbled over, wearing Polli's high heels. Polli tried to get up to take the shoes away from the girl, but could only manage to get on all fours.

[31]For a moment Polli was frightened. Then she realized that, for the first time in years, she had no place to rush to. She rolled over lazily on the floor and licked her paw.

Connect to the Author

Al Carusone has been an ice-cream maker, a nuclear-reactor operator, a science teacher, and a salesman. And he has always loved a good story. "My love of stories goes back to some of my earliest memories," says Carusone. "Nothing quite compared to the delicious contrast between my cozy bedroom and the sense of mysterious adventure in the fairy tales my mother and father read me." Carusone has published three books of fiction.

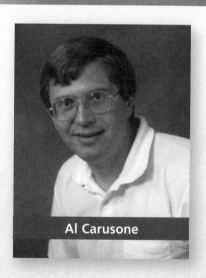

Al Carusone

COMING OF AGE

- In what ways can you connect to someone else's story?
- Why do people tell stories about childhood?
- How can important people or moments shape who we become?

On Turning Ten

by Billy Collins

The whole idea of it makes me feel
like I'm coming down with something,
something worse than any stomach ache
or the headaches I get from reading in bad light—
5   a kind of measles of the spirit,
a mumps of the **psyche**,
a **disfiguring** chicken pox of the soul.

You tell me it is too early to be looking back,
but that is because you have forgotten
10   the perfect **simplicity** of being one
and the beautiful **complexity** introduced by two.
But I can lie on my bed and remember every **digit**.
At four I was an Arabian wizard.
I could make myself invisible
15   by drinking a glass of milk a certain way.
At seven I was a soldier, at nine a prince.

But now I am mostly at the window
watching the late afternoon light.
Back then it never fell so **solemnly**
20   against the side of my tree house,
and my bicycle never leaned against the garage
as it does today,
all the dark blue speed drained out of it.

This is the beginning of sadness, I say to myself,
25   as I walk through the universe in my sneakers.
It is time to say good-bye to my imaginary friends,
time to turn the first big number.

It seems only yesterday I used to believe
there was nothing under my skin but light.
30   If you cut me I could shine.
But now when I fall upon the sidewalks of life,
I skin my knees. I bleed.

Connect to the Author

Billy Collins

© McClatchy-Tribune, 2006

Billy Collins has been called the most popular poet in America. In fact, he served as Poet Laureate of the United States from 2001 to 2003. His warm and witty poems have earned him a huge audience.

Collins was born in 1941. He wrote his first poem when he was 12. Then his father brought home a poetry magazine. Collins was amazed. "The poems sounded cool to me—they sounded like they were talking, the imagery was fresh," he says. "They mentioned cars! I remember reading a poem by Thom Gunn about Elvis Presley, and that was a real mindblower because I didn't know you could write poems about Elvis Presley. I thought there was poetry—what you read in class, you read 'Hiawatha' in class—and then when you left class, there was Elvis. I didn't see them together until I read that poem."

In addition to writing poems, Collins has taught English at City University of New York for 30 years.

Eleven
by Sandra Cisneros

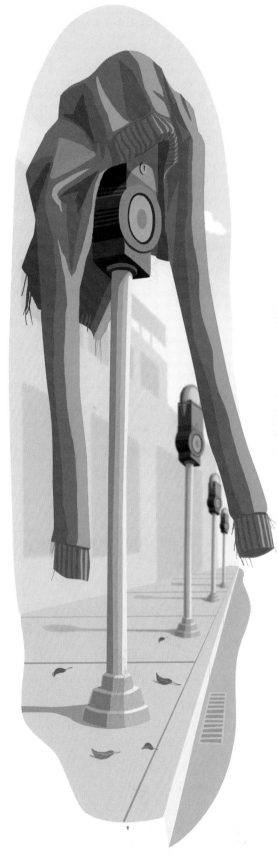

[1]What they don't understand about birthdays and what they never tell you is that when you're eleven, you're also ten, and nine, and eight, and seven, and six, and five, and four, and three, and two, and one. And when you wake up on your eleventh birthday you expect to feel eleven, but you don't. You open your eyes and everything's just like yesterday, only it's today. And you don't feel eleven at all. You feel like you're still ten. And you are—underneath the year that makes you eleven.

[2]Like some days you might say something stupid, and that's the part of you that's still ten. Or maybe some days you might need to sit on your mama's lap because you're scared, and that's the part of you that's five. And maybe one day when you're all grown up maybe you will need to cry like if you're three, and that's okay. That's what I tell Mama when she's sad and needs to cry. Maybe she's feeling three.

[3]Because the way you grow old is kind of like an onion or like the rings inside a tree trunk or like my little wooden dolls that fit one inside the other, each year inside the next one. That's how being eleven years old is.

[4]You don't feel eleven. Not right away. It takes a few days, weeks even, sometimes even

231

months before you say Eleven when they ask you. And you don't feel smart eleven, not until you're almost twelve. That's the way it is.

[5]Only today I wish I didn't have only eleven years rattling inside me like pennies in a tin Band-Aid box. Today I wish I was one hundred and two instead of eleven because if I was one hundred and two I'd have known what to say when Mrs. Price put the red sweater on my desk. I would've known how to tell her it wasn't mine instead of just sitting there with that look on my face and nothing coming out of my mouth.

[6]"Whose is this?" Mrs. Price says, and she holds the red sweater up in the air for all the class to see. "Whose? It's been sitting in the coatroom for a month."

[7]"Not mine," says everybody. "Not me."

[8]"It has to belong to somebody," Mrs. Price keeps saying, but nobody can remember. It's an ugly sweater with red plastic buttons and a collar and sleeves all stretched out like you could use it for a jump rope. It's maybe a thousand years old and even if it belonged to me I wouldn't say so.

[9]Maybe because I'm skinny, maybe because she doesn't like me, that stupid Sylvia Saldívar says, "I

think it belongs to Rachel." An ugly sweater like that, all raggedy and old, but Mrs. Price believes her. Mrs. Price takes the sweater and puts it right back on my desk, but when I open my mouth nothing comes out.

[10]"That's not, I don't, you're not . . . Not mine," I finally say in a little voice that was maybe me when I was four.

[11]"Of course it's yours," Mrs. Price says. "I remember you wearing it once." Because she's older and the teacher, she's right and I'm not.

[12]Not mine, not mine, not mine, but Mrs. Price is already turning to page thirty-two, and math problem number four. I don't know why but all of a sudden I'm feeling sick inside, like the part of me that's three wants to come out of my eyes, only I squeeze them shut tight and bite down on my teeth real hard and try to remember today I am eleven, eleven. Mama is making a cake for me for tonight, and when Papa comes home everybody will sing Happy birthday, happy birthday to you.

[13]But when the sick feeling goes away and I open my eyes, the red sweater's still sitting there like a big red mountain. I move the red sweater to the corner of my desk with my ruler. I move my pencil and books

and eraser as far from it as possible. I even move my chair a little to the right. Not mine, not mine, not mine.

[14]In my head I'm thinking how long till lunchtime, how long till I can take the red sweater and throw it over the schoolyard fence, or leave it hanging on a parking meter, or bunch it up into a little ball and toss it in the alley. Except when math period ends, Mrs. Price says loud and in front of everybody, "Now, Rachel, that's enough," because she sees I've shoved the red sweater to the tippy-tip corner of my desk and it's hanging all over the edge like a waterfall, but I don't care.

[15]"Rachel," Mrs. Price says. She says it like she's getting mad. "You put that sweater on right now and no more nonsense."

[16]"But it's not—"

[17]"Now!" Mrs. Price says.

[18]This is when I wish I wasn't eleven, because all the years inside of me—ten, nine, eight, seven, six, five, four, three, two, and one—are pushing at the back of my eyes

when I put one arm through one sleeve of the sweater that smells like cottage cheese, and then the other arm through the other and stand there with my arms apart like if the sweater hurts me and it does, all itchy and full of germs that aren't even mine.

[19]That's when everything I've been holding in since this morning, since when Mrs. Price put the sweater on my desk, finally lets go, and all of a sudden I'm crying in front of everybody. I wish I was invisible but I'm not. I'm eleven and it's my birthday today and I'm crying like I'm three in front of everybody. I put my head down on the desk and bury my face in my stupid clown-sweater arms. My face all hot and spit coming out of my mouth because I can't stop the little animal noises from coming out of me, until there aren't any more tears left in my eyes, and it's just my body shaking like when you have the hiccups, and my whole head hurts like when you drink milk too fast.

[20]But the worst part is right before the bell rings for lunch. That stupid Phyllis Lopez, who is even dumber than Sylvia Saldívar, says she remembers the red sweater is hers! I take it off right away and give it to her, only Mrs. Price pretends like everything's okay.

[21]Today I'm eleven. There's a cake Mama's making for tonight, and when Papa comes home from work we'll eat it. There'll be candles and presents and everybody will sing Happy birthday, happy birthday to you, Rachel, only it's too late.

[22]I'm eleven today. I'm eleven, ten, nine, eight, seven, six, five, four, three, two, and one, but I wish I was one hundred and two. I wish I was anything but eleven, because I want today to be far away already, far away like a runaway balloon, like a tiny *o* in the sky, so tiny-tiny you have to close your eyes to see it.

Connect to the Author

Sandra Cisneros grew up in two worlds. She was born in 1954 in a poor neighborhood of Chicago. But her father moved the entire family back and forth between Chicago and his hometown in Mexico. Cisneros recalls this existence in stories and poems that reflected her Hispanic culture. "Everything I write is true, but it didn't all happen to me," she says. "I would have to describe it like a cloth in which there are strands which are my own, but there are also strands of other people." Her 1983 book *The House on Mango Street*, about a young Hispanic girl growing up in a barrio, established Cisneros as a major literary figure.

Sandra Cisneros

from Cuba 15

by Nancy Osa

Chicago high school student Violet Paz has just discovered that Abuela, her Cuban grandmother, wants to give her a quinceañero, a coming-of-age party given to girls when they turn 15. Violet has no interest in such an event.

¹**T**hat afternoon, Abuela lay in wait.

²"I don't like to wear dresses anymore," I said, sitting down at the piano in the living room to practice. I trilled over a few keys. "Don't you remember?"

³"No, *mi palomita*," Abuela said, shaking her coiffed, silver-haired head. A Spanish-language magazine sat open on her perfectly ironed lap—her paisley skirt, in swirling shades of green, stayed crisp even though it was made of a shimmery, silky fabric. Abuela always looks as though she's just peeled off the dry cleaner's protective plastic bag. Her raucous makeup is the only chink in her otherwise solid look of togetherness.

⁴"*Ven acá, chica*," she said, beckoning.

⁵When I joined her on the couch, she tapped the centerfold spread in front of us: a backlit photo of a disembodied floor-length evening gown, the kind Cinderella's stepsisters might have worn if they'd had less taste. "This dress, it is the *estilo tradicional*," Abuela said, as though that made it okay.

⁶The dress went from long sleeves to a high neckline in a horrible clash of textures. From its starched, pink taffeta thorax dripped lacy pink ruffles, pink buttons, pink beads. It dripped —pink.

⁷"*Tradicional*," Abuela repeated, tapping the page.

⁸Pink was traditional? I couldn't plead ignorance-as-usual and say *No comprendo*, because this time I understood her Spanish, but only because she'd used a **cognate**. And I only knew what cognates were because Señora Wong had defined them on the first day of class, to demonstrate to us clueless *estudiantes* how much of the language we already knew: *mucho*. So instead I said to my grandmother, "This dress . . . it's . . . nice," and cocked my head at an angle, trying to find some truth to my words.

⁹"*Bueno*," replied Abuela. A bright smile bloomed on her shockingly orange-painted lips. "We plan the *fiestecita* for next *eh*spring. My little Violeta is becoming *una mujer*!" She

mi palomita:
my little dove

Ven acá, chica:
Come here, girl.

estilo tradicional:
traditional style

No comprendo:
I don't understand.

estudiantes: students
mucho: a lot

Bueno: good
fiestecita: little party
una mujer: a woman

sounded so satisfied that I couldn't say no just then. Besides, I'd used up all my arguments already.

[10]I had pointed out that it wouldn't be a real birthday party because I was *already* fifteen years old—that's why she was here in the first place. We had celebrated my birthday the night before. Abuela and Abuelo, Dad's parents, visit us twice every year, in September for my birthday and in May for Dad's. They say those are the only months of the year when the Chicago area is habitable—on account of the snow, the wind off the lake, and, they emphasize, rolling their *r*s, "that *ter-r-r-ri-ble humedad*." Yes, the humidity. And they live in Miami.

[11]But Abuela informed me that the *quince* party need only take place sometime during the year in which one turns fifteen. The girl gets a new dress and a tiara, a bunch of pictures taken in them, and a huge party at a rented hall with all her friends and relatives invited. A *tiara*. These rules had been drawn up in Cuba, and I figured they were pretty strictly enforced, because Abuela seemed to know exactly what she was talking about, and there didn't appear to be much leeway. I was going to have a party in May whether I liked it or not. Judging from the magazine photos, I'd be wearing this pink monster of a dress and a Miss America crown, clutching the arm of some pimply cousin I barely knew, and tottering onto a stage in front of God and everyone else, proclaiming *I am Woman*.

[12]The horror.

[13]How could I tell my own grandmother that I hated dresses, wouldn't be caught dead onstage, and didn't even think of myself as Cuban? I had green eyes and practically blond hair—the same coloring as my Polish American mother.

[14]"Okay, Abuela," I murmured instead.

[15]From the hallway came the singular *veep-veep*! of acetate on acetate. My mom, Diane Shavlovsky Paz, zipped into view.

[16]"Did I hear someone mention a party?" Mom wore a teal, white, and fuchsia "running" suit top decorated with asymmetrical, eye-bruising graphics, and a pair of pale yellow sweatpants outlined with silver piping. Huge clip-on gold hoops hung from her ears; they swung

in aftershock for a full thirty seconds after she sat down across from us, in the white wicker armchair with the red velvet upholstery. She propped her gold open-toed sandals up on the kidney-shaped glass coffee table.

[17]Our house is decorated in Spanish Colonial meets Early Thrift Shop, and so, it seemed, was my mother today. She doesn't always look this good. "Fashion is not my long suit," she'll often say, followed by a pregnant pause while she waits for me to get the pun.

[18]"Your hair looks nice, Mom," I said, trying to **divert** her attention.
[19]"Thanks, Vi. Now, have you set a date yet?"
[20]"A date?" Great. This was beginning to sound like a wedding. And, as I mentioned, my love life lay at an all-time low. They'd have to get me one of those mail-order husbands. Or, if he were coming from

Cuba, I guessed you'd call him a *sail*-order husband. Because of the raft deal.

²¹Abuela doesn't like talking about the rafters. So I didn't tell my joke, though Mom would have loved it.

²²"*Sí*," said Abuela, nodding, "we must make the date for the rental of the hall." She murmured something in Spanish to Mom, who is fluent; I only caught *ella* and *especial*. Then I felt a small yet strong lightning-flash shoot between them, and through the charged air whistling past, I heard Mom say the word. In English. And I knew I was finished.

²³"Planning!" said Mom. "It's all in the planning. We pick the date and work backwards from there." She should know; Mom has planned umpteen grand openings for a restaurant that has yet to make it off the drawing board.

²⁴"Wh-what's to plan?" I asked nervously. "Invite a couple friends, set up a few folding chairs, and bam!"

²⁵"I give you 'bam'!" retorted Abuela. "The *quinceañero* requires *muchos planes*—for the invitations, for the fittings, for to choose the band . . ."

²⁶"And planning," my mother, in her mismatched ensemble, reminded us, "is my long suit."

²⁷There was no arguing that point. Planning was my mother's great hobby. The thing she had trouble with, according to the vocabulary word I looked up because I missed it on the English pretest, was **fruition**. So maybe this shindig would never really happen. It was practically my only hope.

²⁸Abuela had opened her electronic notebook. "The last weekend in May," she said, scrolling through her computerized calendar, "would be *perfecto*."

²⁹Mom reached under a cushion and pulled out our family calendar, the new one from St. Edna's Church that showed a picture of a different local celebrity receiving Communion for each month of the year. From behind her ear, she produced a thick black marker that advertised BUSTER'S MEATS.

sí: yes

ella: she
especial: special

muchos planes: many plans

perfecto: perfect

240

[30]Where had those come from? If I didn't know better, I'd have thought Mom and Abuela had been plotting this ambush for quite some time. Abuela is especially **canny** that way. But Mom wouldn't do that to me. She knows I feel like a dork in

dresses. When I vowed on eighth-grade graduation day never again to be hemmed in by a skirt, Mom agreed. "Everyone's got to develop their own style," she said. So I was sure she'd understand.

[31]She raised an eyebrow at Abuela. "Saturday?"

[32]"*Domingo es tradicional.*"

[33]"Sunday it is!" Mom flipped through the calendar months to May. Beneath the profile of a well-known professional football coach sticking his pink and gray tongue out to receive the Host, in the next-to-last square on the page, she wrote in indelible black ink: VIOLET'S QUINCE PARTY.

[34]So much for Mom's unwavering support.

[35]A nervous chuckle rose up in me, but I refused to let it out. It rattled around inside for a minute, then died. This *quince* business was no laughing matter.

Domingo es tradicional:
Sunday is traditional.

241

Connect to the Author

Nancy Osa

Nancy Osa offers advice on writing and discusses her inspiration for her first book, *Cuba 15*:

"Beginning writers are always told to 'write what you know.' The question is, with limited years behind you, what do you know well enough to write about? Without fail, everyone has a beginning. You might start there. What's your early history, in twenty words or less? I was born in Chicago, and my family moved to the south suburbs when I was five years old. Though I didn't set out to write a book about the area, Chicago and the suburbs are part of the foundation for *Cuba 15*.

"You probably know enough about yourself to begin writing a fictional setting. But I think that a good story entails writing *beyond* what one knows. I like to use realistic details, such as setting, as a jumping off point and then go on to explore mysteries or what-ifs. Though my father is from Cuba, I grew up in a very 'American' household, so in writing *Cuba 15* I first had to admit how much I *didn't* know about Cuba and my family history. As I learned, a book began to take shape. I considered what it would be like to grow up *with* that information. And my main character, Violet Paz, was born.

"Writing about others is a great way to learn, because the questions just keep coming, begging for answers. Considering some questions, however, requires special bravery. Setting this book in and around my hometown helped to bring my fears of the unknown—my Cuban roots, the current relationship between the U.S. and Cuba—down to earth, to make them smaller. And so I was able to address the question of Cuban American identity. The 61,500-word response became *Cuba 15*, and it all started because I wondered about where I came from."

from FLIGHT to FREEDOM

by Ana Veciana-Suarez

In April 1967, 13-year-old Yara García receives a blank diary from her father. As the days and months pass, Yara writes in it the story of her family's flight to Miami from Cuba, along with details of her life in this new and unfamiliar home.

Monday, 11th of September

[1]Patricia, one of the Cuban girls, claims school will get better when I learn the language. On her first day of second grade, she peed in her

pants because she did not know how to ask for the bathroom. Now she speaks English. She has friends. She also has new clothes—not a lot, but some. You can tell the Cubans who have just arrived, she says, by their clothes. They dress old. Old? "*Sí*, old," she said. They dress too formal, like they were in Cuba, the girls especially, with bows in their hair and bobby socks. And they wear the same thing over and over again.

[2]When she was saying this, I fingered my hair bow, and I looked down at my socks. She was describing me to a tee, and my face felt red-hot. Mami makes us dress in nice clothes so that our teachers "receive a good impression." We do not have but two or three outfits of this kind, nice but old and worn. They are always clean even if Mami has to wash them by hand in the bathroom sink.

[3]To be honest, at first I was mortified to find out how everybody regards me. Then I also was upset with Mami. She does not understand how school is different in the United States. But now that many hours have passed since my conversation with Patricia, something else, another feeling, has come over me. I am still angry, but at Patricia. At everybody else, too. I cannot quite explain why, but the thought of these classmates looking down at me makes me so, so angry.

[4]I will show them. Just wait. I am going to be the best student in the class. I will get the highest qualifications of anybody. My marks will be outstanding. I will speak English so well, write it so **eloquently**, that no one will notice the clothes I wear. They will be **mesmerized** by my brilliance. Just wait.

Tuesday, 19th of September

[5]Abuelo Tony told me an interesting thing tonight. After he heard me complaining about school, he took me to my uncle's bedroom and showed me a stack of books on the side of his bed. He said Tío Pablo was studying them all because he wants to be able to be a medical doctor in this country. Though he was a doctor at home, he still has to apply for a license here, which means he has to attend special classes

and take an examination. Abuelo Tony said that if he were stronger and healthier, he would be accompanying Tío Pablo. "Your uncle never gives up, and for that I am very proud of him," Abuelo Tony said.

[6]"It never hurts to study," he said. "Nobody can take away what is between your ears."

[7]Of course he told me this so that I can appreciate the privilege of attending school. That's what he called it, a privilege. I do plan to make good marks, so Abuelo Tony has no need to worry. That way I can show all those classmates, who look at me funny when I can't speak English, how smart I really am.

Thursday, 25th of January

[8]My English is improving day by day. I now have a part in a short play we will perform in class. I speak only a few lines, but I feel proud to have been chosen. At lunchtime Alina and Jane help me memorize my part. At home I practice my lines in front of the mirror. Everyone has noticed how my English is getting better, but sometimes I wonder if that means I will forget Spanish. If I know both languages equally, in what language will I think? How will I dream? How will I pray? Already I know the names for certain things in English but not in

Spanish. I've learned them in school and have to ask Papi or Mami to translate the words into Spanish.

Monday, 12th of February

[9]I have been thinking about what Abuelo said about never forgetting your homeland. Sometimes I worry that I will, because I close my eyes and there are faces and places, even decorations in our house, that I cannot remember in detail. It makes me worry about whether or not I have a home. And I mean *home*, not *house*. I have a house in Cuba, in my neighborhood of La Víbora, but I also have a house here. Which one is really home?

[10]I asked Ileana this after dinner tonight, and she looked at me as if I had just landed in a spaceship. Then she sat close to me on the old pea-green sofa and hugged me. I don't know whatever for, because she hasn't done that in a long, long time. She didn't say anything, just patted me on the back. But finally she spoke, and the more I think about her words, the more I realize she is right. She told me that home is where the heart is. It is where your loved ones are and where you feel comfortable hanging around in your pajamas with curlers in your hair. Well then, that means I have a home here and a home across the ocean there, always there.

Connect to the Author

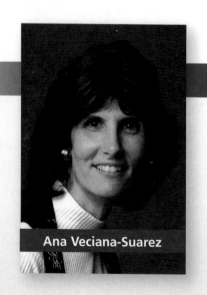

Ana Veciana-Suarez

Ana Veciana-Suarez drew from her own experiences to write *Flight to Freedom*. Veciana-Suarez was born in Havana, Cuba, in 1956. She and her family immigrated to Miami when she was six. Veciana-Suarez has written books for young readers and adults. She currently writes a syndicated column for the *Miami Herald*.

from *Tortuga*

Salomón's Story

by Rudolfo Anaya

This story is from Rudolfo Anaya's third novel, Tortuga. *The novel is about a young boy who has been paralyzed. He is nicknamed Tortuga, which means "turtle," because of the body cast he must wear. While in the hospital, the boy meets Salomón, a* curandero, *or healer, who is also dealing with paralysis. Salomón shares his story with the young boy.*

¹**B**efore I came here I was a hunter, but that was long ago. Still, it was in the pursuit of the hunt that I came face to face with my destiny. This is my story.

²We called ourselves a tribe and we spent our time hunting and fishing along the river. For young boys that was a great adventure. Each morning I stole away from my father's home to meet my fellow hunters by the river. My father was a farmer who planted corn on the hills bordering the river. He was a good man. He kept the **ritual** of the seasons, marked the path of the sun and the moon across the sky, and he prayed each day that the order of things not be disturbed.

³He did his duty and tried to teach me about the rhythm in the weather and the seasons, but a wild urge in my blood drove me from him. I went willingly to join the tribe along the river. The call of the hunt was exciting, and daily the slaughter of the animals with the smell of blood drove us deeper and deeper into the dark river. I became a member of the tribe, and I forgot the fields of my father. We hunted birds with our crude weapons and battered to death stray raccoons and rabbits. Then we skinned the animals and filled the air with the smoke of roasting meat. The tribe was pleased with me and welcomed me as a hunter. They prepared for my **initiation**.

⁴I, Salomón, tell you this so that you may know the meaning of life and death. How well I know it now, how clear are the events of the day I killed the giant river turtle. Since that day I have been a storyteller, forced by the order of my destiny to reveal my story. I speak to tell you how the killing became a horror.

⁵The silence of the river was heavier than usual that day. The heat stuck to our sweating skin like a sticky syrup and the insects sucked our blood. Our half-naked bodies moved like shadows in the brush. Those ahead and behind me whispered

from time to time, complaining that we were lost and suggesting that we turn back. I said nothing, it was the day of my initiation, I could not speak. There had been a fight at camp the night before and the bad feelings still lingered. But we hunted anyway, there was nothing else to do. We were **compelled** to hunt in the dark shadows of the river. Some days the spirit for the hunt was not good, fellow hunters quarreled over small things, and still we had to start early at daybreak to begin the long day's journey which would not bring us out until sunset.

⁶In the branches above us the bird cries were sharp and frightful. More than once the leader lifted his arm and the line froze, ready for action. The humid air was tense. Somewhere to my left I heard the river murmur as it swept south, and for the first time the dissatisfaction which had been building within me surfaced. I cursed the **oppressive** darkness and wished I was free of it. I thought of my father walking in the sunlight of his green fields, and I wished I was with him. But it was not so; I owed the tribe my allegiance. Today I would become a full member. I would kill the first animal we encountered.

⁷We moved farther than usual into unknown territory, hacking away at the thick underbrush; behind me I heard murmurs of **dissension**. Some wanted to turn back, others wanted to rest on the warm sandbars of the river, still others wanted to finish the argument which had started the night before. My father had given me an amulet to wear and he had instructed me on the hunt, and this made the leader jealous. Some argued that I could wear the amulet, while others said no. In the end the jealous leader tore it from my neck and said that I would have to face my initiation alone.

amulet: a charm worn to provide protection against evil or injury

⁸I was thinking about how poorly prepared I was and how my father had tried to help, when the leader raised his arm and sounded the alarm. A friend behind me whispered that if we were in luck there would be a deer drinking at the river. No one had ever killed a deer in the memory of our tribe. We held our

breath and waited, then the leader motioned and I moved forward to see. There in the middle of the narrow path lay the biggest tortoise any of us had ever seen. It was a huge monster which had crawled out of the dark river to lay its eggs in the warm sand. I felt a shiver, and when I breathed the taste of copper drained in my mouth and settled in my queasy stomach.

[9]The giant turtle lifted its huge head and looked at us with dull, glintless eyes. The tribe drew back. Only I remained facing the monster from the

water. Its slimy head dripped with bright green algae. It hissed a warning. It had come out of the water to lay its eggs, now it had to return to the river. Wet, leathery eggs, fresh from the laying, clung to its webbed feet, and as it moved forward it crushed them into the sand. Its gray shell was dry, dulled by the sun, encrusted with dead parasites and green growth; it needed the water.

[10]"Kill it!" the leader cried, and at the same time the hunting horn sounded its too-rou which echoed down the valley. Ah, its call was so sad

and mournful I can hear it today as I tell my story. . . . Listen, Tortuga, it is now I know that at that time I could have forsaken my initiation and **denounced** the darkness and insanity that urged us to the never-ending hunt. I had not listened to my father's words. The time was not right.

¹¹"The knife," the leader called, and the knife of the tribe was passed forward, then slipped into my hand. The huge turtle lumbered forward. I could not speak. In fear I raised the knife and brought it down with all my might. Oh, I prayed to no gods, but since then how often I have wished that I could undo what I did. One blow severed the giant turtle's head. One clean blow and the head rolled in the sand as the reptilian body reared back, gushing green slime. The tribe cheered and pressed forward. They were as surprised as I was that the kill had been so swift and clean. We had hunted smaller tortoises before and we knew that once they retreated into their shells it took hours to kill them. Then knives and spears had to be poked into the holes and the turtle had to be turned on its back so the tedious task of cutting the softer underside could begin. But now I had beheaded the giant turtle with one blow.

¹²"There will be enough meat for the entire tribe," one of the boys cried. He speared the head and held it aloft for everyone to see. I could only look at the dead turtle that lay quivering on the sand, its death urine and green blood staining the damp earth.

¹³"He has passed his test," the leader shouted, "he did not need the amulet of his father. We will clean the shell and it will be his shield! And he shall now be called the man who slew the turtle!"

¹⁴The tribe cheered, and for a moment I bathed in my glory. The fear left me, and so did the desire to be with my father on the harsh hills where he cultivated his fields of corn. He had been wrong; I could trust the tribe and its magic. Then someone shouted and we turned to see the turtle struggling toward us. It reared up, exposing the gaping hole where the head had been, then it charged, surprisingly swift for its huge size. Even without its head it crawled toward the river. The tribe fell back in panic.

[15]"Kill it!" the leader shouted, "Kill it before it reaches the water! If it escapes into the water it will grow two heads and return to haunt us!"

[16]I understood what he meant. If the creature reached the safety of the water it would live again, and it would become one more of the ghosts that lurked along our never-ending path. Now there was nothing I could do but stand my ground and finish the killing. I struck at it until the knife broke on its hard shell, and still the turtle rumbled toward the water, pushing me back. Terror and fear made me fall on the sand and grab it with my bare hands. Grunting and gasping for breath I dug my bare feet into the sand. I slipped one hand into the dark, bleeding hole where the head had been and with the other I grabbed its huge feet. I struggled to turn it on its back and rob it of its strength, but I couldn't. Its dark instinct for the water and the pull of death were stronger than my fear and desperation. I grunted and cursed as its claws cut into my arms and legs. The brush shook with our violent thrashing as we rolled down the bank towards the river. Even mortally wounded it was too strong for me. At the edge of the river, it broke free from me and plunged into the water, trailing frothy blood and bile as it disappeared into the gurgling waters.

[17]Covered with turtle's blood, I stood numb and trembling. As I watched it disappear into the dark waters of the river, I knew I had done a wrong. Instead of conquering my fear, I had created another shadow which would return to haunt us. I turned and looked at my companions; they trembled with fright.

[18]"You have failed us," the leader whispered. "You have angered the river gods." He raised his talisman, a stick on which hung chicken feathers, dried juniper berries and the rattler of a snake we had killed in the spring, and he waved it in front of me to ward off the curse. Then they withdrew in silence and vanished into the dark brush, leaving me alone on that stygian bank.

stygian: eternally dark and frightening; relating to the river Styx in Greek mythology

[19]Oh, I wish I could tell you how lonely I felt. I cried for the turtle to return so I could finish the kill, or return its life, but the force of my destiny was already set and that was not to be. I understand that now. That is why I tell you my story. I left the river, free of the tribe, but unclean and smelling of death.

[20]That night the bad dreams came, and then the paralysis. . . .

Connect to the Author

Photo by Mimi

Rudolfo Anaya

Rudolfo Anaya was born in a small village in New Mexico in 1937. He grew up listening to *cuentistas*, storytellers. "I loved stories," Anaya recalls. "Stories are what the old people told. I was raised on the folktales of the Hispanic New Mexicans." He brings the magical qualities of those folktales into his own writing. "People ask me why I became a writer," says Anaya. "My answer is that I became a writer in my childhood. . . . The characters of my childhood, the family, friends, and neighbors that made up my world, they and their lives fed my imagination."

The Day It Rained Cockroaches

from *The Pigman and Me*
by Paul Zindel

¹The three of us were very excited when we pulled up in front of our new home. There were some unusual things about it, but I've always been attracted to unusual things. For instance, I was the only kid I knew who always liked searching newspapers to find weird news. Whenever I found a shocking article or picture, I'd save it. That week alone, I had cut out a picture of a man who was born with monkey feet, a list of Seventy-Five Ways to Be Richer a Year from

Now, and a report about a mother who sold her daughter to Gypsies in exchange for a theater trip to London. Also, there are ten biographical points about me you should know right off the bat:

1) My father ran away with one of his girlfriends when I was two years old.

2) My sister taught me how to cut out fake coins from cardboard and make **imitation** lamb chops out of clay, because we never had very much real money or food.

3) I once wanted to be Batman and fly off buildings.

4) I yearned to be kidnapped by aliens for a ride in their flying saucer.

5) Ever since I could remember I'd liked to make cyclorama

displays out of shoeboxes and cut out figures of ghosts, beasts, and teenagers to put in them.

6) I once prayed to own a pet gorilla.

7) I used to like to play tricks on people, like putting thumbtacks on their seats.

8) When my father's father was sixteen, he got a job on a Dutch freighter, sailed to America, jumped ship and swam to Staten Island, got married, and opened a bake shop, and he and his wife died from eating too many crumbcakes before Betty and I could meet them.

9) A truck once ran over my left elbow. It really hurt and left a little scar.

10) I am afraid I will one day die by shark attack.

²About anything else you'd ever want to know about my preteen existence you can see in the photos in this book. However, I don't think life *really* started for me until I became a teenager and my mother moved us to Travis, on Staten Island.

³The address of our new home was 123 Glen Street. We stopped in front, and for a few moments the house looked normal: brown shingles, pea-soup-green-painted sides, a tiny yellow porch, untrimmed hedges, and a rickety wood gate and fence. Across the street to the left was a slope with worn gravestones all over it. The best-preserved ones were at the top, peeking out of patches of poison oak.

⁴The backyard of our house was an airport. I mean, the house had two acres of land of its own, but beyond the rear fence was a huge field consisting of a single dirt runway, lots of old propeller-driven Piper Cub-type planes, and a cluster of rusted **hangars**. This was the most **underprivileged** airport I'd ever seen,

bordered on its west side by the Arthur Kill channel and on its south side by a Con Edison electric power plant with big black mountains of coal. The only great sight was a huge apple tree on the far left corner of our property. Its trunk was at least three feet wide. It had strong, thick branches rich with new, flapping leaves. It reached upward like a giant's hand grabbing for the sky.

[5]"Isn't everything beautiful?" Mother beamed.

[6]"Yes, Mom," I said.

[7]Betty gave me a pinch for lying.

[8]"I'll plant my own rose garden," Mother went on, fumbling for the key. "Lilies, tulips, violets!"

[9]Mom opened the front door and we went inside. We were so excited, we ran through the echoing empty rooms, pulling up old, soiled shades to let the sunlight crash in. We ran upstairs and downstairs, all over the place like wild ponies. The only unpleasant thing, from my point of view, was that we weren't the only ones running around. There were a lot of cockroaches scurrying from our invading footfalls and the shafts of light.

[10]"Yes, the house has a few roaches," Mother confessed. "We'll get rid of them in no time!"

[11]"How?" Betty asked raising an eyebrow.

[12]"I bought eight Gulf Insect Bombs!"

[13]"Where are they?" I asked.

[14]Mother dashed out to the car and came back with one of the suitcases. From it she spilled the bombs, which looked like big silver hand grenades.

[15]"We just put one in each room and turn them on!" Mother explained.

[16]She took one of the bombs, set it in the middle of the upstairs kitchen, and turned on its nozzle. A cloud of gas began to stream from it, and we hurried into the other rooms to set off the other bombs.

[17]"There!" Mother said. "Now we have to get out!"

[18]"Get out?" I coughed.

[19]"Yes. We must let the poison fill the house for four hours before we

can come back in! Lucky for us there's a Lassie double feature playing at the Ritz!"

20We hadn't been in the house ten minutes before we were driving off again!

21I suppose you might as well know now that my mother really *loved* Lassie movies. The only thing she enjoyed more were movies in which romantic couples got killed at the end by tidal waves, volcanoes, or other natural disasters. Anyway, I was glad we were gassing the roaches, because they are the one insect I **despise**. Tarantulas I like. Scorpions I can live with. But ever since I was three years old and my mother took me to a World's Fair, I have had nightmares about cockroaches. Most people remember an exciting water ride this fair had called the Shoot-the-Chutes, but **emblazoned** on my brain is the display the fair featured of giant, live African cockroaches, which look like American cockroaches except they're six inches long, have furry legs, and can pinch flesh. In my nightmares about them, I'm usually lying on a bed in a dark room and I notice a **bevy** of giant cockroaches heading for me. I try to run away but find out that someone has secretly tied me down on the bed, and the African roaches start crawling up the sides of the sheets. They walk all over my body, and then they head for my face. When they start trying to drink from my mouth is when I wake up screaming.

22So after the movie I was actually looking forward to going back to the house and seeing all the dead cockroaches.

23"Wasn't Lassie wonderful?" Mother sighed as she drove us back to Travis. "The way that brave dog was able to crawl hundreds of miles home after being kidnapped and beaten by Nazi Secret Service Police!"

24"Yes, Mom," I agreed, although I was truthfully tired of seeing a dog movie star keep pulling the same set of tear-jerking stunts in each of its movies.

[25]"Maybe we'll get a dog just like Lassie one day," Mother sighed.

[26]When we got back to the house this time, we didn't run into it. We walked inside very slowly, sniffing for the deadly gas. I didn't care about the gas so much as I wanted to see a lot of roach corpses all over the place so I'd be able to sleep in peace.

[27]*But there were none.*

[28]"Where are all the dead roaches?" I asked.

[29]"I don't know," Mother admitted.

[30]We crept slowly upstairs to see if the bodies might be there. I knew the kitchen had the most roaches, but when we went in, I didn't see a single one, living or dead. The lone empty Gulf Insect Bomb sat spent in the middle of the floor. My sister picked up the bomb and started reading the directions. One thing my mother never did was follow directions. As Betty was reading, I noticed a closed closet door and reached out to turn its knob.

[31]"It says here we should've opened all the closet doors before setting off the bombs, so roaches can't hide." Betty moaned, her clue to me that Mom had messed up again.

[32]I had already started to open the door. My mind knew what was

going to happen, but it was too late to tell my hand to stop pulling on the door. It sprang open, and suddenly, 5,000 very angry, living cockroaches rained down on me from the ceiling of the closet.

[33]"Eeehhhhhh!" I screamed, leaping around the room, bathed in bugs, slapping at the roaches crawling all over me and down my neck! "Eeehhhhhh! Eeehh! Ehhh! Ehh!"

[34]"Don't worry. I'll get more bombs," Mother said comfortingly as she grabbed an old dishrag to knock the fluttering roaches off my back. Betty calmly reached out her foot to crunch as many as dared run by her.

Connect to the Author

Paul Zindel had a difficult childhood. His parents separated when he was young. His unpredictable and domineering mother was left to support Paul and his sister Betty. They moved often and there was never enough money. "I felt worthless as a kid, and dared to speak and act my true feelings only in fantasy and secret," Zindel remembered in an interview. "That's probably what made me a writer." In college, Zindel majored in chemistry and education. He taught high

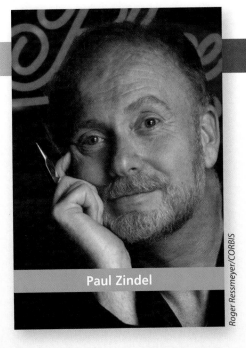

Paul Zindel

Roger Ressmeyer/CORBIS

school chemistry for 10 years. In his spare time, he wrote plays. One of those plays earned him the Pulitzer Prize. After seeing the play, an editor suggested he write a novel for young adults. That novel, *The Pigman*, was considered a huge success. Zindel went on to write dozens of books and plays. He published *The Pigman and Me*, a memoir, in 1992. Zindel died in 2003 at the age of 66.

The Cement Truck

by Laurence Lasky

¹I recall being on the bus, wishing my shoulder was separated, or that my right arm had been plastered to a cast and the cast had a dozen names written on it. "Mr. Kanele," I wanted to say but didn't dare to, "my left ankle is busted," or, "Mr. Kanele, I can't move my right leg." A new thought sprang into my mind. I would arrive at that school, walk up to the nearest wall, and bang my head against it ten or twelve times. This way I would at least sustain a concussion or a brain tumor. Or maybe I could bend my little finger back to my wrist. He wouldn't send a guy out onto the mat with nine fingers. Yes, he would. He would send a one-legged third grader onto the mat if he was presented with the choice of that or a forfeit. "Where's Scutter, my eighty-six-

pound protégé? Hey, Scutter, want to wrestle varsity today?" I could picture him sitting smugly in his English class with his legs tied up in a square knot and with four fingers stuck in his mouth. Nope, it would be against him, me against the world. Maybe I could slash my wrists or slit my throat. That wouldn't work. Nothing would work. Kanele wouldn't accept any excuse I proposed to him.

²Why was I the only guy on the bus changing from rock to petrified wood? All the rest of the hearty wrestlers were talking or singing. How do you account for that? Maybe all wrestlers are idiots. In fact, you have to be an idiot if you're a wrestler. Everybody hates wrestling. Therefore, all wrestlers are idiots. Including me, for being on this ridiculous team.

³"There it is, to the left," said one of the wrestlers.

⁴"Yep, that's South Rock, all right."

⁵I pressed my nose against the window. There it was, ugly and cruel. The bus continued rumbling along, but now I felt each bump kicking my stomach so I could hear it bouncing emptily like a tin can.

⁶Kanele had told me about the guy I was to wrestle. "He's a county

champ, Lasky. A slicker wrestler doesn't exist. He knows every single move in the book. Strong, too. Strong as a bull. You're in for one, Lasky."

⁷That really encouraged me. We would walk into that school, and there he would be. I'd walk up to him and he'd look at me and say, "You know what? You're the sickliest little thing I've ever wrestled. I eat guys like you for breakfast." Just swell. And I would laugh, heh, heh, and say back to him, "Are you on weight? What's your record? Did Yates beat you? Don't you think wrestling is a silly sport? I hate wrestling. Too much callisthenics. I'm going to be a doctor when I grow up." Then he would look at me as if I were a bug. He would shrug his shoulders and say, "That's your problem, buddy." I would watch him stalking off.

⁸By now we were inside the building. Ed Reynolds said, "Hey, some joint here!" Wrestlers must be perfect morons. No one will be able to drag me to that wrestling room next year.

⁹Then Kanele walked up to me. It was rumored that Mr. Kanele was the runner-up in the 123-pound division in the Panama games in 1954. He had a peppery walk, like some bowlegged sailor, and he came up to me and

261

slapped me on the shoulders. "Get ready. Strip down. The weigh-in's in twenty minutes."

[10]I always associated the phrase "weigh-in" with World War Three or Edgar Allan Poe on a chilly December night.

[11]"I thought you said the weigh-in wouldn't be till four?"

[12]"My, you really *are* anxious, Lasky," he said, slapping me on the shoulder.

[13]At wrestling weigh-ins, everybody parades up to the scale nude and one by one they hop on the scale, some keeping their heels off it, some exhaling air furiously, others trying to amputate some useless part of the body. For most of them it boiled down to their heads. Wrestlers are all morons.

[14]County champ was on weight. I was on weight. I wished I wasn't.

[15]He wasn't too overconfident when he stepped on the scale. He hopped on singing, "Row, row, row your boat." Boy, that made me mad. "Buddy," I murmured to myself, "I'm going to beat the daylights out of you." Yes, I was going to beat the daylights out of him. Before twenty million cheering fans. I was going to get him on the mat, whip him into a double-knee-drop leg breaker, and win the gold belt. Everybody would be cheering like crazy. And Kanele would walk up to me and say, "You did it, Lasky, you did it!" And I would say, "I couldn't have done it without you, Mr. Kanele." Then I would be mobbed by a hungry band of autograph seekers and twenty or thirty photographers. Cameras flashing everywhere.

[16]Just before the match, Kanele gave us his usual pep talk. He wasn't one of those I-don't-care-whether-you-win-or-lose-boys-it's-how-you-play-the-game men.

[17]"Listen, you guys. We've lost nine matches in a row. It's about time we saved a bit of our school's honor. Lasky, you start us off. Give the boys a lift by pinning the county champ. Now come on, run out onto that mat."

[18]See, I was going to pin the county champ.

[19]We went out onto the mat, all of us trying to look complicated and important. We looked like a pack of firemen. I felt stupid.

[20]I remember the mat being soft and squishy. While everybody else was deciding what hold to pull, or what reversals to try, or how they were going to take their man down, I was thinking how nice and soft

the mat was. I was also thinking how sick I was. Sick of Kanele, sick of wrestling, sick of all the idiot wrestlers around me, and sick of worry.

21"Listen," I said to myself, "the worst thing that can happen to you is that you'll get pinned in the first period. So what? What's so terrible about getting pinned in the first period? It's been done before. Every member of this team has been pinned in the first period before. Almost every member."

22We sat down in our places and then they came running out onto the mat. The crowd was unlike our crowds. At home matches, we were accustomed to eight people looking down from our side, and two of them were managers, one

was a cheerleader (the one who had drawn the smallest ballot), and two were janitors. Here there were a thousand screaming idiots, all of them completely out of their minds. Everybody was clapping their hands. This I remember. I also remember myself saying, "I got to get out of here."

[23]"Victory! Victory! Victory! Kill these guys! Smash them! Break them! Maul them! Stomp them into the ground."

[24]I was now standing in my corner, Kanele talking to me, and the county champ was standing in his corner, his manager talking to him. "Mr. Kanele, I think my back is brok—"

[25]"What's that, Lasky?"

[26]"Nothing, oh, nothing."

[27]The match is a blurred picture. They always are. I remember going out there and shaking hands with the guy and giving him a pleasant smile which he didn't see and the moron referee tooting his whistle and that monster walking toward me.

[28]Thwap. I was on the mat. He was on me like an octopus. He had my arm, and the other arm. Now the leg and then my head. Then the other leg. Then my nose was pushed into that soft, squishy mat. It was blue-green. The one at the other school was white, but I liked this one better. It was a pretty blue-green. All soft and squishy. You would have liked to step on it; your foot would have sunk in three inches. I wished I could have been rolled up in it and sent bouncing down a hill. On a cool, windy day in April. With swaying trees all around and a little brook at my side.

[29]Then I felt a cement truck on my chest. The referee's hand came down and his whistle blew. But the crowd wasn't there. I looked at Kanele. Kanele looked at me. Agony, agony, agony.

[30]Here it came, the deadly ray gun. His eyebrows were down, his mouth expressionless. I could detect just that little twitch of the upper lip he was so good at. The eyes were fixed, fixed on my eyes. I couldn't avoid them. It was terrible.

[31]"Well, Lasky," said Kanele, "at least you didn't quit." He lied. Boy, did he lie.

WORLD AT WORK

- *What jobs lie beneath the surface of what we see around us?*
- *What inspires people to follow certain career paths?*
- *What special interests or abilities do you have that could lead to a career?*

The Food Stylist's Art

by Doug Stewart

You would not really eat moto oil, but it makes this roasted turkey appear moist and tasty in a photograph.

[1]Has a delectable ice-cream sundae in a magazine ad ever made your mouth water? Well, your taste buds might be in for a surprise if you could take a bite. Advertising professionals know that a scoop of real ice cream melts into a gloopy mess under the hot lights of a photo studio. That's why the ice cream you admired could have been cold mashed potatoes and food coloring.

[2]But wait—isn't the best way to get a delicious-looking photograph of food to prepare something delicious and take a picture of it? Not necessarily, say members of a **bizarre** and highly competitive profession known as food styling. These folks are so persnickety, they can spend a week getting a single meal ready for its closeup. If the food is to appear on a magazine cover or a TV commercial, the effort can earn them several thousand dollars.

[3]"When we can, we go for normal cooking, because that's usually going to look best on camera," says schoolteacher-turned-food-stylist Dolores Custer, "but there are certain foods that just don't behave for us." One of those is ice cream, she says. This is why stand-ins for ice cream are sometimes used when meals are photographed (though only, by law, when ice cream isn't what the ad is selling). Custer's own recipe for guaranteed-not-to-melt ice cream is a pound of confectioner's sugar, a third to a half cup of Crisco, and an equal amount of corn syrup. Yum!

[4]Another problem food is turkey. "If you cook it fully, it gets burnt spots," she says. "Then, after it sits out for half an hour, it wrinkles." Food photographers hate wrinkly turkeys. The solution:

267

Cook the turkey for 40 minutes, pin back the skin if needed, then paint it an attractive roast-turkey color, using cocktail bitters and gravy coloring. Modern stylists frown on old-school tricks like basting a bird with soap, shellac, or motor oil. Still, undercooked turkeys are as much a health hazard as soaped-up ones, so they're tossed out after a shoot. (Most other foods used in photo shoots remain perfectly edible. In New York City, the food-styling capital of the world, a charity called City Harvest collects the leftovers and distributes them to the homeless.)

[5]For the food stylist, patience is a **virtue**. Custer has dumped boxes of corn flakes onto a tray and sorted through them, one by one. "I look for what I call flakes with character," she says, "the ones that curl or twist, because perfect flat flakes don't look very interesting in a photograph."

[6]If this is show business, it's not the glamorous end. Imagine baking 80 apple pies to get one that's good-looking enough for a starring role. Or digging through dozens of chicken pot pies to extract the most succulent-looking pea, the most correct carrot cube, and the most perfect chicken chunk, then placing them by hand on the marquee slice of pie as director and crew wait. Stylists are allowed to handpick the prettiest **morsels** but not to insert them more

To make perfect-looking ice cream, mix confectioner's sugar, Crisco, and corn syrup. Well, at least the sprinkles and the cone are the real deal.

abundantly than the factory does. Also forbidden: Putting marbles in a bowl of soup so that more of the meat and other goodies are forced up to the surface and into camera range.

Perfect flat flakes don't look very interesting in a photograph.

[7]TV commercials where actors delightedly bite into a product are especially taxing for an off-camera cook. "Once they take a bite from a sandwich or whatever's being advertised, it can't be used again, so you have to prepare things in volume," says New York City food stylist Ricki Rosenblatt. "For one bite-and-smile ad, I cooked maybe 300 hamburgers in five hours." (In case you were wondering, the actors spit out the bite after each take. This is how people in food commercials stay thin.)

[8]For location shooting, a food stylist packs more gear than a soldier on maneuvers: bags and backpacks containing toasters, salad spinners, cutting boards, hair dryers (for melting cheese), staple guns, paintbrushes, dental tools, and more. What they don't carry with them, they race out and buy—200 heads of garlic perhaps, in order to find three that are perfectly shaped and blemish-free ("heroes," as they're known in the trade). Veteran stylist Marilinda Hodgdon maintains what she calls a candy library in her New York City home, just in case an art director needs to shoot, say, Halloween candy in March. "I'm not saying it's fresh enough to eat," she says, "but anytime a job calls for candy canes, I have them."

A food stylist's kit might include a staple gun, a jeweler's propane torch, a heat gun, and an iron.

[9]Nothing puts a stylist's ingenuity to the test more than keeping food looking fresh, hot, and scrumptious in a studio as the hours drag on. Ricki Rosenblatt has slipped pieces of dry ice under a pile

269

of smoked ribs to give them a **perpetually** steamy, fresh-from-the-smokehouse look. "For coffee," she says, "I'll use an eyedropper to put little bubbles at the edge of the surface as though the cup was just poured. It's actually detergent." Letting cereal get soggy in milk, of course, is a major styling no-no. "Cereal holds up better if you put it in Elmer's Glue," says Rosenblatt.

[10]These tricks are the **exception**, not the rule, she and other food stylists emphasize. The trend in recent years, especially in fancy food magazines, is to show real, honestly prepared food, as though the photographer were documenting a dinner party. For one thing, the public has become more savvy about what real food looks like. Gluing parsley to a carrot top to make it look healthier isn't going to fool as many people as it once did.

[11]For all the painstaking care that food stylists bring to their

Cereal holds up better if you put it in Elmer's Glue.

work, they sometimes find they don't go far enough. Stylists as a rule may be finicky, but art directors tend to be full-blown obsessives. They're the ones who insist the spaghetti ends be tucked in. Rosenblatt recalls being asked to rearrange the sesame seeds on a hamburger bun. The seeds weren't spaced evenly enough for the director. "I used tweezers and reattached them with airplane glue," she says. "It was a print ad, so no one was going to eat it."

[12]Dolores Custer once prepared a white-chocolate mousse to be photographed. As she was about to plop three raspberries and a piece of mint on top, the art director peered in and noticed,

perhaps for the first time, that raspberries have tiny hairs. The hairs, he decided, had to go. "While everyone waited, my assistant and I took tweezers and pulled off all the hairs on the raspberries," she says. It took 10 minutes per berry.

[13]Custer took the request in stride. She runs workshops around the country on how to make food look good, and she always gives her students a list of **attributes** that every good food stylist should have. "One of the most important," she says, "is a sense of humor."

How to Cook a
Cheeseburger

The first step is to add a little gravy coloring for that just-grilled look.

Next, glue those sesame seeds in a nice arrangement on the bun. Then whip out your hair dryer and melt the cheese.

Sandy Skoglund

Gathering Paradise © 1991, Sandy Skoglund

¹**S**andy Skoglund has always been good at making things. As a girl, she created comic books, designed dresses for her dolls, and sewed her own clothes. She was especially good at drawing **caricatures** of people. To amuse her friends, Sandy often made cartoons spoofing class assignments. One was of George Washington crossing the Potomac, saying silly things shown in balloon captions over his head.

²Sandy did all of these things in spite of a handicap. When she was

three, she became ill with polio, a virus that destroys nerve passages between the brain and muscles of the body. The disease **paralyzed** Sandy's left shoulder and weakened her left arm so much that she had to adapt from being left-handed to using her right hand.

[3]Because of her injury, Sandy felt different from other children. The injury was not obvious, thanks to physical therapy, but Sandy knew it was there. From this experience she became aware of the difference between appearances and reality— between how things look and how they really are. Sandy did not look handicapped, but she was. Even today, she cannot use her left arm to lift heavy things above her head.

[4]Sandy was born in Quincy, Massachusetts, on September 11, 1946. Her father, Walter, ran the family gas station and garage. Her mother, Dorothy, was a nurse. Sandy is the oldest of four children. When she was eight, her father began working as an **executive** for the Shell Oil Company. Each time he was promoted, the family moved —from Massachusetts to Maine to Connecticut. When Sandy was a teenager, his work took the family to southern California.

[5]Sandy remembers how different southern California was from anywhere she had ever been. The sun shone almost every day, and the bright colors of flowers and of red-roofed adobe houses made an impression on her. Some of those vivid colors are in the photographs Sandy makes today.

[6]One summer, Sandy got a job as a waitress at Disneyland. As a child, she had enjoyed comic books, cartoons, and Disney movies. As a teenager working at Walt Disney's amusement park, Sandy saw how convincing fantasy could be to people of all ages. Anything was possible in the make-believe world of Walt Disney.

[7]Looking back, Sandy sees that many experiences she had when she was growing up contributed to the artwork she now makes. But when she was young, she never imagined she would become an artist. It was not until she attended Smith College, a school for women in Massachusetts, that she discovered how much she liked learning about art and art history. For her junior year, Sandy studied art history in Paris at famous places like the Louvre museum and the Sorbonne, part of the University of Paris.

[8]A year after she graduated from Smith College, Sandy enrolled in graduate school at the University of Iowa. There, she studied painting and sculpture and became interested in filmmaking. Once, Sandy shot a

Sandy Skoglund sculpts squirrels from nondrying clay in her studio.

© 1991 Sandy Skoglund

horror movie starring her brother as a dead man who rises from the grave. Sandy made him appear so ghostly that when police drove by and saw him dozing in a car during a break in the filming, they stopped to investigate. They thought he was dead! Sandy had already learned how to make staged scenes look convincingly real.

[9]Throughout her training in art and art history, Sandy had never taken a class in photography. From her experience with making films, she understood the workings of the camera, but she had to teach herself how to make prints in the darkroom. She asked photographer friends for advice and got tips from the local camera store. Sandy picked up the rest of the technical information she needed as she went along.

[10]Among her early images are color photographs of frozen food. In *Peas on a Plate* (1979), she carefully lined up frozen peas to form a diamond on a brightly colored party plate. The plate sits on decorative paper used to cover the inside of kitchen cabinets. The peas are laid out so perfectly that we see them as **elements** in a pattern, not as food.

[11]To get inspiration for these pictures, Sandy looked at color photo ads of food in magazines. The artificial and theatrical quality of these images fascinated her. The advertisements showed products carefully set up in a studio to look their best. Sandy knows, however, that appearances are **deceiving**.

A product never looks as good at home as it does in the ad. Just as Sandy spoofed class assignments with cartoons when she was a girl, she now made pictures that poked fun at the exaggerated staging of advertising photographs.

[12]Starting in 1979, Sandy began arranging entire rooms to be photographed. In one picture, titled *Hangers*, she painted a room in her studio bright yellow and pink, then covered it from top to bottom with blue clothes hangers. Everything is set up for the camera's point of view: The hangers are carefully placed to outline the chairs as though the scene is flat and the hangers were drawn in position. The man in pajamas stepping into the room seems unaware of the strangeness of his surroundings. This is true in many of Sandy's pictures. The people in the pictures do not appear to see the same things we, the viewers, do. We get the feeling Sandy is showing us something special, something only the camera can see.

[13]A year later, Sandy made one of her best known photographs,

Radioactive Cats. She started by spending hours thinking about how to make a photograph of a room full of cats. How many cats would there be? What would they be doing? What kind of room would they be in? Once

Sandy Skoglund prepares a scene to photograph by arranging plastic squirrels she created earlier.

Sandy had an idea of how the picture would look, she got to work.

[14]First, she molded twenty-five cats out of chicken wire and plaster and painted them day-glo green. Next, she built a set, like a movie or stage set. She furnished it with a table, two chairs, and a refrigerator she found in a junk shop. Then she painted everything gray, even the radiator, the floor, and the kitchen window. Sandy positioned the cats around the room

Radioactive Cats © 1980, Sandy Skoglund

and brought in two friends to pose for her. She gave them gray clothes to wear and told them where to sit and stand. Sandy loaded the camera with film and, when everything was just right, she took the picture. All of this work, from start to finish, took about six months.

[15]Over the past twenty years, Sandy has become well known for her **zany** photographs in which animals and foodstuffs reign. Her success is due in part to her resourcefulness. Sandy uses all her skills—as sculptor, painter, cartoonist, and designer—in staging the scenes she photographs. The final image, though, seems to come from the magical world of make-believe. As in a trip to Disneyland, we walk away knowing that we have been somewhere extraordinary. Sandy Skoglund has taken us on a tour of her imagination.

CATASTROPHE!

by Patty Moynahan

"Hello, Mom? It's me, Felicia, and I'll tell you why I'm calling—
Yes, I know it's hard to hear my voice above the caterwauling.
Something strange is going on at Aunt Louise and Uncle Pat's:
I am standing in their kitchen, and the place is full of cats!

5   Cats are crouching in the cupboard, there are felines on the floor.
    Cats are creeping, cats are craning—there are twenty-five or more!
    Cats are poised atop the fridge and perched upon the breakfast table.
    It's as if I'm in a nightmare or a twisted children's fable.

Please believe me when I tell you it's a most peculiar scene,
10   And if *that's* not weird enough, well, all the cats are colored green!
Their tails are pointy fingers, their bodies sleek and longish;
They're like a lab experiment gone horribly wrongish.

    Uncle Pat and Aunt Louise don't seem to mind the cats at all.
    But they're giving me the creeps, and that's why I had to call.
15   Is this real, or am I dreaming? Either way, it's quite disturbing.
    Please come quick, Mom—I'll be waiting for you outside on the curbing."

THE CIRCUIT

by Francisco Jiménez

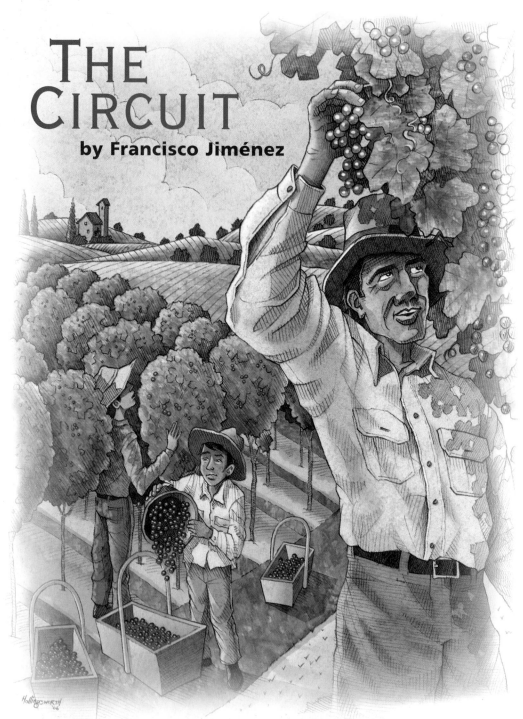

A family of migrant farmworkers finished picking the last of the strawberry crop. Now they are seeking work from a vineyard owner whose grapes are ready to harvest.

¹At sunset we drove into a labor camp near Fresno. Since Papa did not speak English, Mama asked the camp foreman if he needed any more workers. "We don't need no more," said the foreman, scratching his head. "Check with Sullivan down the road. Can't miss him. He lives in a big white house with a fence around it."

²When we got there, Mama walked up to the house. She went through a white gate, past a row of rose bushes, up the stairs to the front door. She rang the doorbell. The porch light went on and a tall husky man came out. They exchanged a few words. After the man went in, Mama **clasped** hands and hurried back to the car. "We have work! Mr. Sullivan said we can stay there the whole season," she said, gasping and pointing to an old garage near the stables.

³The garage was worn out by the years. It had no windows. The walls, eaten by termites, strained to support the roof full of holes. The dirt floor, **populated** by earthworms, looked like a gray road map.

⁴That night, by the light of a kerosene lamp, we unpacked and cleaned our new home. Roberto swept away the loose dirt, leaving the hard ground. Papa plugged the holes in the walls with old newspapers and tin can tops. Mama fed my little brothers and sisters. Papa and Roberto then brought in the mattress and placed it on the far corner of the garage. "Mama, you and the little ones sleep on the mattress. Roberto, Panchito, and I will sleep outside under the trees," Papa said.

⁵Early next morning Mr. Sullivan showed us where his crop was, and after breakfast, Papa, Roberto, and I headed for the vineyard to pick.

⁶Around nine o'clock the temperature had risen to almost one hundred degrees. I was completely soaked in sweat, and my mouth felt as if I had been chewing on a handkerchief. I walked over to the end of the row, picked up the jug of water we had brought, and began drinking. "Don't drink too much; you'll get sick," Roberto shouted. No sooner had he said that than I felt sick to my stomach. I dropped to my knees and let the jug roll off my hands. I remained motionless with my eyes glued on the hot sandy ground. All I could hear was the drone of insects. Slowly I began to recover. I poured water over my face and

neck and watched the black mud run down my arms and hit the ground.

⁷I still felt a little dizzy when we took a break to eat lunch. It was past two o'clock and we sat underneath a large walnut tree that was on the side of the road. While we ate, Papa jotted down the number of boxes we had picked. Roberto drew designs on the ground with a stick. Suddenly I noticed Papa's face turn pale as he looked down the road. "Here comes the school bus," he whispered loudly in alarm. **Instinctively**, Roberto and I ran and hid in the vineyards. We did not want to get in trouble for not going to school. The yellow bus stopped in front of Mr. Sullivan's house. Two neatly dressed boys about my age got off. They carried books under their arms. After they crossed the street, the bus drove away. Roberto and I came out from hiding and joined Papa. "*Tienen que tener cuidado*," he warned us.

⁸After lunch we went back to work. The sun kept beating down. The buzzing insects, the wet sweat, and the hot dry dust made the afternoon seem to last forever. Finally the mountains around the valley reached out and swallowed the sun. Within an hour it was too dark to continue picking. The vines blanketed the grapes, making it difficult to see the bunches. "*Vámonos*," said Papa, signaling to us that it was time to quit work. Papa then took out a pencil and began to figure out how much we had earned our first day. He wrote down numbers, crossed some out, wrote down some more. "*Quince*," he murmured.

⁹When we arrived home, we took a cold shower underneath a waterhose. We then sat down to eat dinner around some wooden crates that served as a table. Mama had cooked a special meal for us. We had rice and tortillas with "*carne con chile*," my favorite dish.

¹⁰The next morning I could hardly move. My body ached all over. I felt little control over my arms and legs. This feeling went on every morning for days, until my muscles finally got used to the work.

Tienen que tener cuidado: You have to be careful.

Vámonos: Let's go.

Quince: fifteen

carne con chile: a mixture of meat and spicy red peppers

[11]It was Monday, the first week of November. The grape season was over and I could now go to school. I woke up early that morning and lay in bed, looking at the stars and **savoring** the thought of not going to work and of starting sixth grade for the first time that year. Since I could not sleep, I decided to get up and join Papa and Roberto at breakfast. I sat at the table across from Roberto, but I kept my head down. I did not want to look up and face him. I knew he was sad. He was not going to school today. He was not going tomorrow, or next week, or next month. He would not go until the cotton season was over, and that was sometime in February. I rubbed my hands together and watched the dry, acid-stained skin fall to the floor in little rolls.

[12]When Papa and Roberto left for work, I felt relief. I walked to the top of a small **grade** next to the shack and watched the "Carcanchita" disappear in the distance in a cloud of dust.

Carcanchita: an old, run-down car

[13]Two hours later, around eight o'clock, I stood by the side of the road waiting for school bus number twenty. When it arrived I climbed in. No one noticed me. Everyone was busy either talking or yelling. I sat in an empty seat in the back.

[14]When the bus stopped in front of the school, I felt very nervous. I look out the bus window and saw boys and girls carrying books under their arms. I felt empty. I put my hands in my pants pockets and walked to the principal's office. When I entered I heard a woman's voice say: "May I help you?" I was startled. I had not heard English for months. For a few seconds I remained speechless. I looked at the lady who waited for an answer. My first instinct was to answer her in Spanish, but I held back. Finally, after struggling for English words, I managed to tell her that I wanted to enroll in the sixth grade. After answering many questions, I was led to the classroom.

[15]Mr. Lema, the sixth grade teacher, greeted me and assigned me to a desk. He then introduced me to the class. I was so

nervous and scared at that moment when everyone's eyes were on
me that I wished I were with Papa and Roberto picking cotton. After
taking roll, Mr. Lema gave the class the assignment for the first hour.
"The first thing we have to do this morning is finish reading the story
we began yesterday," he said enthusiastically. He walked up to me,
handed me an English book, and asked me to read. "We are on page
125," he said politely. When I heard this, I felt my blood rush to my
head; I felt dizzy. "Would you like to read?" he asked **hesitantly**.
I opened the book to page 125. My mouth was dry. My eyes began
to water. I could not begin. "You can read later," Mr. Lema said
understandingly.

¹⁶For the rest of the reading period I kept getting angrier and angrier
with myself. I should have read, I thought to myself.

¹⁷During recess I went into the restroom and opened my English book
to page 125. I began to read in a low voice, pretending I was in class.
There were many words I did not know. I closed the book and headed
back to the classroom.

¹⁸Mr. Lema was sitting at his desk correcting papers. When I entered
he looked up at me and smiled. I felt better. I walked up to him and
asked if he could help me with the new words. "Gladly," he said.

[19]The rest of the month I spent my lunch hours working on English with Mr. Lema, my best friend at school.

[20]One Friday during lunch hour, Mr. Lema asked me to take a walk with him to the music room. "Do you like music?" he asked me as we entered the building.

[21]"Yes, I like Mexican *corridos*," I answered. He then picked a trumpet, blew on it and handed it to me. The sound gave me goose bumps. I knew that sound. I had heard it in many Mexican *corridos*. "How would you like to learn to play it?" he asked.

corridos: narrative or romantic poems turned into songs

[22]He must have read my face, because before I could answer, he added: "I'll teach you how to play it during our lunch hours."

[23]That day I could hardly wait to get home to tell Papa and Mama the great news. As I got off the bus, my little brothers and sisters ran up to meet me. They were yelling and screaming. I thought they were happy to see me, but when I opened the door to our shack, I saw that everything we owned was neatly packed in cardboard boxes.

Connect to the Author

Chuck Barry

Francisco Jiménez

When Francisco Jiménez was 4 years old, his parents brought him and his brother to the United States illegally. They were fleeing the poverty of their small village in Mexico. But without the proper papers, the family had to earn a meager living picking crops. They did not have a permanent home for years. "I came to realize that learning and knowledge were the only stable things in my life," says Jiménez. "Whatever I learned in school, that knowledge would stay with me no matter how many times we moved." Jiménez became a U.S. citizen in 1965 and went on to become an award-winning author and well-respected college professor. He has taught at Harvard, Columbia, and Santa Clara universities.

"Mermaids" Fight to Save Florida Roadside Attraction

by Kimberly Ayers and Boyd Matson
National Geographic on Assignment

A mermaid at the 1961 Weeki Wachee underwater show in Florida comes face-to-face with Wily Willie, the friendly sea monster.

[1]At a west Florida intersection, where the 21st century runs headlong into 1947, is a roadside attraction that must be seen to be believed. There are no Disney cartoon characters or underwater mannequins, but living, breathing, bubble-blowing mermaids just an hour drive north of Tampa.

[2]Weeki Wachee Springs attracts tourists from around the world, and during its heyday attracted celebrities including Elvis Presley. But in

recent times the park has fallen into disrepair and is faced with a few financial and political woes. Now the mermaids—new and old—are fighting to save what they say is a Florida landmark.

[3]The mermaids are highly endangered. Fewer than 20 people in the country do this for a living, and all of them are right here at Weeki Wachee.

[4]"We breathe underwater. That's what mermaids do," said Krista Lewis, a mermaid in training. "We're half fish, half human."

[5]Weeki Wachee is a throwback to an era when vacations meant the parents packing up the car and heading out for a couple weeks for 3,000 miles (4,800 kilometers) of driving around the country. Roadside attractions were the only way to keep kids from having a backseat meltdown.

[6]Weeki Wachee is a theater built into a natural spring—allowing the audience to walk into an underwater world without getting wet. With today's environmental laws, there will probably never be another place like it in the U.S.

A Unique Playground

[7]Clad in their **iridescent** Lycra tails, the mermaids perform choreographed routines and stories and are sometimes joined by fish, turtles, and manatees—creatures that some say inspired the original mermaid legends.

[8]"Sometimes I feel as if I might really be a mermaid. Some days are better than others, and you don't really feel like you need breaths as much as other times," Lewis said. "I love the swimming aspect . . . especially on sunny days, it's so beautiful. And knowing that people in there are watching you . . . sometimes you do feel as though it's like a real thing."

[9]The geology of Florida makes Weeki Wachee a unique playground. The state is a patchwork of springs that **discharge** fresh water from underground aquifers. Weeki Wachee's springs pump out more than 60 million gallons (227 million liters) of water every day—that's 740 gallons (2,800 liters) per second. Diving down a little over a 100 feet (30 meters) into the throat of the spring is like trying to swim headfirst through a Jacuzzi jet.

[10]Manatees and turtles were the only residents of Weeki Wachee until 1947, when an ex-Navy frogman named Newt Perry combined his military experience and a natural

inventiveness to create Weeki Wachee's first underwater show.

Mermaid Recruits

[11]Early underwater performances ranged from feeding fish to drinking from a soda bottle to performing with a submerged circus. It was an underwater **novelty** designed to bring the crowds in off the highway.

[12]"U.S. 19 was just a two lane highway then, very few cars going by. So when we weren't in a show, we'd run out to the road in our bathing suits and we'd beckon them in," said Mary Darlington Fletcher, one of the original mermaids from the 1940s. "So we put on a show for two people in a car. It didn't matter. We didn't need a real good excuse for an audience."

[13]As the performances became more sophisticated, Weeki Wachee's fame grew and so did the crowds. At its height, during the 1960s, the mermaids performed ten shows a day.

[14]Many of the mermaids were first introduced to Weeki Wachee as audience members themselves, just taking a break from the highway. They fell in love with a fantasy on the other side of the glass.

[15]"When I was three years old, I came to the park for the first time. I can remember coming. I fell in love with the mermaids, the bubbles, the spring, everything. I just loved it," said Amy Fobell. At 16, she signed on as a lifeguard at the water park next door. At 18, she auditioned for the underwater show. Now she's living her dream.

[16]"Everybody who leaves for another job . . . wants to keep one foot in the door so they can come back," said John Summers, Weeki Wachee's only merman.

Mermaid Alumni

[17]To experience the freedom of staying underwater without scuba requires learning how to breathe using an air hose. Without masks, mermaids learn to take gulps of air from the hose, balancing the pressure on their ears and sinuses while being **buffeted** by a 12-mile-an-hour (19-kilometer-an-hour) current.

[18]"Breathing off the air hose is really, really hard—just to keep in mind not to breathe in your nose when you're in the water. But after a couple of times you learn your lesson," mermaid Sativa Smith said. The temptation is to take big gulps of air, but that leads to rising and falling very quickly because air increases **buoyancy**. The trick, the mermaids say, is to maintain neutral buoyancy so that one can hover in

Mermaids at Weeki Wachee Springs perform without scuba gear in the underwater theater.

AFP/Getty

place. Letting go of the air hose is the hardest part. It takes most people months of training before they are ready for the show.

[19]"It was very hard in the beginning when I would drop my hose and do a ballet move and then go down and pick up my hose. It was scary," Lewis said.

[20]So just how long can a mermaid hold her breath?

[21]"When I swam in the '60s and '70s and we timed each other, I got a 4:15 [4 minutes, 15 seconds] one time. Yeah, I was really proud of that. But the record is 6:10," said Barbara Wynns, a mermaid alumnus.

[22]Eventually Weeki Wachee became old news. The novelty wore off, and it no longer attracted headlines, investors, or crowds. Many people at Weeki Wachee are worried that the park will soon shut down, a victim of changing times and local politics. But some former mermaids, rather than soaking in a hot tub in a retirement home, have squeezed back into their sequins to breathe life back into the park.

[23]"Wrinkles, cellulite, chubby, whatever—we're ready to go," Wynns said.

[24]Unfortunately the mermaid fantasy is an incurable disease, according to Susie Pennoyer, a senior mermaid who started performing monthly alumni shows in 1997 to help **revive** interest in the park. "It just keeps us healthy, it keeps us vitalized. It's a stress relief. Once a mermaid, always a mermaid."

from *The Beet Fields*

Memories of a Sixteenth Summer

by Gary Paulsen

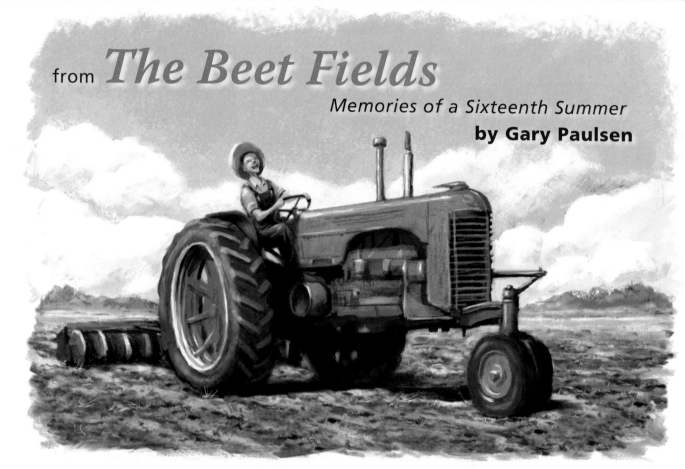

The main character, who throughout the novel is called simply "the boy," has run away from home. He has been weeding with a hoe in the beet fields of North Dakota to earn a tiny wage. But he accepts a new job, driving a tractor, after he catches a glimpse of the farmer's daughter, Lynette, and falls in love.

¹**H**e never once spoke to Lynette.

²Bill set him up in a small trailer next to the machine sheds that had once been used for camping but was now falling apart. It had a bunk across the end covered with mouse droppings and a small table next to the bunk. No lights, no heat, and when it rained it leaked like a sieve.

³"You won't be in here that much," Bill told the boy. "We work all the time summer and fall. You'll be working from light to dark and then some."

[4]Except that it wasn't work, not like hoeing beets had been. It was just sitting driving a tractor. Bill had two large Case diesel tractors and it only took him a few minutes that first day to teach the boy how to refuel and run one of them. He hooked the diesel onto a disc and sent the boy off to work the fields he'd leased.

[5]The fields were a good three miles from his farm and once the boy was there working, Bill kept him there until well after dark. Alice drove out in a pickup and brought him cake and sandwiches for forenoon lunch, a full hot meal in lard buckets for midday dinner, cake and sandwiches again for afternoon lunch and then a full supper, always taken in the field so he could keep working.

[6]He had thought at first they might send Lynette with the food but it was always Alice, always good food, more than he could possibly eat but always Alice. She brought him coffee to drink in a Thermos and he hated coffee but drank it anyway, with sugar she brought in an old peanut butter jar, to keep awake on the droning tractor he was driving.

[7]There were no lights on the tractor, for which the boy was grateful. Just at dark—close to nine o'clock—Bill would come in the pickup and take him back to the trailer. The boy would fall asleep on the bunk, mouse droppings and all. Before daylight Bill would pound on the side of the trailer to wake him. He would just have time to stop at the outhouse, eat a standup breakfast at the tailgate of the truck—a thick-bread sandwich with eggs and bacon between the slices. Then Bill would drive the boy back to the field, dozing all the way, to refuel the tractor and start discing again at first light.

[8]The boy prayed for rain, prayed to get sick, prayed for the tractor to break down, prayed for Bill to get sick, prayed for lightning, prayed for the very earth to swallow the tractor and end the work. But all he got was good weather, the roar of the poorly muffled diesel and the endless, endless North Dakota fields. He thought of many things; he thought of *all* things. Tractor thoughts. And of course he thought of Lynette, though he never saw her. He thought of movie stars and cars he would like to own, a hot rod he would build someday and Hank Williams and he sang, at the top of his lungs, trying to harmonize

with and sing louder than the tractor, he sang every country-and-western song he knew and then made some up and at last, in the end, he came down to thoughts of revenge. He thought of getting even with everybody who had ever done a wrong thing to him—his parents, bullies, life, a teacher who'd hit him, an aunt who'd called him bad names when she was drunk—thought of all the ways he could hurt them and make them know, *know* that they had done him the wrong way.

⁹And still there were more fields. He worked a week, then another, then another with no break and each Monday morning Bill handed him seven crisp five-dollar bills to add to the beet money in his pockets.

He was rich but even if he'd had time off he didn't want to go to town because he was afraid of being found and sent back.

¹⁰He lived for sleep and lived to see Alice coming with the pickup to bring him food. He would try to get her to talk but she walked along the edge of the field while he sat and ate, picking bits of grass and

small flowers until he was done, then took the dishes and leftover food back, all without speaking more than a word or two but smiling at him and nodding and leaving him.

[11]Jail must be like this, he thought after three weeks—except that it doesn't move and they don't pay you.

Connect to the Author

Gary Paulsen didn't meet his father until he was 7 years old. During Paulsen's childhood, his father was an officer fighting in World War II. When the war was over, Paulsen and his mother moved to the Philippines, where he saw his father for the first time.

Gary Paulsen

"After we returned to the States, we moved around constantly," he says. "I lived in every state." The longest time he spent in any school was 5 months.

Paulsen was, in his own words, "a miserable student."

"School was a nightmare because I was unbelievably shy, and terrible at sports. I had no friends, and teachers ridiculed me," Paulsen recalls.

"One day as I was walking past the public library in twenty below temperatures, I could see the reading room bathed in a beautiful golden light," Paulsen says. "I went in to get warm and to my absolute astonishment the librarian walked up to me and asked if I wanted a library card. She didn't care if I looked right, wore the right clothes, dated the right girls, was popular at sports—none of those prejudices existed in the public library. When she handed me the card, she handed me the world. . . . It was as though I had been dying of thirst and the librarian had handed me a five-gallon bucket of water. I drank and drank."

Paulsen ran away from home when he was 14. He traveled with a carnival, worked as a migrant farm hand, and trapped animals for the state of Minnesota. Using money he earned as a trapper, Paulsen enrolled in a small Minnesota college. After college, he joined the Army and worked with missiles. Then, when his tour of duty was over, he took extra classes and became an engineer. When he realized he didn't like the work, Paulsen took a risky step. He applied for a magazine editing job, even though he had no experience. The publisher could tell that Paulsen wanted to learn the business. "I was there for about a year, and it was the best of all possible ways to learn about writing. It probably did more to improve my craft and ability than any other single event in my life."

Paulsen's first book was published in 1966. He continued to write until 1977, when he was sued because of information he included in his book *Winterkill*. He won the suit, but, he says, "the whole situation was so nasty and ugly that I stopped writing."

Following that difficult time, Paulsen returned to trapping to make money. But when a friend brought him four sled dogs, his life changed again. Paulsen fell in love with sledding. He entered the Iditarod, a grueling 1,200-mile race across Alaska.

The race was "a mind-boggling experience," Paulsen says. "You don't sleep for seventeen days. You begin to hallucinate. You are not allowed any outside assistance. If you make a mistake, you are left to die."

His experiences inspired him to write again. The result was his award-winning novel *Dogsong*.

Paulsen says he continues to write for two reasons. "I want my . . . years on this ball of earth to mean something. Writing furnishes me a way for that to happen. Secondly, I have not done anything else in my life that gives me the personal satisfaction that writing does. It pleases me to write—in the very literal sense of the word."

THE ROAD AHEAD

- How do you relate to what you read in previous Expeditions?

- How can a story help you understand yourself?

- Who do you want to become on your road ahead?

It's Just Words

¹"**S**o," my mom says the second I walk in the door, "where have you been? School was out two hours ago."

²"Around," I say. That doesn't go over well, I can tell, but she just shakes her head and turns back to the sink.

³"Did you go to that job interview that Mrs. Barnes set up for you?"

⁴"Yeah, but there's no way I'm working at that bookstore," I say and help myself to some of the carrots she's peeling for soup. The woman is crazy for soup. Makes it every week and then freezes it like we're not going to have any food. Money is tight and all, but I mean, come on. Soup?

⁵"What's wrong with a bookstore?" my mom asks. She stops peeling carrots and sits down at the table with me. "Bookstores are great. They're quiet. They're peaceful. They're not hectic and full of screaming kids." She rubs her temples around and around. "They're quiet," she says again. I figure it was a long day at the daycare center where she works.

⁶"Yeah, they're quiet. They're boring and quiet, and I've got nothing in common with any of those people there."

⁷You should see these bookstore people. All mousy and gray like Mrs. Barnes and always reading something. Except for Camilla. Okay, she's always reading something, but she's not so mousy and gray. She's got short red hair and 12 earrings, and she kind of smiles at me sometimes in the hall at school. Camilla's okay. But, I don't talk to her or anything because what would I say?

⁸Mom is talking, and I realize I have no idea what she's said. I do that a lot, I guess. Tune out.

⁹"What?" I say.

¹⁰"Honestly, Jack. Would you listen for once?" she sighs. "I said that Mrs. Barnes really wants you to take that job. And, wouldn't you like to start saving some real money? You know I can't buy you a car next year. Maybe this would get you started."

¹¹I'll be 16 in three months. Yeah, a car would be good. Not that I've got many places to go, but it would be good anyway.

¹²I'm doing it again. She's talking. I haven't heard a word. So I just

nod my head and say, "Yeah. Okay."

[13]"Really? You'll go?" she asks. She looks surprised in a happy way, and I know I've just agreed to something that's going to kill me. "I have to say that just amazes me. I didn't think I'd ever persuade you to go to a poetry reading."

[14]She looks so happy I can't tell her that she's right, there's no way I'd ever go to a poetry reading. So I just ask, "What time? Where?"

[15]"At the bookstore tomorrow night at 7:30. You're supposed to meet Mrs. Barnes in the parking lot at school at 6:30. She's taking a group on the school bus. I think you'll like this poet. He's . . . different." She gets up and goes back to the carrots. I think she's whistling.

[16]I lay my forehead on the table. Poetry reading? My buddies will

rub this in for days. Me watching some nerd wearing his little glasses, reading his little rhymes about birds and flowers. Why couldn't she pick a ball game or a concert or something, anything, else? Who cares about poetry? It's just a bunch of words that don't make sense.

[17]Before I can think of a way to get out of going, I'm standing in the parking lot with a bunch of kids I don't know. It's 6:30, and of course, Mrs. Barnes is right on time. She drives up in a school bus and opens the door. The others push me in that direction, so I get on the bus. I don't talk to anybody. I've got nothing to say to these people. Bunch of losers going to a poetry reading. I hunch down in a seat by myself and wonder if I can just stay on the bus without Mrs. Barnes noticing.

[18]When we get to the bookstore, there's a bunch of people **milling** around out front like they're waiting for something important to happen. My mom is there with some of her friends. Then I see a flash of red in the crowd, and there she is. Camilla. Reluctantly, I get off the bus with the group. When Camilla smiles and waves, I turn around to see who she's smiling at. Then I figure out it's me. I act like it's no big deal and kind of stroll over to her, but on the inside my **circuits** are buzzing like my head's about to come off. What am I going to say? I can't come up with any words at all.

[19]"Hey, Jack," Camilla says.

[20]"Hey," I say. This is going to kill me, I think, and I'm racking my brain trying to come up with something, anything, to say. How do those smooth guys do it? How do they make it look like the easiest thing in the world to walk up to THAT girl and just start talking?

²¹"Do you know J.T.'s stuff?" she asks.

²²"J.T.?" I say. I sound like an idiot. It's just words, I say to myself. It's just regular words, and they just need to start coming out of your mouth.

²³"Yeah, the poet. He did a reading last month. He's really amazing."

²⁴I laugh. "Right. Can't wait."

²⁵Camilla gets this smirk on her face. "We'll talk after. I'll be interested to hear your **impressions** then. Come on. Let's get seats."

²⁶We sit inside where chairs are lined up in rows. I **lace** my hands behind my head and tip my chair back, ready not to listen to the nerdy poetry guy. Then he walks out, and I'm so startled my chair bangs back down on the floor. This big cool-looking guy wearing a leather jacket and sunglasses pushed back on top of his head walks up to the microphone, clears his throat, and starts to read his first poem.

[27]*There is something sinister about something so simple*
As the way the words can just come tumbling out
Before you even have time to understand what
They mean or what you mean.
Black and white and ugly and pretty and
Gorgeous and frightening and wow and
What happens when you say them
Out loud? And what happens when you
Keep them as **hostages** *inside, waiting?*
For what?

[28]People are clapping, especially Camilla. And me.

[29]The poet reads more, and I listen. When he finally leaves after signing copies of his book, the crowd **stirs** and talks and kind of hums. Camilla still sits next to me, and I hear myself saying to her, "I'm going to start working here."

[30]"Cool," she says. "I'm sure we'll have some of the same shifts. I work most weekends and sometimes after school."

[31]Then we're talking. About the poems. About school. About stuff. The words come out just fine.

Report Card Blues

by Emotion Brown

You got your report card
But you didn't report the news.
And now you're stranded somewhere
Between being secretly excited
5   And openly displaying the blues.

And you choose in school
To just be cool
And keep it on cruise,
Sitting in your seat with your cap pulled low,
10   Pants sagging to the floor
So those As and Bs in your pocket don't show.

And what your homies don't know
Is that you're smart.
And that's not the hard part,
15   Which is the life you're living.
Mimicking radio and television
Is kind of boring—isn't it?

Refusing to take the road less traveled,
Instead of spitting poetry on mics,
20   You'd rather spit on gravel.
But soon it will all unravel.
Because by far those As and Bs in your pocket
Dictate that you're a star.

So rise and shine . . . now.

Connect to the Author

Camika Spencer, also known as Emotion Brown, is deeply involved in the arts as a novelist, performance poet, dancer, and musician. She is a national best-selling author of three novels published by Random House and St. Martin's Press. In her poetry and singing performances, she is known as Emotion Brown, her artistic stage name. A graduate of East Texas State University with a degree in Broadcast Communications, she is currently working on her fourth novel and performing with her band Mo Brown and Company. She also participates in various arts-in-schools programs in Dallas, Texas, where she teaches creative writing, poetry, hip-hop dance, and Visions in Community.

Brian Guilliaux

Emotion Brown

Old Snake

by Pat Mora

Old Snake knows.
Sometimes you feel
you just can't breathe
in your own tight skin.
5   Old *Víbora* says, "Leave
those doubts and hurts
buzzing like flies in your ears.
When you feel your frowns,
like me wriggle free
10   from *I can't, I can't.*
Leave those gray words
to dry in the sand
and dare to show
your brave self,
15   your bright true colors."

Connect to the Author

When she was young, Pat Mora did not appreciate her Mexican heritage. Mora, who was born and raised in El Paso, Texas, grew up in a bilingual household. But she would only speak Spanish at home. At school, she tried to act more "American." She tried to ignore the Mexican part of her culture. But writing helped her understand and embrace her identity. "I take pride in being a Hispanic writer," says Mora. "I will continue to write and to struggle to say what no other writer can say in quite the same way."

Cheron Bayna
Pat Mora

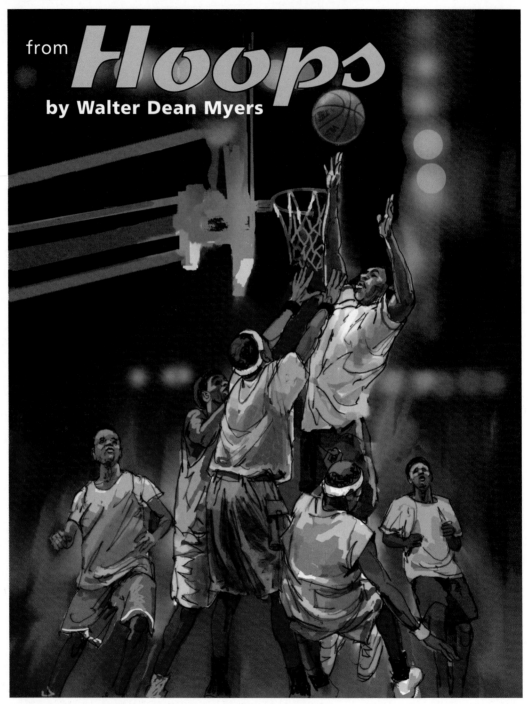

from **Hoops**

by Walter Dean Myers

The first basketball game of the tournament is about to begin.
Lonnie, one of the players, checks out the opposing team, the
Morningside Comanches. He notices that Stealer John, a large and
powerful player, will be playing against him.

¹**W**hen we got to the gym for the first game, there was a crowd there. I was surprised because mostly these **tournament** games didn't amount to much. There were a few white guys in suits—I figured they must have been scouts or something.

²Stealer John got the opening tap and drove right for the basket. He went up and jammed, and everybody on the sideline started calling out his name. It was like a chant. STEAL-LER! STEAL-LER! Paul brought the ball down and tried a behind-the-back pass to Ox, and Stealer **intercepted** the ball and started downcourt again. He slowed the ball up when I got to it. Then he started moving to my right at the top of the key. He pointed to a spot on my right, and I thought that he was pointing to a spot for somebody to set a pick. I looked over, and he faked to my left. Then I jumped to the left and he went around me on the right side and I slipped and he jammed. That was his second jam in a row.

³We went down, and Lenny fed me the ball cutting across the lane. Stealer was on me, but I had half a step on him. I spotted Ox under the hoop, waving his arms. I could have either passed or went for the bucket myself. I went for the bucket. Ox's man, he must have lost Ox, so he switched over on me, came up, and threw my shot away. They scored again.

⁴Paul hit a jumper. Then I stole the ball and got ahead of everybody and went up for the jam and hit the rim. The ball bounced out to Stealer, and he was off. I went after him, and when he put a move on to go around Lenny, I caught up with him. He started a drive, only he dribbled the ball too high and I went for it and got a piece of it and he went into me and we both fell down. They called a two-shot foul on me, and then there's Jo-Jo tapping me on the shoulder and telling me I'm out of the game.

⁵"What did you take me out for?" I asked Cal.

⁶"You're turning your head on defense—"

⁷"I didn't turn my head!"

⁸"I saw you! That's why he got around you!"

⁹"I was going for the steal! You said to look for the ball!"

¹⁰Cal started sounding off at me. His shirt collar was open, and the veins in his neck stuck out. I sat down on the bench and watched as the Comanches ran up and down the court. It was a sloppy game, and they were winning easy. No matter what

Stealer did they were yelling for him. Cal put Lenny on him, and he styled on Lenny like he wasn't even there. Even the referees were cracking on us. Ox was getting some respect around the boards, but Paul was so anxious to make Lenny look good he wasn't doing a thing. At half time they were up 74 to 54.

[11]We went into the locker room and sat down. Cal didn't say anything. He just started getting his stuff together like he was going to leave. Everybody looked at him, but nobody said anything. Then Cal was standing in front of the mirror, picking out his hair, when Ox asked him what he wanted us to do in the second half.

[12]"Do?" He turned around and looked at Ox. "What you asking me for? You playing your own game, ain't you? Everybody's playing for themselves, right? You ain't passing

the ball. I know about playing basketball. I don't know what you're doing out there. Maybe you like the way they are laughing at you."

[13]"You sitting Lonnie out don't help none," Jo-Jo said.

[14]"Lonnie is sweet on Stealer John," Cal said. "You see the way he keeps giving him everything he wants. 'Go by me, Mr. John. Go on to the basket, Mr. Stealer. You want this **rebound**, Mr. John?'"

[15]"Well, look, Cal," I said. "You don't want me playing, I won't play!"

[16]"That's right," Cal said. "Go on home. Because it takes a man to have enough pride to go out there and play the second half like he means it. And I don't think you guys are men enough!"

[17]I walked out and went back into the gym. I wasn't sure what I was

going to do or where I was going. I looked and Ox was with me and so was Jo-Jo. The others started out, too. I went down to the bench and sat on it.

[18]"Where's your coach?" the referee asked.

[19]"He's sick," somebody said.

[20]"Well, let's get going."

[21]I went out on the floor and looked for Stealer John. He wasn't on the court. I looked again. They were starting their scrubs!

[22]Roy got the tap to Jo-Jo, who went all the way down the lane for the quick two. They came down and pulled a nice play with a couple of switches, but the cat that went for the hoop blew, and the rebound came out to Breeze. He brought it to the top of the key and then hit Paul with a bounce pass for another basket.

[23]They went to inbound the ball and Jo-Jo jumped at the guy taking the ball out and the ball came in wild. I got it and hit a short jumper. Then their guy got jumpy and stepped into the court when he was taking the ball out, and the ref turned it over to us on the violation. We scored again, and they called time-out.

[24]"Come on, we got to tighten up," Paul was saying.

[25]I looked over to the scorer's table, and they were bringing their first five back in. I looked over to our bench, and I saw Cal standing behind some other dudes. Okay, he wanted to know what we were made of, he'd find out.

[26]Stealer John brought the ball down, and I kept my hand on him the whole time. He passed the ball off but called for it right back. I was right on him. I didn't let him breathe for a minute. Finally he backed himself into a spot where Paul could double-team him. I saw it and figured he'd move the ball away from Paul and I'd have a chance for it. Paul came over, and I saw his man start to cut towards the basket. Maybe Stealer John would have passed the ball to the cutting man or maybe he would have forced the shot up, but he never got the chance. I had the ball and started down the court. I couldn't hear anybody after me, but I put the ball on the backboard anyway for another **deuce**.

[27]They called another time-out.

[28]"You gonna pay for that, sucker!" Stealer John pointed at me as he went to his bench. It made me feel good that he was mad.

[29]The rest of the game went down . . . without a smile, without a moment everybody's mind wasn't

in it. They were playing ball like they were professionals or something. But we came back slow but steady. People watching got real quiet, and the game was being played by everybody just the way it was supposed to be. When we got six points away, the buzzer went off. We lost.

[30]We got in the locker room, and I was so tired I couldn't even sit down straight. Cal was handing out towels. He gave us some Gatorade and salt tablets, too.

[31]A guy who had been hanging around the gym came in and started congratulating everybody.

[32]"You got a nice team, coach," he said, handing Cal a card. "You got some really classy ball players. You don't mind if I tell them how good I think they were?"

[33]"I mind!" Cal looked at the guy like he had said something about Cal's mama or something. Then he threw the guy's card on the floor.

[34]The guy shrugged and walked out.

[35]Paul picked up the guy's card and looked at it and handed it to Ox.

[36]"Hey, coach." Ox was holding they guy's card. "That was a scout!"

[37]"I don't want any of you guys talking to nobody without clearing it with me first!" Cal said.

[38]"I don't know what you talking about, man," Ox said. "You said this tournament was about having coaches see us, didn't you?"

[39]"Yeah, that's what it's all about," Cal said. There was sweat around his mouth, but the rest of his face was dry. "They all come like Big Daddy, too. But just like every daddy, they got their own family to feed. He's going to tell you anything you want to hear as long as he can get you to play for his team. That's how he gets paid, by delivering the right flesh to the right team. Then, if he can't get what flesh they want, they get a whole lot of backups, just so they can justify their expense account.

[40]"I've seen guys like you thinking that some big school is interested in them because they've talked to a scout. You know for every guy that makes a team some scout has talked to twenty or thirty guys around the country and said the school was interested? You turn down five real chances for some fabulous school and go there to find you going up against a hundred guys just to make the junior varsity. Now can we talk about the game?"

[41]"Yeah, go ahead, man." Paul was already getting into his street clothes.

[42]"Let me ask you guys something."

Cal was stuffing all the towels into a bag. "You guys win or lose out there today?"

[43]"You know we lost, coach," Paul said.

[44]"Did you have to lose?"

[45]No one said anything.

[46]"Who here thinks you lost because the other team was better than you were?"

[47]No one said anything.

[48]"Then let's all have two minutes of silence." Cal stood up and bowed his head. "We got young black men here who choose to lose instead of winning. That's something we should all have a moment of silence for. That's an **opportunity** we let die. Just give me two minutes of silence."

[49]It was a long two minutes. At first it was uncomfortable, then it was embarrassing, and then I started to feel just a little ashamed of myself. After the two minutes were up, Cal told us how proud he was of how we had played the second half. It was too bad, he said, that we didn't think enough of ourselves to win when we had the choice.

[50]By the time Joni and Leora got to the locker room, we were all dressed and ready to go. We went down to the center and drank some sodas . . . that we had stashed there.

[51]"What you guys celebrating?" Cal said.

[52]I thought he was going to get into the thing about us losing again. Ox said he wasn't celebrating nothing, just having a few drinks.

[53]"I'm just trying to relax after the game," Paul said.

[54]"You go tell that to somebody who never played this game," Cal said. "You celebrating what you found out on that court this afternoon. You got yourselves a good team. You know it, the team that beat you know it, and everybody that saw the game knows it. You guys can play some ball, and that's what you're celebrating! Now somebody pass me a cool drink!"

[55]When he said that, when he let it all out, we just tore loose. Because that's what we were thinking to ourselves. We were thinking that we played us some ball. I mean, we played us some B-A-L-L! We might have blown the game, but when we had our stuff together out on the court, it was together! Hearing Cal say it just put the icing on the cake.

Connect to the Author

Walter Dean Myers is best known for his novels about young African Americans in Harlem, a neighborhood of New York City where he grew up. Myers was born in 1937. He moved to Harlem when he was 3 years old to live with foster parents after his mother died. A speech problem left him feeling isolated at school. He turned to writing to express himself.

"Writing seemed, and still seems to be, my major involvement with life," says Myers. "I write to give hope to those kids who are like the ones I knew—poor, troubled, treated indifferently by society, sometimes bolstered by family and many times not. I was a high-school dropout, and I know how easy it is for them to lose their brightness in a web of drugs, gangs, and crime."

Henry Ray Abrams/AP Photo

Walter Dean Myers

Jamie Oliver

Getty

Jamie Oliver prepares one of his recipes on *The Tonight Show with Jay Leno*.

¹Jamie Oliver had it all. He was only 27 years old, but he already owned a beautiful mansion in the English countryside outside London. He drove a flashy sport car. Millions of people in more than 50 countries watched his TV cooking shows. His bestselling cookbooks further fattened his bank account.

²"I could have retired, or just kept doing what I was doing," Oliver says. "I have a wonderful wife and a beautiful little girl, and my house was paid off. But in the end, it was only cooking—not that much of a big deal. I thought, 'There's got to be something more.'"

³Oliver remembered a friend who worked with kids who were struggling in school. She helped them learn to focus by teaching them how to cook. "I felt I could relate to that because I wasn't great at school, but in the kitchen I came alive," Oliver said. "I thought then how fantastic it would be if there was some kind of charity that could help to train youngsters who wouldn't otherwise get the chance, and give them a kick start in the restaurant business."

Preparing for a New Future

⁴Oliver realized that he could use his fame and fortune to help others. He decided to open a restaurant. But this restaurant would be different. This restaurant would not be about making money. It would be about giving **disadvantaged** youths a chance to turn their lives around.

Jamie Oliver talks with chefs-to-be before opening a new restaurant in Amsterdam, The Netherlands.

⁵First, Oliver recruited 15 people between the ages of 16 and 24. Some of the recruits dropped out of school. None had jobs or much hope for the future. Not one of them had any experience cooking, but Oliver was convinced they could learn to be great chefs. "Being a good cook isn't about being born to it," Oliver says. "It's about discovery and growth. I don't believe there is such a thing as a person who doesn't like cooking; they just don't know it yet."

⁶Next, Oliver began training the recruits to be professional chefs. It was **grueling**. Oliver and the recruits worked 60 hours a week for weeks on end. And Oliver wasn't always the happy, cuddly guy he appeared to be on his television shows. He could be demanding and impatient. "Towards the end, it was draining," said Tim Siadatan, who completed the training. "We hadn't had a break for a good part of 18 months."

⁷During the training sessions, a television crew filmed everything. Oliver thought the training would make a great reality TV show. He was right. *Jamie's Kitchen* was a huge hit. Millions of viewers tuned in to watch the drama.

⁸As the training continued, some of the recruits dropped out. "For some, it just wasn't for them," Jamie says. "Some couldn't hack it." But some could. Finally, 10 of the recruits made it through the

training. They were ready to become professional chefs at Oliver's new restaurant. Oliver decided to call the restaurant Fifteen, after the number of recruits at the beginning of training.

A Smashing Success

[9]Fifteen is a bright and cheerful place. Space-age plastic seating surrounds the tables. Hot pink touches and graffiti-style scribbles contrast with warm wooden walls. Hot pink booth seats add splashes of color to the dining room. The word *Fifteen* is painted in hot pink letters on one wall. All the hot pink **decor** is fitting. Fifteen has become one of the hottest restaurants in London.

[10]Food critics loved Fifteen from the day it opened. One raved about "some of the best dishes I have been served in a long time." Another said his pasta dish was "the best I have ever had anywhere." A third critic saved his most **lavish** praise for Oliver himself. "He's got that one

A senior sous-chef works in the kitchen of Fifteen in Cornwall, England.

ingredient that all food needs, but you can't get from a supplier: a big heart," the critic said. The public loved Fifteen as much as the critics did. People had to schedule their visits to Fifteen months in advance to

Sam Morgan Moore

Diners at Fifteen in Cornwall have a clear view of chefs at work in the restaurant's kitchen.

make sure there would be an open table.

[11]Oliver came up with the idea for Fifteen and invested $5 million of his own money. But he shares the credit for its success. "This restaurant is really all about the kids," he said. "The ones we've got now are as sharp as nails. They can tell you about the ingredients, the wines, the shapes of pasta—things that it took me 12 years to learn."

[12]Oliver doesn't make any money from the restaurant. All of the profits are used to help other youths train for restaurant careers. Every year, another group of youths is trained to take the place of chefs who leave Fifteen. The trained chefs have no trouble finding work in other restaurants. The new recruits won't be showing up on television, though. In some ways, the success of the TV show caused problems for a few of the original 15 recruits. "It actually impacts on their

learning," Oliver said. "They start to think they are celebrities without being chefs first." To solve that problem, Oliver no longer films the training. "This time we've worked out who was in it for the cooking and who was in it just to be on TV," Oliver says.

[13]Fifteen has been so successful that Oliver has opened three other Fifteens. He hopes to open branches all over the world. Each restaurant will train underprivileged youths to work as chefs. "And I know for a fact that there are some in the Fifteen **brigade** who are going to go on and make some serious splashes in the restaurant world later on," Oliver says. "And when they are ready . . . we will be able to help them set up their own places, because as far as I am concerned, this is a lifelong project. Wherever these guys end up, we'll never say goodbye. I'll always be there for them."

Oliver's Next Mission

[14]In 2006, Oliver took on a new challenge. He wanted to improve the quality of food served to English school children. British schools were spending less than a dollar per school meal. Many schools didn't even have kitchens. "These are dark times," Oliver said. "We have got some of the most unhealthy kids in the whole of Europe."

[15]To solve that problem, Oliver needed to convince government leaders to spend more money on school food. So he filmed a new television series. This one was called *Jamie's School Dinners*. Like all his shows, it was a big hit. When people realized the state of school food, they demanded that the government do something. Once again, Oliver's efforts paid off. The government increased funding for school food and **banned** the sale of sugary soft drinks and junk food.

[16]Oliver also showed schools how they could make healthier meals. One school that followed his advice saw an immediate improvement in their students. "It has made a huge difference," head teacher Angela Birchall said. "The children have more energy and seem more focused."

[17]With luck, all of England's schoolchildren will soon benefit from Jamie Oliver's energy and focus.

Jamie Oliver's Recipe for
The Best Pasta Salad

Serves 4

11 ounces small shell-shaped pasta
3 cloves garlic
½ pint yellow cherry tomatoes
½ pint red cherry tomatoes
1 handful of black olives, pitted
2 tablespoons fresh chives
1 handful of fresh basil
½ cucumber
4 tablespoons white wine vinegar, or to taste
7 tablespoons extra-virgin olive oil
sea salt and freshly ground black pepper

Bring a large pan of salted water to a boil. Throw in the pasta and cloves of garlic, boil until *al dente*, drain, and run under cold water to cool. Put the garlic to one side to use for the dressing. Put the pasta in a bowl. Chop the tomatoes, olives, chives, basil, and cucumber into pieces about half the size of the pasta, and add to the bowl. Squash the garlic cloves out of their skins and mush in a mortar and pestle. Add the vinegar, oil, and seasoning. Drizzle this over the salad, adding a little more seasoning to taste.

GARLIC

CHIVES

Michael Paul/StockFood Creative/Getty

BASIL AND
CHERRY TOMATOES

Teubner/StockFood Creative/Getty

Golden Glass

by Alma Villanueva

¹It was his fourteenth summer. He was thinning out, becoming angular and clumsy, but the cautiousness, the old-man seriousness he'd had as a baby, kept him contained, ageless and safe. His humor, always dry and to the bone since a small child, let you know he was watching everything.

²He seemed always to be at the center of his own universe, so it was no surprise to his mother to hear Ted say: "I'm building a fort and sleeping out in it all summer, and I won't come in for anything, not even food. Okay?"

³This had been their silent communion, the steady presence of love that flowed regularly, daily —food. The presence of his mother preparing it, his great appetite and obvious enjoyment of it—his nose smelling everything, seeing his mother more vividly than with his eyes.

⁴He watched her now for signs of **offense**, alarm, and only saw interest. "Where will you put the fort?" Vida asked.

⁵She trusted him to build well and not ruin things, but of course she had to know where. She looked at his dark, contained face and her eyes turned in and saw him when he was small, with curly golden hair, when he wrapped his arms around her neck. Their quiet times —undemanding—he could be let down, and a small toy could delight him for hours. She thought of the year he began kissing her elbow in passing, the way he preferred. Vida would touch his hair, his forehead, his shoulders—the body breathing out at the touch, his stillness. Then the explosion out the door told her he needed her touch, still.

⁶"I'll build it by the redwoods, in the cypress trees. Okay?"

⁷"Make sure you keep your nails together and don't dig into the trees. I'll be checking. If the trees get damaged, it'll have to come down."

⁸"Jason already said he'd bring my food and stuff."

⁹"Where do you plan to shower and go to the bathroom?" Vida wondered.

¹⁰"With the hose when it's hot and I'll dig holes behind the barn," Ted said so quietly as to seem unspoken. He knew how to slither under her, smoothly, like silk.

¹¹"Sounds interesting, but it better stay clean—this place isn't that big. Also, on your dinner night, you can cook outdoors."

¹²His eyes flashed, but he said, "Okay."

¹³He began to gather wood from various stacks, drying it patiently from the long rains. He kept in his room one of the hammers and a supply of nails that he'd bought. It was early June and the seasonal creek was still running. It was pretty dark out there and he wondered if he'd meant what he'd said.

¹⁴Ted hadn't seen his father in nearly four years, and he didn't miss him like you should a regular father, he thought. His father's image blurred with the memory of a football hitting him too hard, pointed (a bullet), right in the stomach, and the

punishment for the penny candies—a test his father had set up for him to fail. His stomach hardened at the thought of his father, and he found he didn't miss him at all.

15He began to look at the shapes of the trees, where the limbs were solid, where a space was provided (he knew his mother really would make him tear down the fort if he hurt the trees). The cypress was right next to the redwoods, making it seem very remote. Redwoods do that—they suck up sound and time and smell like another place. So he counted the footsteps, when no one was looking, from the fort to the house. He couldn't believe it was so close; it seemed so separate, alone—especially in the dark, when the only safe way of travel seemed flight (invisible at best).

16Ted had seen his mother walk out to the bridge at night, looking into the water, listening to it. He knew she loved to see the moon's reflection in the water. She'd pointed it out to him once by a river where they camped, her face full of longing. Then, she swam out into the water at night, as though trying to touch the moon. He sat and glared at the fire and roasted another marshmallow the way he liked it: bubbly, soft and brown (maybe six if he could get away with it). Then she'd be back, chilled and bright, and he was glad she went. Maybe I like the moon too, he thought, **involuntarily**, as though the thought weren't his own—but it was.

17He built the ground floor directly on the earth, with a cover of old plywood, then scattered **remnant** rugs that he'd asked Vida to get for him. He **concocted** a latch and a door, with his hand ax over it, just in case. He brought his sleeping bag, some pillows, a transistor radio, some clothes, and moved in for the summer. He missed no one in the house but the dog, so he brought him into the cramped little space, enduring dog breath because he missed *someone*.

18Ted thought of when his father

left, when they lived in the city, with forty kids on one side of the block and forty on the other. He remembered that one little kid with the funny sores on his body who chose an apple over candy every time. He worried they would starve or something worse. That time he woke up screaming in his room (he forgot why), and his sister began crying at the same time, "Someone's in here," as though they were having the same terrible dream. Vida ran in with a chair in one hand and a kitchen knife in the other, which frightened them even more. But when their mother realized it was only their **hysteria**, she became angry and left. Later they all laughed about this till they cried, including Vida, and things felt safer.

[19]He began to build the top floor now but he had to **prune** some limbs out of the way. Well, that was okay as long as he was careful. So he stacked them to one side for kindling and began to brace things in place. It felt weird going up into the tree, not as safe as his small, contained place on the ground. He began to build it, thinking of light. He could bring his comic books, new ones, sit up straight, and eat snacks in the daytime. He would put

in a side window facing the house to watch them, if he wanted, and a tunnel from the bottom floor to the top. Also, a ladder he'd found and repaired—he could pull it up and place it on hooks, out of reach. A hatch at the top of the ceiling for leaving or entering, tied down inside with a rope. He began to sleep up here, without the dog, with the tunnel closed off.

[20]Vida noticed Ted had become cheerful and would stand next to her, to her left side, talking sometimes. But she realized she mustn't face him or he'd become silent and wander away. So she stood listening, in the same even breath and heartbeat she kept when she spotted the wild pheasants with their long, lush tails trailing the grape arbor, picking delicately and greedily at the unpicked grapes in the early autumn light. So sharp, so perfect, so rare to see a wild thing at peace.

[21]She knew he ate well—his brother brought out a half gallon of milk that never came back, waiting to be asked to join him, but never daring to ask. His sister made him an extra piece of ham for his four eggs; most always he ate cold cereal and fruit or got a hot chocolate on the way to summer school. They treated Ted somewhat

like a stranger, because he was.

^{22}Ted was taking a makeup course and one in stained glass. There, he talked and acted relaxed, like a boy; no one expected any more or less. The colors of the stained glass were deep and beautiful, and special —you couldn't waste this glass. The sides were sharp, the cuts were slow and meticulous with a steady pressure. The design's plan had to be absolutely followed or the beautiful glass would go to waste, and he'd curse himself.

^{23}It was late August and Ted hadn't gone inside the house once. He liked waking up, hearing nothing but birds—not his mother's voice or his sister's or his brother's. He could tell the various bird calls and liked the soft brown quail call the best. He imagined their taste and wondered if their flesh was as soft as their song. Quail would've been okay to kill, as long as he ate it, his mother said. Instead, he killed jays because they irritated him so much with their shrill cries. Besides, a neighbor paid Ted per bird because he didn't want them in his garden. But that was last summer and he didn't do that anymore, and the quail were proud and plump and swift, and Ted was glad.

^{24}The stained glass was finished and he decided to place it in his fort facing the back fields. In fact, it looked like the back fields—trees and the sun in a dark sky. During the day the glass sun shimmered a beautiful yellow, the blue a much better color than the sky outside: deeper, like night.

^{25}He was so used to sleeping outside now he didn't wake up during the night, just like in the house. One night, toward the end when he'd have to move back with everyone (school was starting, frost was coming and the rains), Ted woke up to see the stained glass full of light. The little sun was a golden moon and the inside glass sky and the outside sky matched.

^{26}In a few days he'd be inside, and he wouldn't mind at all.

Connect to the Author

Alma Villanueva was born in 1944 and raised in San Francisco by her grandmother, her mother, and her aunt. She wrote poems as a teen, but she didn't begin to write seriously until she was almost 30. Since then, her writing has won many awards. But perhaps even more rewarding are the personal thanks she has received for her work. She recalls a student who wrote to thank her for her poem "Mother, May I?" "I never imagined that I'd receive a letter like hers," Villanueva says. "Writing takes all your courage—to stand by your work and see it through to publication—courage and luck (and discipline, discipline, discipline). But, imagine, someone understanding what you meant to say . . . someone saying thank you."

Leon Canerot

Alma Villanueva

Life Doesn't Frighten Me

by Maya Angelou

Shadows on the wall
Noises down the hall
Life doesn't frighten me at all
Bad dogs barking loud
5 Big ghosts in a cloud
Life doesn't frighten me at all.

Mean old Mother Goose
Lions on the loose
They don't frighten me at all
10 Dragons breathing flame
On my counterpane
That doesn't frighten me at all,

I go boo
Make them shoo
15 I make fun
Way they run
I won't cry
So they fly
I just smile
20 They go wild
Life doesn't frighten me at all.

Tough guys in a fight
All alone at night
Life doesn't frighten me at all.

25 Panthers in the park
Strangers in the dark
No, they don't frighten me at all.

That new classroom where
Boys all pull my hair
30 (Kissy little girls
With their hair in curls)
They don't frighten me at all.

Don't show me frogs and snakes
And listen for my scream,
35 If I'm afraid at all
It's only in my dreams.

I've got a magic charm
That I keep up my sleeve
I can walk the ocean floor
40 And never have to breathe.

Life doesn't frighten me at all
Not at all
Not at all.
Life doesn't frighten me at all.

Legend of the Nine Suns/The Bridgeman Art Library/Getty

Connect to the Author

As an African American girl in a small southern town in the 1930s, Maya Angelou's future was limited by boundaries set by others. Backbreaking work, low pay, and no respect were a part of her experience. But she refused to be defined by the racist and sexist attitudes she faced. Instead, she became a singer, dancer, actress, and movie director—and a great storyteller. Encouraged by her friends, Angelou began writing about her childhood. When these stories were published in *I Know Why the Caged Bird Sings*, she was immediately recognized as a major literary voice. Though her stories, poems, and essays focus on her life, they also shed light on us all. "In all my work, what I try to say is that as human beings we are more alike than we are unalike," Angelou says.

Getty

Maya Angelou

Smithsonian National Air and Space Museum

Bessie Coleman

from
*American Profiles:
Women Aviators*

by Lisa Yount

[1]Bessie Coleman was born on January 26, 1892, in a dirt-floored cabin in Atlanta, Texas. She was one of 13 children. Her family moved to Waxahachie, a small town near Dallas, in 1894. There her father, George, bought a small plot of land and built a house.

[2]George Coleman was almost a full-blooded Indian. In 1901, when Bessie was nine, he moved to Oklahoma, which was then called Indian Territory. He felt he would be better treated there than he had been in Texas. Susan, Bessie's mother, refused to go with him and was left to raise her last four daughters alone. Bessie, the oldest, took care of the younger girls while Susan worked as a cook and housekeeper.

[3]"My mother's words always gave me the strength to overcome obstacles," Bessie Coleman said later. Susan Coleman could not read or write, but she was determined that her children would "be somebody." She borrowed books from a library wagon that went

327

through the community once or twice a year. Bessie loved these books. "I found a brand new world in the written word," she said.

[4]Bessie finished high school, a rare thing for an African American girl in those days, and vowed to go on to college. She washed and ironed to earn tuition money. In 1910, she enrolled in Langston Industrial College (now Langston University) in Oklahoma, but she had enough money for only one semester. After that she had to return to Waxahachie.

Bessie Coleman's French flying license, dated June 15, 1921

Smithsonian National Air and Space Museum

[5]After working and saving for several more years, Bessie Coleman moved to Chicago in 1915. At first she stayed with Walter, one of her older brothers. She worked as a manicurist, caring for the fingernails of customers at the White Sox Barber Shop.

[6]The United States entered World War I, and two of Coleman's brothers went to fight in France. "I guess it was the newspapers reporting on the air war in Europe . . . that got me interested in flying," Coleman recalled later. "All the articles I read finally convinced me I should be up there flying and not just reading about it."

[7]At first that goal seemed impossible. Only a few flying schools in the United States admitted women, and none would accept an African American woman. But during her search for flight training, Coleman made an influential friend. He was Robert S. Abbott, founder and editor of the *Chicago Weekly Defender* newspaper. Abbott suggested that Coleman get her pilot training in Europe, where prejudice against women and African Americans was not as great as in the United States.

[8]Coleman won her pilot's license from the *Fédération Aéronautique Internationale* on June 15, 1921.

[9]Coleman had "grand dreams," not

only for herself but for her people. "I decided blacks should not have to experience the difficulties I had faced, so I decided to open a flying school and teach other black women to fly." She knew this task would not be easy.

[10]To start her flying school, Coleman needed money. She planned to earn it in the same way most young pilots did in the early 1920s. She would become a "barnstormer," doing stunt flying in air shows and taking paying passengers up for short rides.

[11]After a second trip to Europe for advanced training, Coleman made her first air show flight at Curtiss Field near New York City, on the Labor Day weekend of 1922. Several thousand people attended the exhibition, which was billed as "the first public flight of a black woman in this country."

[12]"Queen Bess" amazed the crowds at her air shows with aerobatic stunts. They included loops, spirals, and low dives. She always made sure her audience got its money's worth. When a woman she had hired as a parachute jumper lost her nerve, Coleman found another pilot to fly the plane, strapped on the parachute harness, and made the jump herself.

Bessie Coleman stands in front of her airplane.

[13]Coleman also became known as "Brave Bessie"—for good reason. In one exhibition, her plane's motor died when she was at the top of a loop. Instead of curving over gently to complete the circle, the plane started to dive.

[14]Coleman had to turn the dive into a landing. Landing a Jenny was not easy, since the plane had no brakes. It just had to roll to a stop. Even after she straightened the plane out, Coleman knew she was coming in much faster than she should.

Smithsonian National Air and Space Museum

Fortunately, that particular field had a long runway. The Jenny finally stopped with just 200 feet of runway left.

[15]The crowd cheered, thinking the whole thing was part of the show. Only Brave Bessie knew how close to disaster she had come.

[16]Coleman's luck did not always hold. In an exhibition in southern California in 1923, her Jenny crashed and she suffered several broken ribs and a broken leg. But Brave Bessie sent a telegram from her hospital bed: "Tell them all that as soon as I can walk I'm going to fly!"

[17]In fact, Coleman was not able to fly again for almost two more years. By the end of 1925, she wrote her sister that she had almost enough money to open her flying school. First, however, she would make another tour in Florida.

[18]As part of her Florida tour, Coleman planned to perform in an air show for the Negro Welfare League of Jacksonville on May Day of 1926. She had just made the final payment on a new Jenny. A white mechanic, William Wills, flew the plane from Dallas to Jacksonville. He had to make two unscheduled landings on the way because of engine trouble.

[19]Early on the morning of April 30, Coleman and Wills took the Jenny up for a test flight. Wills was in the pilot's seat. Coleman was planning to make a parachute jump during her May Day exhibition, and she wanted to study the area to find a good jump site. She did not fasten her seat belt because she was too short to see out of the plane when she was strapped in. She also did not wear her parachute.

[20]After circling over the racetrack where Coleman would perform, Wills began to fly back to the airfield. Then the plane suddenly speeded up and went into a dive. At 500 feet above the ground it turned upside down, throwing Coleman out. She was killed when she hit the ground. The Jenny crashed into a nearby field, killing Wills as well.

[21]Following a memorial service in Jacksonville, Coleman's friends took her body to Chicago. Over 5,000 people attended her funeral. She was buried at Lincoln Cemetery.

[22]Ten years after Coleman's death, Robert Abbott wrote an editorial in the *Chicago Weekly Defender* that said in part, "Though with the crashing of the plane life ceased for Bessie Coleman, she inspired enough members of her race by her courage to carry on in aviation, and what they accomplish will stand as a memorial to Miss Coleman."

Vocabulary

A

accept	to agree to
accessible	easy to reach or get to
accident	a wreck
accomplish	to do with success
accustomed	used to
ache	to hurt
activity	something you spend time doing
adapt	to change something to suit new conditions
admire	to look up to
advertise	to tell about a product or event to get people to buy it or go to it
advice	an idea put forward about what someone else should do
advise	to tell someone what you think he or she should do
afternoon	the time of day between morning and evening
aisle	a row or passageway
alter	to change
ambitious	hard to do or achieve
ancient	very, very old
annoying	causing a little bit of anger
antique	an old and valuable object
anxious	worried or afraid
applaud	to praise
appreciate	to understand fully
aquatic	having to do with water
argument	statements used to persuade someone
arrange	to put in order
assignment	a task you are given to do
assist	to help
assume	to guess, sometimes wrongly
attempt	to try
attract	to draw something closer
attribute	a quality or feature
audience	a group of people who watch or listen to a performance
avoid	to keep away from
aware	having knowledge about something because you notice it or see that it is happening

B	**ban**	to state that something must not be done
	benefit	to help
	bevy	a group
	biohazard	something harmful to living things
	bizarre	very strange or odd
	brigade	a group of people who have a common goal
	brilliant	very clever
	buffeted	blown around by something
	bulge	a part that swells outward
	buoyancy	the ability to float
	burst	to open or break apart suddenly
	bury	to put in the ground
C	**campaign**	a planned set of activities to reach a goal
	canny	clever
	capable	being able to do something
	carcass	a dead body
	caricature	a funny drawing of someone
	character	the qualities that make a person different and special
	circuit	the path an electrical current follows
	clasp	to hold tightly
	clench	to hold tightly
	coax	to get a person or an animal to do something
	cognate	a word that is similar to a word in another language
	compelled	moved to do something because you think you must
	competition	a contest
	complaint	a statement that shows unhappiness
	complexity	the quality of being difficult or complicated
	compose	to write
	conceal	to hide
	concentrate	to give all your attention to something
	conclude	to use facts to decide something
	concoct	to invent
	condition	state of health
	conduct	to carry out
	confine	to keep in one place
	conserve	to save
	constant	always happening

construct	to build
contain	to have within
contemplate	to look at and think about
contents	things held inside something else
cooperate	to work together
crew	a group of workers
critic	a person who finds fault with someone or something
cumbersome	awkward to carry because of shape, size, or weight
D **daily**	every day
dangling	hanging
deceiving	misleading
decision	a choice
decor	the style or look of all the things in a room or house
decoration	something added to make something else attractive
dedicate	to set something apart in memory of certain people or events
defend	protect from danger
denounce	to reject
derail	to keep something from happening as planned
descend	to go down to a lower level
desperate	in great need of help
despise	to dislike very much
detail	a small part of something larger
determination	the quality of deciding to do something and then doing it no matter what
deuce	two points
development	the process of making or improving something
device	a tool that does a certain job
devote	to give your time or energy to something
digit	any of the numbers 0 through 9
disadvantaged	worse off than others
disagree	to have a different opinion
discharge	to put out
discovery	something new that has been learned
disfiguring	spoiling how something looks
disguise	a change in looks to keep from being recognized
display	to show
dissension	disagreement and argument

	disturb	to bother
	divert	to make something go in another direction
	doomed	sure to die or be destroyed
	dread	deep fear
	droning	a low, dull noise that goes on and on
E	earnest	serious
	eerie	strange and frightening
	elegant	stylish or graceful
	element	one part of a larger whole
	eloquently	clearly and beautifully
	emblazoned	printed
	endure	to go through something because you have to
	engage	to make something happen or to keep something happening
	enormous	very, very large
	enthusiasm	great interest
	essential	very important
	establish	to set up or start
	examine	to look closely at someone or something
	exception	something that is not included in a general statement or rule
	executive	a leader of a business
	expense	cost
	export	to sell to another country
	expose	to make someone aware of something
	express	show or tell
	extraordinarily	in a very unusual way
F	fabulous	very good
	fame	the state of being well-known
	familiar	well known
	famine	a food shortage resulting in widespread hunger
	fearful	afraid
	festival	a celebration
	filter	to seep or pass through slowly
	fond	having a liking for
	foreign	relating to another country
	fortunate	lucky
	frantically	in a quick but disorganized way
	frequent	close together

	fruition	a hoped-for outcome
	furiously	with great energy, effort, or speed
G	**gear**	the tools needed for an activity
	giddy	unsteady, as if you are about to fall
	gnashing	the act of pressing together with force
	grace	smooth, beautiful movements
	grade	a slope
	grating	a flat metal frame with bars across it, used to cover an opening
	grueling	very difficult and tiring
	grumble	complain in a low voice
H	**hangar**	a large building in which airplanes are kept
	heave	to push, pull, or lift something very heavy
	heir	someone who has the right to receive another person's property when that person dies
	hesitantly	in a shy or doubtful manner
	hideous	very ugly or hard to look at
	hind	back or rear
	horrible	very bad
	hostage	someone who is being held against his or her will
	humanity	the group made up of all people
	hustle	to move quickly with a purpose
	hysteria	uncontrolled panic
I	**ideal**	the best possible person or thing
	identity	who someone is
	idol	a famous person who is greatly admired by fans
	ignore	to pay no attention to
	illegal	not within the rule of law
	illuminated	lit up
	imitation	fake
	immediate	at once
	immense	great or huge
	impress	to make an impact on
	impression	thought and opinion
	incredible	hard to believe
	indigo	a dark, purplish blue
	individual	a person
	initiation	the process of becoming a member

	inspire	to make someone want to do something
	instant	a short period of time
	instinctively	without thinking it through
	interact	to talk or spend time with
	intercept	to catch a ball that was thrown to someone on the opposing team
	investigate	to look carefully at the details of something
	involuntarily	without meaning to
	involve	to have as a part of something
	iridescent	having rainbow colors that seem to move and change
	irregular	not following the usual pattern
K	**knowledge**	possession of facts and ideas
L	**lace**	to wind or twist together
	lapse	a momentary slip or failure
	lavish	given in large amounts
	legend	a story that is most likely untrue
	leisure	free time
	loll	to sit or lie in a relaxed way
	lurch	to move in a jerky, swaying fashion
	lurk	to wait in a threatening way
M	**maintain**	to keep something going
	major	big; important
	marvel	something amazing
	mature	adult
	meanwhile	at the same time
	merge	to blend or combine
	mesmerized	so interested that you cannot think of anything else
	microscopic	tiny; too small to see without a microscope
	mill	to wander without purpose
	misleading	giving someone a wrong idea
	monitor	to watch or keep track of
	morsel	a small piece
	mysterious	hard to explain or understand
	myth	a story that tells how something came to be
N	**native**	born in a certain place
	natural	in or from nature
	necessary	needed
	necessity	something needed

	neglect	to fail to do something
	nervous	worried; frightened
	nervousness	a feeling of worry or unease
	nonsense	something silly or untrue
	notify	to let someone know
	novelty	something new and interesting
O	objection	opposing opinion
	obsessed	to think about someone or something all the time
	opportunity	a chance
	opposition	a group who is against something
	oppressive	heavy; like a burden
	ordinary	common; usual
	organize	to make sure all parts of something are in place
	original	first
	overcome	to struggle against and win
P	panic	a sudden feeling of great fear
	paralyze	to cause the loss of feeling or movement in a part of the body
	patience	the ability to stay calm when something takes a long time
	peer	to look carefully at something hard to see
	perpetually	always
	persuade	convince; talk into
	pleasure	a feeling of happiness
	populated	filled with
	possible	able to happen
	precisely	in an exact or correct way
	premium	something that is wanted or needed, but hard to get
	preschool	younger than school-age
	prey	an animal that is caught and eaten by another animal
	professional	relating to a person's work
	promote	to help something take place or do well
	prompt	quick; speedy
	pronounce	to say
	propose	to suggest or put forth
	prosperous	having a large amount of money or resources
	protection	something that guards or keeps safe
	prune	to cut or trim
	psyche	your mind or spirit

	purpose	reason for
Q	quality	how good or bad something is
R	rank	foul-smelling
	realize	to see or to understand
	rebound	to catch a ball that has bounced off the backboard or rim of the basket
	recently	happening not long ago
	recommend	to suggest that something or someone would be good
	reflect	to show
	regret	to wish something had not been said or done
	relief	less stress or pain
	relive	to think about a past event
	remind	to make a person think of something or someone
	remnant	a scrap or small piece
	remote	far away
	request	the act of asking
	resemble	to look like
	result	outcome; something caused by something else
	reveal	to let others know something
	revenge	the act of getting even with someone
	revive	to make something popular again
	ritual	a service or ceremony
S	sacrifice	to give up
	savage	fierce
	savor	to enjoy something as much as you can
	scamper	to run or move playfully
	scary	causing fear
	scramble	to move quickly
	secure	safe
	seek	to try to find
	settle	to accept
	shallow	not deep
	simplicity	the quality of being easy or uncomplicated
	sincere	honest
	snowboarder	one who slides down a snowy slope on a narrow board
	social	having to do with people living in groups
	solemnly	in a very serious manner

	solution	a way of dealing with a problem
	starvation	not having enough food to live
	stir	to move about
	strut	to walk in a proud way
	suggest	to state as a good choice
	suspense	a state of nervous waiting
T	technological	related to tools made by humans for certain tasks
	tempt	to cause someone to want to do something
	thrilling	very exciting
	thunderstorm	a storm with thunder, lightning, and rain
	tolerate	to put up with
	tournament	a sports event made up of rounds of games
	typical	like most others
U	unable	not able to do something
	underprivileged	having less than others do
	unexpected	coming as a surprise
	urge	to encourage someone to do something
V	vanish	to disappear
	virtue	a good quality
	visible	can be seen
W	wistful	deep in sad thoughts over something that cannot be had
Z	zany	strange and funny